Talking
with
Psychopaths
and Savages

**MASS MURDERERS
AND SPREE KILLERS**

Born in 1948 in Winchester, Hampshire, Christopher Berry-Dee is descended from Dr John Dee, Court Astrologer to Queen Elizabeth I, and is the founder and former Director of the Criminology Research Institute (CRI), and former publisher and Editor-in-Chief of *The Criminologist*, a highly respected journal on matters concerning all aspects of criminology from law enforcement to forensic psychology.

Christopher has interviewed and interrogated over thirty of the world's most notorious killers – serial, mass and one-off – including Peter Sutcliffe, Ted Bundy, Aileen Wuornos, Dennis Nilsen and Joanna Dennehy. He was co-producer/ interviewer for the acclaimed twelve-part TV documentary series *The Serial Killers*, and has appeared on television as a consultant on serial homicide, and, in the series *Born to Kill?*, on the cases of Fred and Rose West, the 'Moors Murderers' and Dr Harold Shipman. He has also assisted in criminal investigations as far afield as Russia and the United States.

Notable book successes include: *Monster* (the basis for the movie of the same title, about Aileen Wuornos); *Dad Help Me Please*, about the tragic Derek Bentley, hanged for a murder he did not commit (subsequently subject of the film *Let Him Have It*) – and *Talking with Serial Killers*, Christopher's international bestseller, now, with its sequel, *Talking with Serial Killers: World's Most Evil*, required reading at the FBI Behavioral Analysis Unit Academy at Quantico, Virginia. His *Talking with Psychopaths and Savages: A Journey Into the Evil Mind*, was the UK's bestselling true-crime title of 2017; its successor volume, *Talking with Psychopaths and Savages: Beyond Evil,* was published in the autumn of 2019. In 2020 a new edition of his *Talking with Serial Killers: Dead Men Talking* appeared and the same year saw the publication of his latest book, *Talking with Serial Killers: Stalkers.*

https://www.christopherberrydee.com/

Christopher Berry-Dee

Talking
with
Psychopaths
and Savages

A study of the most dangerous and
unpredictable of all crimes

JB

First published in the UK by John Blake Publishing
an imprint of Bonnier Books UK
4th Floor, Victoria House
Bloomsbury Square,
London, WC1B 4DA
England

Owned by Bonnier Books
Sveavägen 56, Stockholm, Sweden

www.facebook.com/johnblakebooks
twitter.com/jblakebooks

First published in paperback in 2021

Paperback ISBN: 978-1-78946-422-1
Trade paperback: 978-1-78946-421-4
Ebook ISBN: 978-1-78946-423-8
Audiobook ISBN: 978-1-78946-424-5

British Library Cataloguing-in-Publication Data:
A catalogue record for this book is available from the British Library.

Design by www.envydesign.co.uk

Printed and bound in Great Britain by Clays Ltd, Elcograf S.p.A.

1 3 5 7 9 10 8 6 4 2

John Blake Publishing is an imprint of Bonnier Books UK
www.bonnierbooks.co.uk

For mathematician, astronomer, astrologer, teacher, occultist, and alchemist, Dr John Dee (13 July 1527–1608 or 1609).

Contents

Prologue

He who fights with monsters might take care lest he
thereby become a monster. And if you gaze for long
into an abyss, the abyss gazes also into you.

FRIEDRICH WILHELM NIETZSCHE: GERMAN PHILOSOPHER

In the process of researching and writing this book, your
author became a very angry man. 'Furious' would be nearer
the mark. Allow me to explain why.

For many decades I have been studying, corresponding
with and interviewing the human pond scum that are
psychopathic sexual serial killers – with a few mass murderers
and one-off killers thrown into this homicidal mix. So I more
or less understand what makes most of them tick.

Furthermore, I understand the serial killers' sexually driven
motives far better than most, because I haven't just read about
this murderous breed then lectured about them – as many do
from some lofty lectern without meeting even one of them

– I have actually gained access to the dark abyss of their twisted minds. I have touched them, felt their evil tentacles of thought insidiously worming their way into my own head. By doing so, one starts to think as they do. However, as Friedrich Nietzsche ominously points out above, this can be a very dangerous exercise indeed.

To put it succinctly, I haven't merely looked at the T-shirts; I own a whole collection of them, some thirty at last count, that being the number of serial killers I have met, interviewed, corresponded with. But never have I become angry with any of these monsters; not once have I allowed my emotions to cloud my judgements, as shockingly heinous as these offenders' crimes have been. It's almost as if I have ice instead of blood, running through my veins, as if I wrap up my own emotions and feelings snug and warm so that the horrific events – often gleefully, gloatingly revealed to me by these twisted men and women – don't affect me.

After boasting about his rape and murder of young women and two little schoolgirls (the latter, as he exclusively revealed to me on camera, he anally abused postmortem), the priapic, Cornell University-educated Connecticut serial killer Michael Bruce Ross said to me, 'I really am such a nice guy.' Then he giggled, before bursting into hysterical laughter. Ross, aged forty-six, was executed by lethal injection at Somers Correctional Institution on Friday, 13 May 2005. And I can assure you that I have heard far worse than what he told me – many times over.

Yet I reiterate, I have never got angry with any serial killer… not even close to it. My 'anger management' seems to be well under control when I deal with the most God-awful of murderers most foul. I put it down either to being very thick skinned, or perhaps to my service in HM Royal Marines 'Green Beret' Commandos. And to be truthful I also think that I am a very nice guy, too.

But mass murderers are an altogether different breed to serial killers, as we shall learn later, and it is in this connection that I became so enraged when I started to write this book.

In a nutshell, and despite many experts claiming otherwise, society can never stop a person from metamorphosing into a sex-crazed monster such as Ted Bundy or Peter Sutcliffe. Yet many societies could, if they had the will and the balls, significantly reduce the chances of a mass murderer running amok with a firearm. But they do not, and without dressing this up in PC speak, I say that legislating politicians who permit their citizens easy access to guns have blood on their own hands.

Sexual serial killers use just about every abhorrent method known to man to torture and kill – employing everything from firearms, knives and strangulation to bludgeoning, caustic fluids, electrocution, dismembering victims while they are still breathing or setting them on fire while they are still alive; more often than not there is rape involved, too. Needless to say, many serial killers – including Michael Ross, for example – commit necrophiliac acts on the corpses. Some serial killers may use a gun to finally dispatch their victims, but they do not use explosive devices as domestic mass murderers sometimes do. Mass murderers and spree killers do not include rape, or torture, in their homicidal repertoire. They do not stalk their victims, as serial killers are so inclined to do over days, sometimes even months on end – because serial killers get a perverse kick out of stalking their prey, while mass killers do not.

As I hope this book will clearly illustrate, with very few exceptions mass murderers use high-power military-assault-style weapons and are often 'tooled-up' with handguns as well. Therefore, the antidote to their heinous acts at first blush seems clear to me: ban this type of gun. We Brits did it, so did the Australians, more or less in a heartbeat!

The second reason I was furious is because as a former Marine I have witnessed bombings and mass shootings at first hand. I know all too well the devastation caused by bombs and firearms. I know exactly how it feels to pull the trigger of arguably the finest battle rifle ever made – the 7.62mm L1A1 Self-Loading Rifle (SLR); to feel the recoil punch of the stock in one's shoulder as a round zips down range at over 1,800 ft per second, to lift one's human target clean off their feet and soon into a coffin, then into a hole in the ground. So why in God's name are some governments, specifically the USA's, allowing lethal weapons such as AR-15s to be purchased as easily as armchairs, with their gun controls as slack as a hooker's morals?

Just as I had reached the point of no return in my tirade (around halfway into the book you now hold in your hands), I realised that I had an anger-management problem vis-à-vis mass murders and firearms control. So I hit the pause button to reboot and to think again.

I cannot say that I had some sort of God's-light-shineth-upon-thee epiphany. In fact, it was YouTube that brought me to my senses, to a place of calmer waters. Why? Because millions of law-abiding citizens in the USA and other countries across the world enjoy as a 'hobby' the fun of firing red-hot lead at targets and taking such weaponry out to hunt game.

A note to the USA's National Rifle Association (NRA): please read that well, and what follows too. For online, I viewed numerous videos of young, fresh-faced lads out in the fresh air with their dads popping away at feral wild boar – a pest in Texas – or even buck deer when a pot shot looked on the cards. This *is* a healthy father-and-son pursuit, much like in the UK when dad takes his boy fishing with rod and line. Except there is a much smaller bang for one's buck, excuse the pun, when reeling in a 1.5-kg sea bass than when bringing down a truly pissed-off 120-kg Hogzilla – one furious enough to ram his tusks into that place where the sun doesn't shine.

Then I thought about all the feral kids roaming the streets at night in the UK with zero parental control. Their fathers drunk as skunks, sponging off the 'social', with mums getting a hiding from them every five and twenty minutes. I would put money on it that those boys would love to have quality dad-and-son time fishing out on some beach. Better still, hunting in the backwoods: a campfire, chewing the fat with other kids and like-minded dads, skinning and butchering the beast out in the wild to bring some fresh meat home for supper. Instead, they eat crap pizza, available in eight-packs for a quid and with as much nutrition as a piece of cardboard.

There was another angle, probably the most important, that occurred to me too: there are always two sides to any debate, especially regarding firearms control. Considering the ever-escalating firearm mass murder rate in the USA, we need to think more about the innocent victims and the grieving next of kin of those involved in mass-murder shootings. Their voices have to be heard, too. They have to be taken into account when discussing mass murder, *inter alia*.

> The easy availability of weapons like this [high-powered military grade firearms], which have no purpose other than killing human beings, can all too readily turn the delusions of sick gunmen into tragic nightmares.
>
> *Time* Magazine, 24 June 2001

As for the motives and the anger that fuels these low-life mass killers, I more or less deliberately ignore other books that regard it as of social interest to delve into their back histories – their 'narratives'. I partly set aside the well-meaning psychiatrists and psychologists and the 'lefties' who suggest that when one suspects that a person with access to firearms might be going off of the rails, 'early intervention' is an option to be considered. For do we live in a Utopian society? No, we do not. This book discusses this controversial matter in, I hope, some depth.

As my tens of thousands of readers across the world know, I do not mince my words; purely because I am like you. *We* say it as it is, do *we* not? No political spin; no confusing psychobabble from *moi*. Domestic mass murder does exactly what it says on the tin. So let's prise open the lid and see what is inside.

I leave you with a note of gratitude to David J. Krajicek,

author of *Mass Killers: Inside the Minds of Men Who Murder* (2019). His book is exceptional, and although we may agree or choose to disagree on various issues, I believe that he and I sing from the same hymn sheet. His book has been of mega assistance to me in writing mine. Thank you, David. Thank you very much indeed.

Introduction

America… just a nation of two hundred million
used-car salesmen with all the money we need to
buy guns and no qualms about killing anybody else
in the world who tries to make us uncomfortable.

HUNTER S. THOMPSON, AMERICAN JOURNALIST AND WRITER:
AUTHOR OF *FEAR AND LOATHING IN LAS VEGAS*

With the Prologue done and dusted, this book is now your road trip into the murky world of mass murder, and you are about to join me after I extend this most cordial invitation: 'Welcome, folks. I am your guide.'

Your ticket is this book, yet this journey will not be some kind of enjoyable visit to a fictional, criminological Disney World, where fantasy reigns supreme. No buttering things up, no political correctness, no layer cake with an icing of bullshit to sweeten the facts.

And why? Well, fellow travellers, we are soon going into

the sickening, very real world of bodies blasted to pieces, crimson-red bloody remains, limbs, guts, grey spongy brain matter, shattered white bone – all the results of mass shootings and domestic bombings. Innocent lives lost; men, women, children, even unborn babies blasted away. This is what happens to those victims caught up in mass-murder events. We must also take into account the insufferable grieving of those left behind, their unrelenting tears, broken hearts, shattered dreams. And the injured, their bodies and everlastingly disfigured, their minds traumatised forever. I truly hope this book speaks for them, too.

> Michael was quiet and polite. He was as good as gold… wouldn't hurt a fly.
>
> Marjorie Jackson, school caretaker:
> on British spree killer Michael Ryan.

Let's use our imagination now. I'd like you to look out of our imaginary coach window at those trees over there. Imagine that it is a fine, sunny day, and auburn-haired Susan Godfrey, aged thirty-three, has just finished taking her two adorable children, four-year-old Hannah and two-year-old James, for a picnic.

It is about 12.30pm.

Look, there is Susan packing away the picnic things.

Now watch as a man dressed in black slowly creeps up to her. Slung across his shoulder is an AK-47-type assault rifle loaded with armour-piercing bullets. In his hand is a Beretta semi-automatic 9mm pistol. He orders Susan to strap the children into the car, which she does, but you can see that she is terrified. He then marches her away with the children screaming out for her.

Deep in the woods, about a hundred yards from the car, this stranger orders Susan to turn her back to him so he cannot see her face, then he fires... can you hear the shots? Because there are fifteen high-velocity rounds being fired at point-blank range into her back. She falls down, dead.

By the grace of God, the children have been left unharmed. They will be found wandering around confused, scared, crying amongst the trees some time later.

Of course, if you actually witnessed this in real life this would be your worst Stephen King-type of nightmare come true. Yet this is what happened to Susan Godfrey when she took her two children to Savernake Forest, seven miles from the sleepy market town of Hungerford, on Wednesday, 19 August 1987. And if it had been your wife or sister, this terrible thing would haunt you to your own dying day. Furthermore, there seems to have been no motive for this savage murder. Susan was not sexually assaulted. No connection between her and her killer would ever be found. There was no evidence to suggest that Ryan had stalked Susan, because he had been in the forest since mid-morning. A local lad had heard a burst of automatic gunfire from there at around 10.30am. The police could only speculate that she had surprised him during his target practice. Maybe a bullet had ricocheted too close for comfort, so Susan decided to hastily pack up and leave, perhaps to report Ryan to the police. If she'd done that, he would have lost his firearms licence and his arsenal of guns. She had to die, and once that deadly deed was done there could be no turning back.

* * *

Before I was commissioned to write this book, my editor-in-chief asked what experience I had regarding mass murder. That was a valid question, because one cannot put one's heart and soul into a project – any project – unless one has some understanding of what one is writing about, no matter what the subject may be. I write this book with a few dreadful first-hand experiences of shootings and bombings that still haunt me today. There are many awful memories, but one is inclined to block them from one's mind because they are too horrific to even think about these days, let alone relate, as I sit at my desk now. However, I can confirm that I served three tours in Northern Ireland while serving with 45 Commando, HM Royal Marines. On my second tour, I was badly injured. I spent a month in the Queen Elizabeth Hospital, Belfast, after which I was taken by Saracen armoured car to Musgrave Park Hospital, where I stayed another six weeks before being airlifted by an RAF 'Andover' to RAF Brize Norton, then by Westland Wessex helicopter to the Royal Naval Hospital Haslar in Gosport, Hampshire. Then, after a lengthy period convalescing, and getting the best treatment pretty much anywhere in the world, I was released and returned to duty. I will use this opportunity to tell you about 'Blood Friday', the devastation wrought by a series of at least twenty explosives, mostly car bombs, planted by the IRA in Belfast, Northern Ireland, during 'The Troubles'.

The date was 21 July 1972. All of the devices exploded within the space of eighty minutes and were mainly targeted at infrastructure, especially the transport network, and including the main bus station – an incident that I immediately attended. Nine people were blown to pieces at the Belfast bus station: five civilians, including a little lad selling newspapers, along with two British soldiers, a Royal Ulster Constabulary (RUC) reservist, and a member of the Ulster Defence Association (UDA). A further 130 were injured in the same incident, with many maimed for life.

At this time I was based at Flax Street Mill along the Crumlin Road in north-west Belfast. We had seen plenty of shootings – civilians, men, women and kiddies, police officers and troops shot to death – but never bombing carnage like this. Upon my arrival at the bus station, with the dull thump of bombs still exploding around the city, I witnessed a RUC officer on bended knees and sobbing his heart out. In his hand was a bloodied shovel. On the ground was a black, plastic bin liner. All around him over some distance were the bits and pieces of the young newspaper boy. It looked like a display from a butcher's shop blown to smithereens.

Shortly thereafter, I had to visit the Queen Victoria Hospital. Here, amongst a red sea of casualties, was quite the most beautiful girl, aged about seventeen, drenched in her own blood. A six-inch nail had been blown straight into her jaw. It was still in-situ, as the medical staff figured out what to do next. She didn't cry. There were no tears at all. She was in shock, but it was evident that she would be terribly disfigured for life. God bless her.

Therefore, as a former Royal Marine, it goes without saying that I have, like so many other servicemen and women, seen the results of bomb blasts and firearm wounds on living human flesh. I know precisely the devastation explosives and bullets can cause. And I will add this: faced with determined, well-trained hot British fire, the cowardly IRA ran a mile.

Now, please, please think again about that young girl with the nail in her jaw. Imagine if she had been *your* daughter. Give a thought to that little newspaper boy, blown to pieces. Imagine if he had been *your* son. Every time some scumbag commits a domestic bombing or a mass shooting, think how you would feel if you lost someone very precious to you, or that they were maimed for life. Would you care a jot if the killer had had a dysfunctional childhood, that he had run amok because he harboured some vendetta against his estranged wife, or that he wanted to take revenge on society because he had been sacked from his place of work and didn't receive his last wage packet on time? Would you be even remotely interested in any of the upside-down, all-too-often often differing professional psychiatric opinions given later, concerning the killer's state of mind? I bet, like me, you wouldn't.

So, to pull no punches, in this book I want you to be sickened to the stomach. Because if you manage to meld the hopefully 'educational experience' of this read with the shock horror, let me tell you that *your* views matter, as you will see as we go along our way. If I have made any errors, those mistakes are mine and mine alone.

But let's cheer ourselves up a bit now, for we are heading off to the USA. When we arrive it will be just two days before the Fourth of July, 1995. Oh, and bring your packed lunches with you. It's a long drive along Mass Murder Road, with a lot of unpacking to do at various stops before we reach our destination.

CHRISTOPHER BERRY-DEE

UK AND PALAWAN, PHILIPPINES

1

Waco, TX

The Second Amendment is on the line. Criminals won't give up their guns, and to protect myself I'm not going to give up mine.
RESIDENT OF AUSTIN, TEXAS: TO THE AUTHOR

Waco, in the 'Lone Star State'. Many years ago, I visited the Texas Ranger Hall of Fame and Museum, out on the Texas Ranger Trail, close to the Brazos River.

They have a real fondness for museums, do our American cousins. I read somewhere about the 'American Museum Museum', though I am not sure exactly where the place is. They even have a Colonel Sanders Museum in Watterson Park, Kentucky, for KFC aficionados, and it gets rave reviews. Can you imagine 'The British Fish and Chip Museum', or a permanent 'Bangers and Mash Display' in the British War Museum, because this porky delicacy has its origins way back in World War I? (If you are an American reader and you want to know a thing or two about the latter, please look up

1

the Thompson House website Bangers and Mash: a History – you will never look back!)

All that said, if ever you are in Waco, and you have a big thing about fizzy pop, why not visit the history and memorabilia exhibited at the soft drinks bottling plant, built in 1906, now the 'Dr Pepper Museum & Free Enterprise Institute' on 300 South 5th Street. For it is just a short stroll from the aforementioned Texas Ranger exhibition, where you will see lots and lots of guns. Here, one can also take in the venerable history of an elite law-enforcement outfit dating back to the first days of the Anglo-American settlement of what is today the state of Texas.

My guide around what's commonly called Los Diablos Tejanos, aka The Texas Devils Museum, was a big guy: ruddy faced, thinning silvery white hair and a well-cultivated paunch. He stands a ramrod-straight 6ft 5in in his leather-tooled, Cuban-heeled boots. He's a retired Texas Ranger but he still wears the signature cream-to-white Western hat, an immaculate starched white shirt, black suit and corded leather American gold-eagle bolo.

'Tex' is the spitting image of John Wayne starring as Rooster Cogburn in the movie *True Grit* – as, it has to be said, was my old pal, the legendary US Marshal Mike McNamara, who sadly is with us no more. Tex's handgun is holstered, but Texas Rangers – even those well past their service sell-by date – may carry just about any sidearm they choose, so he pulls out of his holster a heavy .38-calibre chrome-plated six-shot revolver. It has an engraved ivory grip. Quite obviously, he keeps his gun well oiled, for the chamber spins around and around with reassuring watch-like clicks. It's loaded with live rounds, too, because hot-blooded Texans never fire blanks.

'You've always carried that?' I ask.

'*Yes*, sir!'

'Why not an auto?'

Measuring me through squinting azure eyes, this gritty guy says: 'Autos can jam. Most shootings take place up close, an' if you need *more* than six bullets then *you are* dead... *sir*!' Tex's face is law-enforcement weathered. He has 'Don't f*ck with me' writ large from head to toe. He's made his point.

I liked this don't-shit-over-me guy very much. I mean I liked him very much indeed, just as I did most of the other cops I met in the Lone Star State: the legendary US Marshal brothers Mike and Parnell McNamara, and sheriffs like Larry Pamplin out of Marlin County, who, incidentally, ended up locked up in his own jail for 'misappropriating victual funds meant for the prisoners'. Then we have the guys from Alcohol, Tobacco & Firearms (ATF), Special Weapons & Tactical (SWAT), the FBI, dedicated homicide detectives such as Austin homicide cop Tim Steglich, state troopers, and countless more. And this is just Texas, for I have been all over the USA, meeting some amazing law-enforcement officers along the way. And they all told me, in so many words: 'For Christ's sake, we should never sell high-powered firearms to civilians. Many are redneck assholes and can start a small war.'

Actually many assholes have done so. And they still do.

With that said, many US policemen are assholes themselves; small-minded, totally unfit, morally and religiously bigoted, pimple-faced, overweight rednecks who would serve society better if they'd stayed working in their Mom and Pop's shoe store on, say, Main Street, Crap Creek, Nevada. But give them a gun and a Maglite, hey bro, they are good to go. They'll put holes into any black guy who looks at them twice; even just the one glance sometimes is enough.. That's very often the American way, you see. But please don't just take my word for it: go online and search for YouTube videos about US cops killing innocent citizens. They will blow your mind.

I should emphasise here that most US cops stick by their motto 'To Protect and to Serve'. They are community men: family guys who do barbeques, love taking their fresh apple-pie-making wife and their equally fresh-faced kids around swap meets. They do Sunday church, afterwards spending an inordinate amount of time in 400-acre shopping malls. Big time they celebrate the Fourth of July, Thanksgiving, Labor Day. And in Texas the men call their spouses 'Ma'am'. I like this as well.

I like apple pie. Even more so when one mysteriously appears still hot on your open kitchen windowsill, all wrapped up tight in red-and-white gingham check cloth. Kind of homely, is that. Kind of neighbourly, too. You don't get any of this where I live along the UK's south coast. If you do buy one of 'Mrs Crampton's Home-made Apple Pies' from your local superstore, it will probably get nicked out of your trolley before you even reach your parked car. But, here's a thing. One can network in the States – gain access to almost anything and everything – because US law enforcement love being on TV, and showing off their hardware. It's in their cowboy genes, you see, way, way back before Roy Rogers and his 15.3-hands-tall palomino horse, Trigger.

So, there I am, in Washington State, and in passing I ask a US Marshal if he had any contacts down in Texas. He says,

4

'Yes, sir!' He picks up a phone, and within a few minutes he tells me that in Waco he has buddies who do great alligator steaks. 'You're welcome to go visit there,' he says. 'US Marshals Mike and Parnell McNamara, will be expecting ya.' That's kind of homely law enforcement if you ask me, helped by the fact that American cops seem to love Brits. I can't say I have always found the same in the UK.

That's how I ended up in Waco, and wound up visiting the Texas Ranger Hall of Fame and Museum, out on the Texas Ranger Trail. Actually, it's not a 'trail' in the true dusty, cactus-bordered, tumbleweed Lone Ranger-and-Tonto sense. It's more of a road that services the American Football Coaches Association, the Umphrey Law Center – Lot # 59 and the Texas Ranger place of worship, where I would see all those guns.

But many, many other guns, in their hundreds of thousands, get into the wrong hands. So the genesis for this book started in Waco, TX, with a big guy wearing a white cowboy hat showing me lots of them, after which he said:

In the Second Amendment of the Constitution, our forefathers gave the people the right to keep and bear arms. But that was back then. Times have moved on, sir.

These days we hand out lethal weapons like sweets... even to kids... to people who know no better, even total nut jobs. Anyone can now get hold of a firearm and blow lots of innocent people away, an' it's gonna get worse.

Mass killings can only escalate, and you know

what? The politicians don't give shit, an' it's us cops who have to clean up the fucking mess.

Thank you for visiting with me at the Texas Ranger Museum.

Ya'll have a nice day!

Two days later, while I am eating alligator steak with US Marshal brothers Mike and Parnell McNamara, the fifty-one-day Waco Siege comes up in conversation. As far as domestic mass murder and massacres are concerned, this one really does take some beating.

In short, David Koresh's cult, the 'Branch Davidians', were quartered at the Mount Carmel Center, just off US-84, at Axtell, about fourteen miles east of Waco. And, as we all should know, while minding their own business – OK, Koresh and his folk were stockpiling illegal weapons, but they were not murdering anyone, or posing the slightest threat to human life – the FBI, US Marshals Service, ATF, and loads of local law enforcement moved in on some pretext to evict them and take away their guns (which the Second Amendment of the Constitution of the United States permitted them to own). This all gave rise to two firefights. The end result being that the entire place was burned to the ground: 4 agents were killed, 16 wounded, with, on the other side, a total of 82 men, women and innocent kids wiped out – all ending on Monday, 19 April 1993. In short, fellow travellers, this was a mega massacre and law enforcement pretty much kicked it off. You can find the full history behind this 'gunfight at the Branch Davidian Corral' on the internet – if you want to. But that's the USA, you see.

During my US travels I have visited numerous crime scenes, popped tops off bottles of Bud and chewed the fat with attorneys and judges, and listened to a great deal of Johnny Cash on the car radio. This book initially takes you to the USA then across the world, for this is *our* journey with many have-to-be-humorous-to-lighten-the-load moments, as well as plenty of sickening twists and turns. And hopefully a few insights into the minds of mass murderers and spree killers along our way.

We will examine large-scale homicides committed by lone killers – those who explode out of the blue to wreak carnage on innocent fellow citizens. And we will try to understand, if only a tiny bit, the hatred-filled, maladjusted psychopathological mindsets of these people – often teenagers of loving, or more often of plumb dumb, parents – who felt inexorably compelled to commit blood-bath atrocities beyond anyone's comprehension. Only the post-mortem photographs, the grieving next of kin's suffering and the precious white headstones set deep in clipped, lush, green grass, can portray the true meaning of the mass murder that has become epidemic in America today.

And we must ask ourselves: why?

2

A Rage to Live

No beast is more savage than man when possessed with
power answerable to his rage.
PLUTARCH (LUCIUS MESTRIUS PLUTARCHUS, AD 46–AFTER AD 119):
GREEK-BORN ROMAN BIOGRAPHER AND ESSAYIST

I think that Plutarch had something here. We might add 'there's a sort of rage a man feels when he's been deceived where he most trusted. It compares to no other anger,' the words of the American novelist Orson Scott Card. However, this book is not about people who have been deceived, it is about those who, in their own twisted psychopathologies, *perceive* they have been deceived. There is an almost convoluted yet distinct distinction here. It's those whose perceived emotions are sparked by some small sleight, then fester, intensify like the gathering winds of an emotional tornado, until they spin out of control and these individuals wreak havoc and death on those whom they imagine have done them wrong, when the opposite is true. And in most cases, killing entirely innocent men, women and children who get in their way, out of misplaced revenge.

> I don't think about the end game. I've got lots to occupy my mind. It's the rage that keeps me going.
> Terry Pratchett (Sir Terence David John Pratchett, OBE, 1948–2015)

For many decades I have been studying serial killers; I have met, and/or corresponded with, more than thirty of them. And without exception, their motives are largely driven by an underpinning social grudge, metamorphosing into the sex killings of their chosen victim type; most often they visit upon their prey a fury of unleashed homicidal sado-sexual rage.

You may question why I use a humorist's quote above, but Sir Terry Pratchett inadvertently hits the nail on the head as far as mass murderers are concerned. For they don't care about the end game either – it is the rage that keeps them going.

Let's not confuse ourselves. For the mass murderer and the spree killer are very distinct from the serial killer in many patently obvious ways, although even today the most eminent psychologists and psychiatrists, even the police themselves, often get it wrong, being unable to differentiate between the two. Thus 'mass murderer', 'spree killer' and 'serial killer' erroneously become one and the same.

Many wrongly categorise Theodore Robert Bundy (1946–89) as a mass murderer when, in fact, he was a sado-sexual necrophile serial killer, because the FBI definition of a serial killer describes, amongst other things, 'an offender who kills three times or more times with a cooling-off period, which can last days, weeks, months, or even years, in between the events'.

Oops, and before an eagle-eyed reader jumps down my throat, I should add that recently the FBI decided to merge the definitions of 'serial killer' and 'mass murderer', although God only knows why. In fact, when I asked the FBI for an explanation, they didn't seem to know either. Therefore, I will keep things as they were: a sort of previous status quo, if you like.

Bundy's serial-killing career probably started during the 1970s. He confessed to thirty murders (the true number may never be known) and carried on committing sado-sexual homicide until he was finally arrested in 1978, which is precisely why I have highlighted the 'cooling-off' periods in-between each kill event, above. Furthermore, to reinforce the adjective 'serial', it refers to repeatedly committing the same type of offence, and typically, following a similar characteristic, predictable behaviour pattern, to which I will add the two prime motives – sexual gratification and hatred – into the mix.

One of the most notorious mass murderers in US criminal history – a man who has, without doubt, inspired scores more abject losers to commit similar atrocities – is the 'Texas Tower Sniper', aka Charles Joseph Whitman (1941–66). For his dreadful sins, Whitman has since become a post-mortem cult-type figure, someone with whom we will spend more time later, but here is a taster of what we're dealing with.

On Monday, 1 August 1966, after stabbing to death his

mother and then his wife, this twenty-five-year-old former US Marine ascended the 307-ft University of Texas Tower in Austin. When he arrived at the 28th-floor observation tower, he started randomly shooting – killing 17 people and wounded 31 others before he was shot dead by police and a former military civilian volunteer.

> The people were lying on the ground crying out, 'Please don't shoot me.' But he still shot them in their heads.
>
> Survivor Chris Grant to the *El Paso Times*

Then we have the mass murderer Patrick Crusius (b.1998).

NB: if my memory serves me correctly, as of Tuesday, 3 September 2019, Walmart had discontinued sales of handgun and 'short-barrel rifle' (.223in and 5.56mm calibre) ammunition, also politely requesting that their customers refrain from 'openly carrying firearms' in their stores.

OK, Walmart's genuine announcement – let's say that it was a post-mass-murder epiphany as in a wake-up call – came after a mass shooting claimed seven lives in Odessa, Texas. It followed the two other back-to-back shootings the previous month, one of which actually occurred at a Walmart store, in El Paso, Texas.

It was the morning of Saturday, 3 August 2019. The store, located near the Cielo Vista Mall, 7101 Gateway West Blvd, El Paso, became a scene of utter carnage when twenty-one-year-old Patrick Crusius opened fire with his Wassenaar Arrangement semi-automatic rifle (more commonly known as the WASR-series rifle, manufactured in Romania by the long-established Cugir Arms Factory). Twenty-two shoppers died, with twenty-four more people seriously wounded. In the aftermath, Walmart stated that it was to focus on selling only hunting rifles and related ammo. Currently a Mr and Mrs Garcia are suing the retail giant on the grounds that it: 'failed to provide adequate security to prevent the attack'.

According to the lawsuit, Guillermo and Jessica Garcia were shopping with their two children when they were shot and 'gravely injured'. They argue that Walmart should have had security at the store's entrance, and around the common areas as a 'visible security presence that would have stopped the shooter from entering the store and killing all those people'.

In the UK, we don't have Walmart, but we have plenty of other major stores that have never sold firearms, bullets or material for making pipe bombs, to my knowledge, for that is the British way.

There are countless stores in the USA where, if one shoplifts, one will be instantly collared by armed security with about twenty police vehicles turning up, light bars flashing, guns drawn. Then one is hauled off to face summary justice and, on conviction, time in jail.

In the UK, things are more genteel. The security officers will invite the thief to come to the office; ask him or her if they would like to have a cup of tea to settle the nerves (health and safety, etc), then call the police, who *might* turn up a week later. If one is an out-and-out recidivist, then one might face a grumpy beak sometime in the distant future while the Magistrates' Court gets its act together, get bail to allow one to commit even more offences, rob a few pensioners. The upshot being a few weeks of community service gardening at an old folks' home, whose residents suddenly lose all their most valuable possessions. That's the British way: too much consideration for the little shit who for the thirtieth time has promised he'll turn over a new leaf, and no consideration for the victims. I tell you what they need is a damned good hiding – so sayeth me!

One example of a notorious UK mass murder is the Dunblane Primary School massacre of Wednesday, 13 March 1996. Thomas Hamilton (1952–96) shot sixteen children and one teacher dead before turning a gun on himself. This was a headshot, which should have saved the psychiatrists and psychologists a lot of time in trying to figure out what made his brain tick: a totally redundant exercise, that, because it didn't exist any more. Nevertheless, the shrinks came up with a lot of paperwork and even more of nothing else. Obtuse? Of course I am being obtuse, and the reason why will soon become apparent. We will meet the late Mr Hamilton shortly; however, with just these few examples we can already identify fundamental differences in the execution of the offences and the motives behind them. Bundy's underlying motive was primarily sadistic sexual gratification, while the reasons for the Whitman and Hamilton mass killings were non-sexual, but rather born from an underpinning grudge, metamorphosing into the murder of their unlucky victims.

At this point it would be remiss of me not to mention another type of monster who seems to sit on the fence between the serial killer and mass murderer: the 'spree' or 'rampage killer'. For the sake of yet more justifiable nitpicking, this label is often confused with either serial killers or mass murderers. Well, we can rule out *any* similarity between the words 'spree' and 'serial' in a heartbeat. In the context of homicide the compound noun 'spree killer' might be defined as: 'a person who kills a number of people during a short period of time in close proximity in a frenzied, random, and apparently unpremeditated way'. We can call this person a 'rampage killer' too. This sounds very much like a mass murderer, does it not? Yet I'd argue that we need to take a closer look. To prove my point, let's look at the example of a true spree killer, Michael Robert Ryan (1960–87).

On Wednesday, 19 August 1987, twenty-seven-year-old Ryan (whom we briefly met earlier) roamed around the historic British town of Hungerford in the County of Berkshire, randomly and fatally shooting seventeen people, including a police officer, before killing himself. Fifteen other people were wounded. Perhaps a simpler way of saying this is: Ryan went on an armed 'walkabout', while Hamilton committed his crimes at a single location (a school). In Ryan's case there was *no* cooling-off period between the events. His was a continuum: a rampage of shootings, using a Chinese variant of the AK-47, all executed over a period of a few hours at various locations not far from each other.

For the record (and here is the knockout blow), it was determined after a lot of expensive psychiatric rummaging around inside the mind Ryan once had that his motive was 'inconclusive'. The psychiatrists (and I quote) 'thought' that Ryan had a 'mental illness'. '*Perhaps suspected* acute schizophrenia *and/or* psychosis' (my italics). There's a lot of post-mortem conjecture going on here, with 'thinking' and 'perhaps' topped up with 'suspected'. No firm diagnosis! In fact, although I am being unprofessionally glib here, if Ryan was as nuts as the medical people think he may have been, what were police doing giving him a licence to own a small arsenal of military-grade firearms in the first instance?

And this is the bit I don't get. Twenty-seven-year-old homegrown Michael Ryan owned... wait for it... a 12-gauge shotgun, two rifles, the aforementioned AK-47, three handguns including a 9mm pistol and an American-made M1 carbine. What was that all about? Well, it was *about* the UK gun laws of the time licensing him to own enough firepower to commit a spree-killing event! We will examine Ryan in more detail soon enough, but it is correct to say that he had passed all of the stringent background checks: he had no criminal record, he was a loner (we cannot hold that against him), notwithstanding the fact that one has to question the mentality of any person who has the need to amass so many firearms and keep them in their bedroom. Not even members of the SBS, SAS, or US Navy SEALS, are permitted to do that!

* * *

On the quiet morning of Sunday, 30 April 1989, in the Tyneside resort of Whitley Bay, twenty-two-year-old civil servant Robert Sartin (b.1968) shot seventeen people during a fifteen-minute attempt to commit spree-killing carnage in the sleepy village of Monkseaton.

Picking up his father's double-barrelled side-by-side shotgun, Sartin left his home and ran amok. Unlike Ryan, who used high-powered firearms, it is perhaps fortunate that during his ballistic bender Sartin was armed only with a shotgun, otherwise the death toll might have equalled that of Ryan's. Sadly as it was, just one man, a Mr Kenneth Mackintosh, aged forty-one, died from injuries caused by Sartin's gunshots. A witness saw him begging for his life before Sartin shot him in the chest, saying, 'Now, it's your day to die,' before continuing on before being arrested by a brave, unarmed police officer.

We can simplify the distinctions between a serial killer, spree killer and mass murderer by using the following examples of a Mr A, Mr B and Mr C. Let us assume that they each have the same firearm – an AK-47 in this instance, with fifty rounds apiece – and each kills ten people:

1. Mr A: is an armed 'serial killer' who shoots his ten victims, at different locations, over a period of a year with cooling-off periods in between the events.
2. Mr B: is a 'mass murderer'. He is static and randomly shoots all of his ten victims at one single location, in one event, within a period of, say, thirty minutes.
3. Mr C: is a 'spree killer', aka a 'rampage killer', who walks around an area, such as a small village, randomly shooting all of his ten victims in a continuum of events as they come into his sights.

* * *

There comes a point when the only way you can make a statement is to pick up a gun.

> Sarah Moore, who attempted and failed to
> assassinate US President Gerald Ford in 1975,
> as widely reported in the press.

The [mass-murder] killings are thus also a form of 'suicide note', literally so with most mass murders, who expect to die before the day or week is out; metaphorically so for most serial killers, who sacrifice the remainder of their lives to the 'cause'...

> Professor Elliott Leyton: *Hunting Humans –*
> *Inside the Minds of the Real Life Hannibal Lecters*
> (2001)

Therefore, we can say that despite their differing motives, the mass murderer and the spree killer do have several things in common – one of which is, more often than not, a 'death wish', as Professor Leyton so neatly explains.

For my part, and I cannot emphasise this enough, these mass and spree shooters know that the second they squeeze the trigger there can be no turning back. The bullet leaves a gun muzzle faster than a genie leaves a bottle and you cannot put either back from whence they came.

For his part, the serial killer is a homicidal games player who tries to pit his wits, his over-inflated opinion of his self-perceived intelligence, against the police with a twisted 'catch me if you can' attitude. He gloats over the media publicity his murders attract, whereas the mass murderer and the spree killer totally understand, whatever their state of mind, that any publicity they receive could most likely be post-mortem. In many cases, they have been nobodies in life. Yet there is a growing phenomenon in which dead mass killers attract a following, becoming elevated to cult status amongst a growing faction of very angry males and some women.

In a nutshell, most of these homicidal offenders are committing a type of 'suicide by cop', a subject we will examine later. It helps to explain why mass murderers and spree killers are mentally wired up in a totally different way to serial killers, being as different as teacher's chalk from strong blue-vein cheese, or, for that matter, a hefty pint of Farmer's Armpit real ale and a flute of the finest – and most expensive – champagne.

3

La-La Land

I raped and strangled her. I dragged her under my rig
to grind off her face and prints.
KEITH HUNTER JESPERSON: LETTER TO THE AUTHOR

Readers, there is a truck stop coming up where you can disembark, stretch your legs, take a leak and perhaps 'tis best not to talk to strangers, Keith Hunter Jesperson (aka the 'Happy Face Killer'; b.1955), who murdered eight victims, was an interstate trucker. He met most of his victims at truck stops just like the one we are at now. He has featured prominently in several of my books. A prolific letter writer, he boasts about how he gave Angela Subrize a ride, then raped and killed her. Thereafter, he tied up her corpse, lashed it with rope to the rear axle of his rig than dragged her some twelve miles until all that was left was the end of the frayed rope.

What stretches my mind to breaking point is that Keith is inundated with women who are besotted with him. Photos, some almost pure porn, along with pledges of everlasting love and support pour into his prison mailbox every month. He actually sent me a photo of a letter from an admirer with what appeared to be a red lipstick imprint on the paper.

Jesperson boasted: 'That's not lipstick, it's menstrual blood!'

In their own warped way, some women and some men – we call them 'murder groupies' – are attracted to those who commit mass murder whether the man is already dead or still in prison someplace, and they don't give a damn about the blood and suffering that has been caused. Is it not a shocking indictment that people from different societies around the world are living in a homicidal hate-filled La-La Land where they find so much pleasure in a mass murderer's actions that they are driven to commit the same atrocities themselves?

* * *

Truck stop over with, for now we must move on to the place signposted 'La-La Land' in our schedule. I pledged from the outset that I would mainly ignore the writings of others, but at this juncture I am obliged to take a diversion from the original route, for the roadside marker directs me to Bruce Porter.

Author of *Blow*, *Snatched* and *The Practice of Journalism: A Guide to Reporting and Writing the News*, Porter has written a very insightful foreword to the aforementioned *Mass Killers: Inside the Minds of Men Who Murder*, by David J. Krajicek. He notes that Krajicek points to 'signposts' that should alert school councillors, teachers and child welfare workers, not to mention mothers and fathers and siblings, all of whom might have the chance to intervene on behalf of a friend or a relative before a killer's instincts explode. To some extent Porter and Krajicek may well be correct, for there are often plenty of signs to indicate that a person may be going off the rails. But how does one deal with someone whose emerging mass killer's instincts *might* explode? Well, let's face facts here: removing any opportunity of this person getting hold of firearms in the first instance seems one of the best bets to me. However, one cannot sanction a person based solely on a suspicion about them, simply because the US Constitution says as much − freedom of speech and thought, as rightly it should be. And this also applies to the UK and most of the other countries in the world, it seems to me. For example, one should not call emergency paramedics just because one suspects that a person might suddenly fall down a flight of stairs and break a leg. One only calls the medics when someone has actually taken that most inconvenient of plunges.

Krajicek's line of thinking is that: 'The signposts that should alert them to something bad coming round the bend are often plain to see. Very few of these high-casualty sprees are impulsive. Killers in this class do not snap.' Without trying to nitpick here, spree killers are not mass murderers in the technical sense, as outlined earlier. Nor do *all* mass murderers or even spree killers 'plan their assaults for months, even years, drawing up detailed battle plans and accumulating expensive weaponry,' as Porter suggests, for statistics tell us that most of these types do indeed suddenly 'snap' and go ballistic with no pre-planning whatsoever. Where I do partly agree with Krajicek is when he writes: 'Less obvious but equally important *is that the approaching "event" creates an emotional state of mind in the killer* that approaches a deep religious awakening,' adding: 'journals and videos left by many of these killers suggest burgeoning acute euphoria as the deadly date approaches, an emotional state that experts often see with suicidal people – like Christians approaching the rapture. *In their minds, the path forward is finally clear. Despair is coming to an end, and a twisted form of immortality is at hand*' (my italics in both cases).

There is a lot to unpack there. Despite any perhaps well-founded suspicions people *might have* that someone who has firearms is going off the rails and into some kind of homicidal mass murder 'La-La Land', until that person commits his act, or is armed and on his way to do the deed, there is little to nothing law enforcement can do about it. Which leaves the 'prevention is better than the cure' scenario presented by Krajicek, now almost tipped upside down.

So why do we attach so much curiosity, and pay so much attention, to serial killers and not mass murderers or spree killers? That is another issue I need to raise here. In cinematic terms, there are countless silver-screen or indie movies, or made-for-TV programmes, either based on true crime, factional, or totally pie-in-the-sky fictional inventions, that include serial murderers in their plots. *The Silence of the Lambs* is not about mass murder, nor is the film *Se7en*, two examples among many more in the same genre. The reason, it seems to me, is that a singular mass-murder or spree-killing event cannot inspire a 'catch-me-if-you-can' thriller-chiller that puts bums into pseudo-velvet cinema seats. Thus, there is no opportunity to engage in one's most popular movie-going feast: a bucket of overpriced popcorn, swigging down a gallon of our most popular fizzy drink, and becoming so terrified by the on-screen butchery that the contents of one's stomach finds itself all over the people sitting in front. Yuck! There is no killer v. cop interplay of homicidal snakes and ladders, either, such as there is between Dr Hannibal Lecter and the rookie FBI agent, Clarice Starling.

The other important aspect missing from many mass-murder and spree-killer cases is that more often than not there is no arrest, namely because the offender has been shot by police or committed suicide. Therefore, no lengthy trial, no colourful ambulance-chasing attorneys and morticians, no stern, no-nonsense judges, no guilty verdicts where the victims' next of kin scream, 'Fry him!' as the guilty guy shouts, 'Judge I hope you die of cancer.' There are no decades of appeals. There's no waste of taxpayers' money. No death sentences Stateside, upon which the media ravenously feed. No gleefully printed articles telling us what the killer ate for his last meal, his last contrite, mumbling words. Simply put, when a mass murderer or a spree killer commits his crimes, more often than not all of that is airbrushed out!

We get too much Bible-thumping, let's-forgive-the-killer-for-his-sins claptrap dished out these days. But watch out for the moment when anti-death penalty, quasi-religious leanings are upended after one of their kiddies gets his or her head blown off. Actually, I think US gun shops must thrive on mass murders, because after such terrible incidents these neurotically driven people go out and buy even more guns and boxes of ammo to protect themselves – and this is a fact.

To summarise: an imaginative screenplay writer can pretty

much invent any type of serial killer plot to keep viewers glued to their seats. But it is nigh-on impossible to make a blockbuster out of a mass-murder event, because the opening scene would be followed in a heartbeat by the finale.

* * *

In Timothy James McVeigh (1968–2001), we have a mass murderer who, with others, carried out the Oklahoma City bombing on Wednesday, 19 April 1995. This was a single truck-bomb explosion set off in front of the Alfred P. Murrah Federal Building, killing 168 people and injuring over 680 others. Amongst his bitter motives was seeking revenge against the US government for the aforementioned Waco siege exactly two years previously. Aged thirty-three, McVeigh was executed by lethal injection at the Federal Correctional Complex in Terre Haute, Vigo County, Indiana, on Monday, 11 June 2001. Below are his last words, a hand-written transcript of the poem 'Invictus' (1875) by William Ernest Henley, and I am referring to them for a very good reason:

> *Out of the night that covers me,*
> *Black as the Pit from pole to pole,*
> *I thank whatever gods may be*
> *For my unconquerable soul.*

> *In the fell clutch of circumstance*
> *I have not winced nor cried aloud.*
> *Under the bludgeonings of chance*
> *My head is bloody, but unbowed.*

LA-LA LAND

Beyond this place of wrath and tears
Looms but the Horror of the shade,
And, yet the menace of the years
Finds and shall find me unafraid.

It matters not how strait the gate,
How charged with punishments the scroll,
I am the master of my fate:
I am the captain of my soul.

And, fellow travellers, you might ask: 'So what?'

Do any of the victims of this man's bombing atrocity truly care two hoots who skippered his obnoxious soul? Do we really think that in some Utopian world psychiatrists, psychologists and social scientists – after reading a famous Victorian poem turned to a killer's self-serving purposes, and *inter alia* the inane scribblings or writings and videos that so many other killers spew out before committing mass murder – can magically analyse this stuff hoping to spot any other emerging mass killers and intervene before the genie blasts out of the bottle? Because this is the way retro-examining a killer's back history seems to be going.

But why study mass murderers and spree killers at all when their homicidal intent is always present in them, will always be so, with so many more to come in the future. Once the bullets leave a muzzle, or the bomb fuse goes 'fizz', there can be no reversing anything at all. To even start to imagine that there is an upfront fix-all, or that we can 'intervene' beforehand when someone is suspected of going off the rails, as some social scientists believe is a way forward... well, I think otherwise. Mass murder using high-powered firearms is on the increase, with incidents becoming almost weekly events in the USA. But once a mass murder has been committed, the horse has already bolted. These killers strike out of the blue. Can there really be some kind of antidote, one that will easily and reliably reduce the frequency of such awful events? Um... yes, there is, actually: take automatic firearms off the streets, as we Brits did years ago! Any bickering from gun owners we took on the chin as easy as pie. The Americans? Well, fifty per cent of them still believe that the ownership of military-grade guns, and selling even more firearms after an atrocity, is the right way to go.

Even the finest academic minds on our planet will never be able to understand the socially mixed up, totally and irrevocably screwed psychopathology of these highly dangerous people, simply because these killers cannot even understand themselves. Every time one imagines a solution *might* have been found, one inevitably find oneself still left out in space, parked up on Planet Ignorance.

There are a number of first-rate authors and psychiatrists and psychologists who maintain that serial killers, spree killers and mass murderers have specific, biological and genetic make-ups that can be identified as early as five years of age. I partly agree with this. However, often these academics overstep the mark with an upside-down ideology, which posits that if we spot someone with such traits, we should inform someone in our Utopian society to 'intervene' in an attempt to prevent that person from 'going live', or as I prefer, from 'going ape!' This is the idea that David Krajicek seems to hold on to, and even to suggest as a way forward, but sadly, although it's an admirable thought, it has to be nothing more than a pipe dream.

Generally speaking, as we have come to understand, with a mass murder there is a definite beginning and a chiselled-in-headstone fixed end, with absolutely nothing, except slaughter, in between. With rare exceptions, there is no 'cooling-off' period during which our fictional cops are able to try and run the killer down, as in the chiller movie *Se7en*; there is zilch intrigue, no Hercule Poirot, no Lieutenant Columbo, no CSI stuff. All we have is some guy. More often these days, it's some American hot-wired-to-kill school kid waking up one morning, attending classes armed with a firearm and blasting away his fellow pupils and teachers because he doesn't like to do his homework, because his mates allegedly bullied him, or because he thinks Adolf Hitler was the dog's bollocks.

Yes, this type of event really hits the primetime media news in a big way, at least for a respectfully short time. And after an appropriate period of mourning, you get Texas lawmakers introducing a whole raft of 'House Bills' like these – and these *are* facts:

1. Armed marshals at schools.
2. Guns can be carried in foster homes.
3. Firearms can be held by tenants in *all* rented apartments.
4. Residents no longer to be charged with a crime for carrying a handgun while evacuating from a state or local disaster area.

5. Allowing possession of firearms at churches, synagogues or other places of worship, unless the priest says it's not OK.

So, let's summarise. As an impertinent Brit, I can imagine the following scenario:

One has bought one's spoilt-brat twenty-year-old son – who has an extreme history of depression and early psychological counselling, who is utterly obnoxious and a school bully – a Kalashnikov and 500 rounds of ammo to please him. But, oh dear, he can't take it to school any more because the place is surrounded by armed guards wearing kit that would make any SWAT officer green with envy. Hey, even the teachers are wearing body armour and packing heat, too. But at least the wife can openly carry her .44-calibre Magnum revolver in the foster home where she works, and the other children can keep a small arsenal in their rented digs in case the landlord kicks up a fuss about the noise.

Luckily, in the UK we don't have county or local disaster areas – not too often anyway, so widespread looting is absent – but at least I and my entire brood can attend church services carrying some flowers and not be tooled up; that would never do, would it? Moreover, if one of my children could not pay their rent to a landlord, at least he will live long enough to issue recovery proceedings in the County Court, and not immediately end up in a coffin.

As for schooling: in the UK we do not require armed SWAT-dressed rednecks patrolling the playground to eyeball parents when they pick up their kids after class. The nearest we get to that is a 33-stone music teacher-cum-doctor's receptionist, Ms Hilda Blodgett, whose sucked lemon expression and laser-intensive gaze can crack a walnut at twenty yards – and that's through her bottle-glass-bottom spectacles – because that's the British way, you see! We don't need wannabe SWAT guys outside our schools, do we? We have the likes of Ms Blodgett, or the ever-smiling gate keeper at my young son Jack's school, whom Jack calls 'Steve', as he leaves the gates following a doff of his cap.

But I have, as I often do, digressed. To refocus: the suicide-by-cop motive behind the Odessa mass shootings was that thirty-six-year-old Seth Aaron Ator (1982–2019) had just been fired (so to speak) from his job at Journey Oilfield Services the previous day. To express his dissatisfaction at summarily receiving his cards because he was an idle trucker, he suddenly got busy and drove over a hundred miles from his home to Odessa. And at a traffic stop, which had been set up after he himself had tipped off the FBI that he was going on a rampage, he opened fire with an AR-style semi-automatic rifle, beginning a terrifying 10-mile rampage in which he killed 7 people, wounding another 20 others between the ages of fifteen and fifty-seven, including three cops as well as a seventeen-month-old girl who sustained injuries to her face and chest. These victims, who were mostly Hispanics, had never heard of Journey Oilfield Services; they didn't know that Mr Ator even existed. Indeed, the world only found out who he was after he had been shot dead outside a movie theatre. Of note: Ator didn't spend weeks, months or years planning his event; he simply flipped and waged some payback time twenty-four hours later because hadn't yet been paid his wages. The fact he had been arrested in 2002 for criminal trespass and evading arrest didn't prevent him from illegally obtaining a gun, thus not being checked out through the National Instant Criminal Background System, although nobody seems to know where he got the gun from in the first place.

The Second Amendment of the United States Constitution, reads:

> A well-regulated Militia, being necessary to the security of a free State, the right of the people to keep and bear Arms, shall not be infringed.

Oops-a-daisy! Hold your horses here, for guess from whence that idea was poached? It was influenced by the 1689 English Bill of Rights: an Act of Parliament that dealt with personal defence for Protestant English subjects. It might appear that we Brits have a lot to answer for when it comes down to gun ownership in a roundabout kind of way – the notable difference being that in the UK these days it's hard enough trying to get a shotgun licence to shoot clay pigeons, let alone the pesky, grubby feathered ones that crap over our parked cars; and neither kind are even edible, come to that. More to the point, when was the last time anyone saw an AK-47 being used on a pheasant shoot? This would greatly upset Her Majesty, with Ma'am saying: 'Oh, that is not on, Philip! Now, flush Prince Andrew from that covert.'

We Brits use a modicum of common sense, not large helpings of gross stupidity. And to lighten the load, here is a fabulous example of True Brit common sense coming from Del Boy in a 1986 episode of TV's *Only Fools and Horses* entitled 'A Royal Flush', where he brings a pump-action shotgun to His Lordship's shoot.

> Rodney: Oi! Where did you get that gun from?
>
> Del Boy: Iggy Higgins.
>
> Rodney: Iggy Higgins robs banks.
>
> Del Boy: I know. But it's Saturday… [In those days banks were closed on Saturdays.]

Back we must scoot to the subject of mass murder and spree killing, to ask ourselves why is it that millions of citizens in the so-called 'Land of the Free', a wannabe Utopian world, live in a continuous state of paranoia? The Small Arms Survey states that out of an overall population of approximately 327.2 million (according to the US Census Bureau, 2018), US civilians own circa 393 million firearms (and that's just the 'legally owned' weapons), which is a staggering 46 per cent of the worldwide total of civilian-held firearms.

What a damning indictment of a civilised country that boasts of its citizens being free.

4

The Star-Spangled Banner

*I could stand in the middle of [New York's] Fifth Avenue
and shoot somebody, and I wouldn't lose any voters.*

US PRESIDENTIAL NOMINEE DONALD TRUMP,
SPEAKING IN IOWA, 2016

Thank the Lord that the Americans (citizens, police *and* military) never got their hands on what is arguably the finest battle rifle ever made: the 7.62mm L1A1 SLR. Please follow me here, as the subject becomes very bleak indeed.

As a Royal Marines Commando, I carried the semi-automatic, wood-stock version – the weapon would later have matt-black pebble-grain composite furniture – with its gas-operated, tilting breechblock, and the 20-round magazine we only filled with 18 cartridges. It was chambered to let loose 7.62x51mm NATO rounds downrange at a muzzle velocity of 2,700 ft/s over an effective range of 875 yds (800 metres).

Unlike the original FN FAL battle rifle, on which it was based, the L1A1 was built to Imperial measurements, and it served for decades. It was used throughout the Suez Crisis, in Northern Ireland and the Falklands Conflict, where, ironically, British troops fought Argentinian troops armed with fully automatic FAL rifles.

And we still won!

The L1A1 SLR was, and still is in some parts of the world, a rifle that truly did the business. Although it was a tad heavy at 9.56 lb, all an enemy could realistically do when fired upon was to use concealment. This Mother-of-all-Rifles could punch a bullet through almost any cover, for this was not a firearm intended to wound. Every shot was a kill shot, no matter where on the body the target was hit. Perhaps a small penetration going into the front of the chest, to blast a dinner-plate size gaping hole out of one's back. Even if struck in the leg or an arm, the victim would suffer a bullet-shattered bone, muscles torn to shreds with shock from haemorrhaging most likely resulting in death shortly thereafter. Fire a round into a watermelon and watch how it explodes – that's what it will do to a human head. Such was its mega power of the L1A1. Indeed, on one occasion an armed IRA terrorist was running away and, after failing to yield on order, he was hit by a single shot from one. The impact was so powerful that he carried on 'dead-man running' some twenty feet before he hit a wall – the blood splatter and brain matter went fifteen feet high. I mention this because firearms such as the L1A1 are designed to kill. I mean, what would be the point in letting rip with a 7.62mm general-purpose machine gun

(GPMG), to knock down a whole group of heavily armed enemy only for them merely to get back up again?

Now I turn to the US-made .35-calibre Remington Marlin 336C lever-action rifle. This was the firearm that mass murderer Ronald 'Butch' DeFeo Jr (b.1951) used to blast his family of six to death at point-blank range while they slept in their beds during the night of Wednesday, 13 November 1974. My book *Talking with Serial Killers* (the first of this series) documents this 'Amityville Horror' massacre in detail (it later inspired the book and movie of the same name), and yes, I have interviewed DeFeo in prison, too. So let's put this particular firearm into some gruesome perspective, just as we have done with the L1A1 SLR.

The .35-calibre Remington Marlin is one of the rifles of choice for taking deer, bear, elk and even moose. Depending on the load, most .35-calibre rounds travel at around 2,100 ft/s (just 500 ft/s slower than the L1A1 SLR), with a .35-calibre round generating around 1,900 ft-lbf of energy.

To make this all the more interactive for you, and for you to get a better sense of the power of this rifle and the noise it generates, please look up the video 'Marlin 35 Remington Range 2' on YouTube. Then imagine these shots being fired, at point-blank range, into two sleeping adults and four kids, inside any house at night.

To reinforce my point, here is the slightly abridged medical examiner's report of the DeFeo mass shooting:

- In the master bedroom, Ronald DeFeo Sr had been shot twice in the lower back. The bullets went through a kidney and spine. One stopped in the neck and the other ploughed through the body and onto the mattress. At autopsy the medical examiner, Dr Howard Adelman, determined that death was most likely instantaneous, since he had stayed on the mattress and did not crawl out of bed.

- Sleeping next to her husband, Louise had been shot twice. The gunfire that had killed her spouse seems to have awakened her, and she was turning in bed towards the doorway from where the shots had been fired. The first bullet entered her back, exited through her chest, re-entered her left breast and wrist before stopping in the mattress. The second bullet destroyed her right lung, diaphragm and liver. Death most likely occurred in a matter seconds, since she never put up any signs of a struggle.

- Marc DeFeo and John DeFeo had each been shot once in their backs. From the evidence, the medical examiner determined that their killer stood less than two feet from the boys when he discharged the rifle. Bullets penetrated the heart, lungs, diaphragm and liver of each victim. In addition, John's spinal cord was severed, causing involuntary movements of his lower body.

- Allison DeFeo had also been shot once. Like her mother, she had awakened and turned her head towards the doorway. The bullet smashed upward from her left cheek to her right ear, entering the skull and brain. The bullet exited, hitting the wall, then bounced on the floor, where it came to rest. Death was instantaneous. Powder burns on and around

Allison's eyes indicated that she was awake at the time and staring down the barrel of the rifle.

- Dawn DeFeo had been shot once, too. Her older brother had stood less than three feet away and fired at the back of her neck. The bullet entered the left ear and collapsed the left side of her face. Brain particles splatted the pillow and the sheets were covered with blood and feathers.

If you have the stomach for it, you can find the shocking scenes-of-crime photographs on the internet, but they are not for everyone, not least those with an iffy, delicate disposition. Oh, and 'Butch' DeFeo owned a 12-gauge shotgun *and* a .22-calibre rifle as well as the punchy Remington. He kept them not in a locked gun cabinet, but in cardboard boxes in his basement living space at the family home: 112 Ocean Avenue, Amityville on Long Island, New York.

Here, we might also usefully refer to the Avtomat Kalashnikova model 1947 (AK-47) 7.62x39mm infantry-type assault rifle more normally associated with the hands of guerrillas and child soldiers. This weapon fires ammo at a combat rate of fire of up to 600 rounds a minute. It is known as the 'Widow Maker'. Compare this weapon and its muzzle velocity to the L1A1 SLR, then imagine what horrific damage this can do when fired into parents and their innocent little kids out shopping in the close confines of a mall, a burger outlet, or inside a church.

In America, they have previously handed out these lethal weapon in untold numbers, simply because that is in line with the aforementioned Second Amendment of the United States Constitution. So what about the victims' rights?

To help to answer this question, I momentarily turn to the guidance of a moral sage – one Al Nolf, former Senior Chief Petty Officer (E–8) at the US Navy from 1968 to 1989. On 1 September 2018, he stated on the Q&A website *Quora*:

> Freedom of Religion. Americans are Free to worship in any way they please. They can even choose not to worship at all, or select Satan as their deity of choice. (Just try that one in the Middle East!)

> Freedom of Speech (and Expression/Press). Americans have an absolute guaranteed right to express their individual point of view, even take out a full page in the newspaper to defame the President if they wish. (Try that in North Korea, Iran... or see if you can publish a page defaming Queen Elizabeth in Britain, or in China: Xi Jinping.)

But here's the good bit:

> Freedom to Bear Arms. A 21-year-old American can walk into a gun store (or Sporting Goods retailer), purchase the gun of his/her choosing, ammunition, & a holster, and walk out. (Many countries around the globe, you cannot do that.)

Yes, dear reader. I understand that I am labouring the point here. But what follows is worth a read, too, for Mr Nolf reminds us that:

> In America we have a US Constitution and a 'Bill of Rights' that guarantees rights and benefits second to none in the world. Our young have been raised having taken them so much for granted, that they are not even aware that other countries don't enjoy the same benefits and standards of living with which they were raised.

Ending, he says:

> People really don't know 'why' America is called 'The Land of the Free' anymore. They have no vision of history, misunderstand the present and are not willing to make a meaningful contribution to the future.

You might wish to re-read Al Nolf's comments to let his words of 'wisdom' really sink in, and perhaps his other observations too. Because he, being a former Chief Petty Officer in the US Navy, can also advise you how to restrain a female appropriately if she needs to be taken away by security. At the same time he can answer questions online, such as this one from an idiot: 'Should I carry a bulletproof vest in the back of my car?'

Al's answer, posted on Wednesday, 4 September 2019, reads: 'No. Having a vest in the back is like saying: "If I'm going to be in an accident, I'll put on my seatbelt." You either have it on when it's needed or you don't. It's your choice.'

'Have it on when it's needed?' begs the question, 'How in God's name will you know when you are about to be shot at?' Anyway, thanks, Al, for confirming that kids as young as twenty-one can arm themselves with a small armoury; soon perhaps we can have kiddies wearing toddler-size, army-grade Kevlar bulletproof vests and diapers while in their strollers, too?

Thank heavens we live in the UK and have no desire to defame our Queen. We don't have to go shopping for bulletproof vests, even less keep them in the boots of our cars, nor do we have to wear body armour while driving to the local greengrocers for some carrots.

If you ask me, it seems that the US Constitution and the Bill of Rights need a bit of tweaking, for this was all put together during the late eighteenth century, an era as different from the early twenty-first century as a flintlock musket is from a full automatic assault rifle.

I shall return to the Bill of Rights in due course.

5

Sandy Hook, Newtown, Connecticut

Serial killers are lame. Everyone knows that
mass murderers are the cool kids.
ADAM LANZA: THE SANDY HOOK MASS MURDERER,

ONLINE IN 2011

Newtown came about because of the British. Being the settling colonists that we were, circa 1707, some folk from Stratford, England, bought several parcels of land from the Native American Pohtatuck tribe. These were basically a peaceful people; although it has to be said that from time to time there were a few squabbles between them and other tribes, only for things to be settled by getting stoned smoking peace pipes in a badly ventilated tepees. It seems that most native deaths were brought about not by bows and arrows but by the diseases and maladies the British and other colonists like the French and the Spanish had imported with them. And here we are now, in a quiet Newtown suburb called Sandy Hook.

Qui transtulit sustinet
Connecticut's Latin state motto: 'He who transplanted still sustains.'

With a present population of around 29,000, Sandy Hook has a history well worth reading. Its notable residents have included Dr James Purdy – no relation to the London firm James Purdey & Sons, who have been specialising in high-end bespoke sporting shotguns and rifles since 1814. A freed slave himself, Purdy helped slaves escape to Canada in the 1850s and came to the aid of the victims of smallpox – imported into North America by European colonists in the seventeenth century – during the American Civil War of 1861–5. Others include Charles Goodyear, who in 1839 developed the vulcanisation of rubber; Joseph F. Engelberger, who has been dubbed the 'Father of Robotics'; and Suzanne Collins, author of book series *The Hunger Games*. Indeed, numerous highly talented people have been born, raised and parked their cars in Newtown and Sandy Hook over the decades. Who would not be attracted to a US state with nicknames such as 'The Nutmeg State' and 'The Land of Steady Habits'? I would, for sure.

And, isn't 'Sandy Hook' such a pretty little village name, conjuring up peacefulness, contentment and large helpings of 'all is peaceful with the world'? It sounds like a long way from other places in the USA, where one might certainly anticipate dark deeds taking place. Dodge City, Kansas, springs to mind, with its 'Boot Hill', 'Fort Dodge Jail' and 'Gunfighters' Wax Museum' 'featuring life-size sculptures of legendary figures Wyatt Earp and Sitting Bull'. There is none of that in Budleigh Salterton, I can assure the reader of this. And what about Tombstone, Arizona, with its very own '1878 Boot Hill Cemetery', where some very dead outlaws are allegedly buried, or the 'historic replica gallows on Allen Street'? One can even visit the replica 'Streets of Tombstone Theatre' which re-enacts the famous 1881 cowboy gunfight at the OK Corral. Note of historic interest: cowboys or gunslingers were never buried while wearing their boots, as these were purloined by the undertaker to help meet his undertakings.

I have to ask myself why do re-enactments at all when you can see the real thing very much on a weekly basis all over America? Watch any news channel on the internet or official download on YouTube and you'll see shootouts happening pretty much every day, all perfectly captured on police dash cams or from the cop choppers and news station helicopters clattering around overhead. One gets none of this in the UK.

There is even the bullet-ridden 'Bird Cage Theater' in Tombstone, which goes to prove how appreciative the audience was of the acting abilities of the thespians whose careers appear to have been short-lived. It is claimed that some of their ghosts still haunt the place. Indeed, I think that local legend has it that one actor playing the part of a gunslinger, ill-advisedly pointed a fake pistol in the general direction of the gun-toting, whisky-soaked paying public, who took fright and opened up with a hail of real hot lead.

Goodness gracious me! Can you imagine this happening during the early days in the Odeon, Walton-on-Thames?

Backing onto the lush Treadwell Memorial Park, the Sandy Hook Elementary School takes the state's motto 'He who transplanted still sustains' to the heart of its children's education. This resonates with all of us when we consider our own children's formative and elementary years of schooling, and how precious our kids' lives are. But not to the twenty-year-old Adam Lanza (1992–2012) who, on Friday, 14 December 2012, shot his mother to death at their home then went on to shoot and kill twenty-six people, including twenty Sandy Hook Elementary School first-graders between the ages of six and seven – the others were members of staff – before turning a gun on himself.

Lanza's weapons of choice were a Bushmaster XM15-E2S rifle and a Glock 20 SF handgun, and this incident remains the deadliest mass shooting at either a high school or a grade school in US history. At the time of writing it is the fourth-deadliest mass shooting by a single gunman in the Land of the Free's history, too.

I think I speak on behalf of all of the victims' families when I say as a former law-enforcement officer that none of us are one bit interested in Lanza's state of mind. We're not interested in what the shrinks or politicians say. They just blow smoke. I am telling you that they'll be arming the teachers next. That's the mess my country is in and it's gonna get a lot worse.

Former Connecticut State Police Detective, Michael 'Mike' Malchik: interview with the author

My dear late friend the legendary homicide detective Mike Malchik cleared up more cold-case murders than any police officer in the state's history. Notably, these include the arrest of the now-executed serial killer Michael Bruce Ross, and of the serial killer James Allen Paul (b. 1947, died in prison 2000) – both of whom I have interviewed, while from Ross I extracted two cold-case admissions of murder, too. (See my book *Talking with Serial Killers* for an account of his life and crimes.)

As for Lanza's motive in committing mass murder, I have to refer back to Mike Malchik's comments to me, all of which I entirely agree with. He said it as it is, no punches pulled. After all the smoke and mirrors of political brinksmanship, the debates, the promises to ban semi-automatic military-type firearms, and the bald-faced lies, nothing much has changed, as the mass-murder calendar so reliably informs us to this very day. And not just in the USA but throughout some of Europe, too.

As in the aftermaths of all such horrific mass-murder and spree-killing events, there was the inevitable enquiry into how and why Lanza ran amok in Sandy Hook, with a detailed November 2013 report issued by the Connecticut State Attorney's office, concluding that Lanza acted alone. Wow! So no big surprise there, then! As to why he murdered his mother (four gunshots to her head) then targeted the school, that report offered no clues.

However, another report, issued in 2014, this time compiled by the Office of the Child Advocate (a very lengthy document it is too, so no room for it in this book), summarised that amongst a whole raft of other mental issues,

Lanza did have Asperger syndrome and as a teenager suffered from depression, anxiety and obsessive compulsive disorder. But it concluded rather lamely that 'these issues had neither caused nor led to his murderous acts' and ended with the patently obvious, 'his severe and deteriorating internalised mental health problems [...] combined with an atypical preoccupation with violence [...] *[and] access to deadly weapons* [...] *proved a recipe for mass murder*' (my italics).

Perhaps I am being simple-minded here, but so what? One might reasonably assume that there must be millions of teenagers across the world suffering similar negative mental issues as young Lanza, but they don't all kill their mother then run amok with lethal firearms and kill a whole bunch of kiddies and their teachers, do they? Not all, not even most of them... but, as we shall see later, some do.

It is a fact that one cannot realistically commit mass murder, or wander off out someplace to wantonly kill on such a large scale, armed merely with a knife. Neither can one commit such a murderous undertaking using one's bare hands or a ligature. I truly believe that we can all agree on this – well, I hope we can – so this leaves would-be perpetrators of mass atrocity with a choice of, broadly speaking, a bomb, a truck, poison or firearms. The latter, of course, applies in the case of the Sandy Hook Elementary School killings.

So where did Lanza get his two weapons? In this instance, it was from his fifty-two-year-old mom, Nancy. Yep, mommy owned a Bushmaster XM-15, a model similar to an AR-15 semi-automatic military rifle/carbine, and she had the top-performing Austrian-made Glock recoil-operated pistol, too. And for what reason, you might ask. If one of my divorced mumsie neighbours, with her mentally disturbed, hyper-wired-up son who was into kiddie porn, and who plastered photos of past mass-murder events over his bedroom wall, was living a few doors down, and I learned that she owned a Bushmaster and a Glock pistol, I would move post-haste. Wouldn't you?

In the interest of giving my readers a little more information, and with no expense spared, I looked up the FBI's most recent, and fairly reliable, 2019 crime statistics issued annually for Newtown, Connecticut. Overall there had been a drop in crimes, with levels reaching the lowest point since 1967. In an effort to avoid criticism from eagle-eyed readers, I hasten to add that these FBI crime statistics are compiled on a 'voluntary issued basis'; they are not mandatory and therefore are not exactly 100 per cent accurate, US-wide.

Nonetheless, it has to be said that fifty-one-years of decreasing crimes is quite a remarkable achievement. Arrests had also dropped by 41 per cent since 2009, with a predicted 6 per cent fewer arrests compared to 2017. Indeed, the FBI's Uniform Crime Reporting Programme confirmed that in the period in question there had been no homicides, 6 reported rapes, 2 aggravated assaults, 14 burglaries, 77 larcenies (the most common being shoplifting, with an average value of $165 lost per theft), 6 motor vehicle thefts plus a reported case of arson. So, when one takes a peek at Newtown's crime statistics, and compares them with those of other individual states, and then the national US rate as a whole, it's quite obvious that the Nutmeg State is one of the safest places in the country. So much so that Connecticut's prison population has dropped by 4,097 (23 per cent) inmates since 2011. Indeed, Connecticut is on track to cut its prison population by half within a few years. So, successful has this model been, other states are looking to Connecticut as an example of smart policy reforms and the positive impact they are having.

More to the point, the Sandy Hook district comes out top of Newtown's safest areas to live. Statistics show that a resident has a mere 1-in-2,524 (0.39 per cent) chance of becoming a victim of violent crime in Newtown, while in Connecticut overall there is a 1-in-439 (2.28 per cent) risk. The country's national median is 4 per cent.

Now, if Mrs Lanza had been living in Detroit, Michigan, then I could understand why she might need to own powerful firearms, simply because the violent crime rate in Detroit is a staggering 2,123 crimes per 100,000 people. But she wasn't – she lived in sleepy Newtown, Connecticut.

The Connecticut gun laws of the time stated that while Lanza was old enough to legally carry a 'long gun', such as a shotgun or a rifle, he was too young to own or carry handguns, which kind of makes some sense to me. That said, a rifle is a rifle and they can be deadly accurate, powerful and lethal. But what does not make any sense – unless one lives on another planet far away from our own, or believes that President Donald Trump is 'The Second Coming' – is the fact that the FBI have files (1,500 pages in total) on young Lanza. To kick things off, there was evidence that amongst numerous other 'faults', he had an 'unhealthy interest in young children that could be categorised as paedophilia – but no proof existed that he had acted on it'.

The Feds also learned that Lanza had compiled a spreadsheet that 'meticulously documented hundreds of mass murders and spree killings'. Furthermore, a young woman who knew Lanza very well gave evidence that he believed that mass murders were 'a symptom of a broken society', and that during the school shooting he may have believed he was saving children from the 'harmful influences' of adults. There was a lot more to this report but some of it, along with many names, had been redacted.

Can you see a parallel with the aforementioned Michael Ryan here? It is all 'maybes' and 'may have believed'. You might rightly ask: why did Lanza not kill adults only, instead of also murdering little children?

In keeping with the sentiments expressed by the late Mike Malchik, let's say it as it is. Here we have a single mom, living in one of the safest towns in the country, who according to the American Constitution had 'the right to carry and bear arms'. And, the bottom line is that Nancy Lanza had a delinquent youth with a whole compendium of mental shortcomings residing between his ears; more than enough to keep the shrinks at the Office of the Child Advocate busy for two whole years trying to figure out how he had previously been wired up – an exercise that was a total waste of money and time.

The psychiatrists asked themselves whether Lanza's problems were issues of nature v. nurture, or nature and nurture, perhaps a diet deficiency, or even bad potty-training as an infant, while they thumbed through the then current *Diagnostic and Statistical Manual of Mental Disorders*, published by the American Psychiatric Association. Just like the FBI's final 1,500-page report, no investigative agency could come up with anything other than a million-dollar zilch.

Before I end this piece on this, the most tragic of mass murders in US history, I would like to bounce the following back to my readers, by asking this simple, open-ended question. You – being a loving and responsible single mother or father – raise a youngster with, sadly, a completely dysfunctional mental narrative such as that of Adam Lanza. Would you leave any sort of firearm lying around your home – be it paintball gun, long gun or shotgun – let alone a Glock pistol, or an army-type assault rifle with boxes of ammo? Answers please to the FBI, although there is a distinct probability that they will never reply.

At the time of writing (November 2019), I note that the US Supreme Court has ruled that a lawsuit against the firearm manufacturer Remington Arms, based in Madison, North Carolina – brought by families affected by the 2012 mass shooting in Newtown – could move forward. The justices rejected an appeal from Remington Arms, who had argued that the company came within the provisions of a 2005 federal law, which prevents lawsuits against firearms manufacturers when their products are used during the commission of crime.

This is a fascinating case as far as I am concerned, with the prosecution and defence both putting up their own good legal arguments in equal proportion. The 2005 Protection of Lawful Commerce in Arms Act (PLCAA) gives gun makers and dealers sweeping protections from prosecution. It's an act – as might seem blatantly obvious – totally supported by the NRA and other gun-rights advocates, to prevent lawsuits they fear could help cripple the firearms industry.

Prior to this legislation, lawsuits against the gun industry have generally failed. Nevertheless, the industry was, and remains very worried that a successful case might eventually break through. Therefore, since that law was passed, it has been repeatedly cited by courts to dismiss litigation against gun manufacturers and dealers.

According to an article on the *Vox* website by German Lopez, dated Tuesday, 12 November 2019:

> The families behind the lawsuit pointed to exceptions to legal protections in the PLCAA, including for gun makers and dealers that violate state marketing laws. The families argued that their lawsuit fell within the exceptions, so enabling them to sue Remington for what they described as irresponsible marketing... . Remington argued that the Connecticut Supreme Court interpreted the exceptions too broadly, and appealed its case to the US Supreme Court. Now that the appeal has failed, the lawsuit will proceed in the lower courts.

We will see a similar Florida case in Steelman v. Garcia Gun Center & Ithaca Gun Company later in this book. More broadly, gun-control advocates have pushed to *totally ban* assault weapons. As might be expected, research by the pro-gun lobby indicates such a ban would not have a 'significant impact' on overall gun violence because most US killings are carried out with handguns.

With the US Supreme Court having now ruled in favour of the Sandy Hook litigants, the case will now go back to the lower court for a ruling, and don't expect Congress to pass an assault weapons ban anytime soon. As things stand, the court's order allows the lawsuit filed in the Connecticut State Court by a survivor and relatives of nine victims who died to go forward.

6

Freddie Flintlock

At the time America's forefathers, aka 'The Framers', were framing the US Constitution, almost the only firearms in existence were the 'Long Land' pattern 'Brown Bess' muzzle-loading smoothbore flintlock muskets. The musket appears to have been a British invention and an import, although I expect my French readers will frantically disagree, adding *'Va te faire foutre!'* or something like that. Nevertheless, its rate of fire was restricted: it could only fire a single ball, or a cluster-style shot of multiple projectiles giving the weapon a 'shotgun' effect, before it needed reloading.

Using ball ammunition, the musket was effective on a man-sized target at up to 50 yards (46m); all pretty much hit and miss at 100 yards, but to be frank with you, anything further away was purely speculative, a bit like a shot in the dark. With considerable fiddling about, reloading time in expert hands took around twenty seconds, and an ordinary soldier could shoot three times a minute – that's if a bouncing cannonball hadn't taken his head off during the interim.

Long rifles – so named not just from their length, but because the barrels were rifled with spiral lands and grooves to impart spin on the ball, thus affording greater accuracy – were an American design of the eighteenth century, and were produced by individual immigrant German gunsmiths living in Pennsylvania. Known as 'Pennsylvania Rifles', these were mainly used by snipers and light infantry throughout the Revolutionary War of 1775–83. An effective battle range of up to 300 yards became achievable, the downside being that the reloading time with this rifle was similar to that of the musket, achieving, in favourable conditions, a rate of fire at about three shots a minute.

The flintlock pistols of this age enjoyed effective ranges only out to about sixty feet, at best. Therefore, they would have been entirely unsuited for a sole person mass shooting on a grand scale – one like the aforementioned Sandy Hook shootings, for example.

Assuming one didn't have a flintlock pistol with two, three, four or more barrels for multiple shots (there were some), loading time even for experts on the battlefield took just over fifteen seconds. If you were not an expert, had fumbling fingers and it was raining, making keeping your powder dry your number-one priority, while you were simultaneously shitting bricks as the enemy – fixed bayonets and whites in their eyes – bore down on you, loading time was likely far longer than fifteen seconds. Perhaps even long enough to beat a hasty retreat!

Sadly, however, and lacking a crystal ball, when the Founding Fathers gave people the green light to bear arms there was no way in a million years they could have imagined that this licence would carry forth down the centuries. Or that it would later give US citizens the inalienable right to buy and bear military-style assault rifles firing up to 600 hundred rounds a minute over distances thought pie in the sky in the eighteenth century.

Similarly, as their home-made aircraft momentarily went airborne, brothers Wilbur and Orville Wright could never have envisaged that less than a century after they bounced a few hundred yards on what amounted to a glorified kite, Concorde would be whizzing around the world at 2,179 km/h – not a couple of feet above terra firma but at 60,000 ft (over 11 miles up). From up there, one can see the curvature of the Earth, and *not* just the Kitty Hawk hedge directly in front of the nose of the Wright Flyer's pilot – stalwart Orville himself, whose twelve-second flight in the Flyer marked the first sustained flight in a heavier-than-air contraption.

Using the great gift of hindsight, maybe giving American citizenry the right to buy and carry arms was not such a bright idea after all. I hazard a guess that as these gents in their powdered wigs, breeches and waistcoats sat around a table at night, candles spluttering low with their shadows dancing on the walls, they might have passed around a flintlock pistol, while collectively agreeing that it would be impossible to commit mass murder with a muzzle-loading, single-shot weapon like that.

What we *do* know is that between 1980 and 2018 mass shootings in the USA have risen from 25 incidents to 160 per annum, although in 1995, according to at least one source, only three mass shootings took place. Quite why this anomaly occurred I cannot tell you. The issue may be that the precise inclusion criteria for mass shooting are hotly disputed. In the USA there is no broadly accepted definition of a mass shooting, although it seems pretty obvious to me, and I hope to you, too. *Inter alia*: that if a person goes out heavily armed, lets loose a shower of lead with the intention of killing a lot of people in a single incident, with others wounded adding to the toll, then that is a mass murder. Yet confusion still reigns supreme amongst people well paid to spend decades up to their academic necks searching for exact definitions.

'Confusion' is the American way. Yet, not to be thwarted, a non-profit research group called The Gun Violence Archive defines a mass shooting, as an 'incident in which four or more people, *excluding* the perpetrator(s), are shot in one location at roughly the same time' (my italics). I wonder if there is a Gun Violence Archive Museum someplace in the USA. Tombstone, Arizona, perhaps?

The Congressional Research Service (CRS), however, thins that out a bit – considering what it defines as 'public mass shootings' its definition excludes ' ... the survivor impact – lightly injured, seriously wounded, left permanently disabled and even traumatised for life'. In other words, *it only considers victims as those who are killed to the exclusion of any other individuals who are wounded, maimed for life, or who die sometime later from their wounds*. Perhaps there should be a Congressional Research Service Hall of Fame, as well?

According to The Gun Violence Archive, the Sandy Hook massacre wouldn't be defined as mass murder, when applied to some of the injured victims.

So imagine that your loved one has been maimed for life, or died some time later from gunshot wounds following a mass-shooting event. But they aren't defined as the victims of mass murder, although they may have been emotionally traumatised for life or passed away as the result of their wounds, say a month or even a year later.

To muddy things even further, *The Washington Post* and the magazine *Mother Jones* (*MoJo*), use similar topsy-turvy criteria, with *MoJo* acknowledging that their definition 'is a conservative measure of the problem, as many rampages with fewer fatalities occur'. Do they heck. Mass shootings are now an almost weekly ritual; meanwhile, even a rare bilateral US House of Representatives does very little except sit on the fence. But to be fair to these congressmen, like political lemmings they have to follow the Second Amendment come what may, even if their fellow Americans are being shot down in droves during mass-murder events on a regular basis.

Still, help is allegedly at hand. The definition of mass murder from the crowd-sourced Mass Shooting Tracker project – 'four people shot (including wounded) in one incident regardless of the circumstances' – is perhaps more on target than that of the Gun Violence Archive. Elsewhere, though, the Stanford MSA Project throws its spanner into the works, with 'three plus people shot in one incident, at roughly the same time, excluding organised crime, as well as gang-related and drug related shootings'.

I can mostly live with that last criterion. Because if mobsters, Yardies, Crips, Bloods and drug dealers want to blast each other away, that's fine by me – perfect, to the degree of heaven-sent, as it effectively represents the in-house culling of a violent, extremely antisocial species. Think, for example, of the St Valentine Day's Massacre on Thursday, 14 February 1929 at 2122 North Clark Street, Chicago.

This particular antisocial event took place when seven members and associates of Chicago's 'North Side Gang' were lined up against a wall of the Lincoln Park Garage and shot to death by four unknown men, two of whom were dressed as cops. A most agreeable occasion for one side, not so much the other side, which occurred when normal people were sending cards and costly bunches of flowers to others without revealing who had sent these tokens of affection. (Which all defeats the object, if you ask me – and, yes, I do sound very much like the grumpy Victor Meldrew from the British sitcom *One Foot in the Grave*, don't I?)

As impertinent as this may sound, especially coming from a British criminologist, I think that the CRS has got itself into a pickle with the part of its definition of mass shootings that reads 'the survivor impact – lightly injured, seriously wounded, left permanently disabled and even traumatised for life'. For those unfortunate people are being bluntly informed by the CRS that they were not involved in a mass shooting, although many more folk in their immediate proximity were shot dead.

I think this is ridiculous. On many occasions, a mother has been carrying a child when both were hit. The child dies and the mother survives. Yet, as the CRS has it, the child has been the victim of a mass shooting, the mother not!

I am now looking at the total number of mass-shooting victims in the USA from January 2019 through to the following August (and that year is not over yet, as I type):

- January x 28 incidents: 48 killed, 86 wounded.
- February x 22 incidents: 38 killed, 68 wounded.
- March x 21 incidents: 13 killed, 89 wounded.
- April x 34 incidents: 23 killed, 136 wounded. One of which took place at a school, another at a place of worship.
- May x 43 incidents: 40 killed, 181 wounded. One of which took place at a school.
- June x 48 incidents: 40 killed, 217 wounded.
- July x 52 incidents: 50 killed, 202 wounded.
- August x 49 incidents: 89 killed, 240 wounded. Five of which took place at schools and one at a place of worship.

Clearly, the US mass-shooting trend is on the up and up, with occasional dips in between. On the other hand, when one sees that 297 men, women and children have been shot dead in mass shootings in 8 months, with a further 1,519 wounded – many to suffer lifelong mental and physical trauma – it becomes blindingly obvious that anyone who believes that he's living in the Land of the Free is out of touch with reality. If one has to wear a bulletproof vest, carry a pistol for protection when attending church or going to school, believes an assault rifle is a must-have when shopping at a mall or while tucking into a meat-filled bun with fries on the side at a burger outlet, or go just about anywhere else in the USA, then one is living in fear. Furthermore, if one needs to hoard in one's home the sort of high-power semi-automatic arms used by the military – and for what reasonable purpose? – then one is not only over-the-top neurotic but must be suffering from incontinence on an almost hourly basis.

Well, consider this. In 2018 alone, 11,984 people (and the meter is still running at the time of writing as the figures I'm using only cover from January to October) were killed by firearms in the States. It seems politicians from both the Democrats and Republicans have signally not been up to the task of coping with the plague of gun violence. It's no wonder that the cops have itchy trigger fingers.

'Tis no surprise that when officers pull a vehicle over for a traffic violation, they have one hand on their sidearm. Indeed, there are plenty of examples on YouTube showing fatal shootouts in which police are killed by some driver, or vice versa, during traffic incidents. Here, in the UK, if a motorist is stopped for some reason the bobby will be as chilled out as can be, with an:

''Ello, 'ello, Iggy, and what are *we* up to then? And where is your shotgun?'

'It's Saturday, guv. The banks are closed, so I lent it to Del Boy.'

In 2018 alone – which included the carnage at a synagogue in Pittsburgh, Pennsylvania – there were 47,200 gun-related incidents with 12,000–plus deaths. This breaks down as more than 32 deaths a day. Moreover, these shocking figures do not include the 22,000 gunshot suicides; of the total fatalities, 548 were young children while 2,321 were teenagers.

THE PITTSBURGH 'TREE OF LIFE' MASSACRE

HIAS [the Hebrew Immigrant Aid Society] likes to bring invaders in that kill our people. I can't sit by and watch my people get slaughtered. Screw your optics, I'm going in.

ROBERT BOWERS: POSTING ON THE ONLINE 'GAB' FORUM SHORTLY BEFORE THE ATTACK

The mass shootings on Saturday, 27 October 2018 in Pittsburgh, Pennsylvania, occurred at the Tree of Life – also known as the L'Simcha Congregation – in the Squirrel Hill neighbourhood, while Shabbat morning services were being held. Eleven elderly people were shot dead, seven were injured.

The suspected shooter, armed with an AR–15 SP1-style Colt semi-automatic rifle and three Glock .357 SIG handguns (types 31, 32 and 33) was Robert Gregory Bowers (b.1972). This forty-six-year-old was arrested and charged with sixty-three federal crimes, some of which are capital offences. The trial has yet to take place, but if he is convicted the chances are high that he may be executed by lethal injection.

Sadly, the word count allocated to me for this book forbids a fuller account of Mr Bowers's somewhat antisocial history, all of which can be found online. But he certainly seems to have taken full advantage of living in the Land of the Free, being a right-wing extremist, neo-Nazi white supremacist and vehement Holocaust denier. Yet despite advertising all of these interests on the internet, and stating that he wanted to kill Jews and favoured lynching, not one single person, not one single blogger, brought this man's apparently homicidal intentions to the attention of US law enforcement for even one attempt at 'intervention'. And why should they?: Mr Bowers had the legal right to keep and bear arms and the right to freedom of speech, too. And what if someone had informed the authorities? What would have happened then? I reckon the advice might have been along the lines of:

Um, so what? Mr Bowers does have the right to free speech, you know. He has the right to bear arms. He has every right to be a neo-Nazi and deny anything he doesn't like. So, even if he wants to hang himself, that's f*ck all to do with you, sir.

Thank you for calling the FBI. Have a nice day, now.

7

The University of Texas Tower Massacre, Austin

*I don't quite understand what is compelling me to type
this note. I have been to a psychiatrist. I have been having
fears and violent impulses. I've had some tremendous
headaches in the past [...]*
*After my death, I wish an autopsy on me be performed to
see if there's any mental disorders [...] I hate my
father with a mortal passion [...] I intend to kill my
mother and my wife after I pick her up from work.
I don't want her to have to face the embarrassment
my actions will surely cause her.*
Life is not worth living.

CHARLES WHITMAN: SUICIDE NOTE WRITTEN THE EVENING BEFORE
HE WAS SHOT DEAD ON MONDAY, 1 AUGUST 1966

Born on Saturday, 24 June 1941 in Lake Worth, Florida,
Charles Joseph Whitman seemed at face value to be the All-
American Boy; the sort of good-looking chap that you would

have been pleased to greet when your daughter introduced him as her first date. As a youth, Charles was a model son: intelligent; an Eagle Scout; an accomplished pianist; altar boy at the local Catholic church and very popular amongst his peers. So later, millions of people across the USA and around the world would suck their thumbs and wonder: what the hell went wrong?

For go wrong he most certainly did.

> I taught all my boys to use guns [...] Charles from the age of two. All of them are good.
>
> Charles Adolphus Whitman Jr, father of
> Charles Joseph Whitman

Without question, Mr Whitman was a strict disciplinarian to his three boys; a man who used violence to impose his rules around the family home, even abusing his wife as well. It is said that this 'discipline' negatively affected his eldest lad, Charles; however, Whitman Senior did try to instil into him a need to be the best in all things he turned his hand too. After graduating from high school seventh in a class of seventy-two students in June 1959, the eighteen-year-old enlisted in the US Marines. Joining a force of some 182,000 fighting men and women, Cadet Marine Whitman took his oath to honour the US Marine Corps motto 'Semper Fidelis' (Latin: 'Always Faithful') and he soon jolly well pissed all over their parade. Alas, though, his father didn't learn about this recruitment for some time, and when he heard of his son's actions he telephoned a branch of the federal government to try to have the enlistment cancelled.

His request fell upon deaf ears. His son won a US Navy and Marine Corps Force's scholarship programme to study engineering at the University of Texas, and it was here that he met his future wife, Kathy. They married in August 1962.

So far, so good – until, that is, the proverbial hit the fan. In December 1964, Whitman was court martialled for gambling and moneylending (loan sharking). His academic work suffered; his scholarship was immediately withdrawn; he was dismissed from the Marines.

Quite what his father made of this state of affairs we will never know. However, it had been drilled into young Whitman to succeed at everything, so he went back to university and, impatient to get on well, he overloaded himself with classes in an attempt to obtain his degree more quickly. Adding to this pressure, at the same time he began studying to become a real estate agent, all of which he hoped might help him and his wife prosper. Needless to say, this merely added another stress string to his already taut mental bow. And, as we all know, strings can, without warning, snap.

The precursor came about during March 1966, when Whitman's parents split up. Margaret left her vicious husband because she could no longer tolerate his habitual violence. In fact, Whitman had driven to his boyhood home in Florida to bring his mother back with him to Austin – to a place of safety, where he was now living. But then his father was on his son's back again, frequently phoning to attempt to persuade him to bring his terrified wife back home, and this affected young Whitman greatly.

He had an already established short fuse, and his temper

now grew worse. He feared that he would take out his anger and frustrations on his own wife, Kathy – whom, it has to be said he adored. Sadly, however, by now he had already struck her a few times, so he began confiding in his close friends that he intended to leave her; that he had an urge to climb the university tower in Austin armed with a deer rifle. He told his pals that he wanted to shoot people, but his buddies talked him out of it, as did a university psychiatrist in whom Whitman had confided.

> Man is basically a battlefield. He is a dark cellar in which a well-bred spinster lady [the superego] and a sex-crazed monkey [the id] are forever engaged in mortal combat, the struggle being refereed by a rather nervous bank clerk [the ego].
>
> Don Bannister: clinical psychologist, gently mocking Freud's vision

At this point in Charles Whitman's life we might almost understand where he is at. Undoubtedly he was an articulate, intelligent young man striving to better himself, to live up to the high expectations his strict father expected of him. And despite having now been thrown out of the Marine Corps, he had picked himself up and marched on. He was also bright enough to understand that there was something wrong going on inside his head. He told a few friends that he suffered constant, severe headaches; an evil voice was telling him to kill people while his good self was desperately fighting against it. I have interviewed a number of serial killers who say that they have experienced similar mind splits – a sort of Dr Jekyll and Mr Hyde interference. And I vividly recall the serial killer Michael Ross telling me this while he was on Connecticut's death row:

> I felt like a spider trying to climb up a glass window. I wanted rid of the terrible thoughts inside my head but as soon as I got near to the top I fell down again. An' it was like having an obnoxious neighbour who kept coming round uninvited and getting on my nerves. When I was under medication this neighbour lived down the hallway and left me alone. As soon as the medication was stopped he came back again.

Whitman knew that he was on the verge of doing something terrible. He loved his mother and adored his schoolteacher wife, who also worked part time as a telephonist to supplement the family income. But the evil thoughts inside his mind were winning. He knew what he had to do, but he had to do something to shield Margaret and Kathleen from the shame his future actions would bring about.

He would have to kill them first.

* * *

Margaret Whitman was forty-four years old when she was murdered by her son. She was plump, greying and bespectacled, the abuse she had suffered for twenty-six years at the hands of her husband having ensured that she looked much older than her years. A shy, polite lady, she had worked as a cashier since her son had brought her to Austin.

During the late evening of Sunday, 31 July 1966, Whitman

drove to his mother's apartment at 1212 Guadalupe Street. Here, after a brief struggle in which Margaret's fingers were broken when her hand was slammed in a door, her now crazed son stabbed her in the chest, then killed her instantly with a shot to the back of her head. He picked up her body, placed it onto the bed then pulled up the covers. Before he left, he wrote a note attacking his father, adding, 'I love my mother with all my heart.' Then he rearranged the rugs to cover the bloodstains on the carpet.

Kathleen Whitman, *née* Leissner, was just twenty-three years old when her husband murdered her. The daughter of a rice grower, she had graduated from the University of Texas in 1964. Around 3 a.m. on 1 August, Whitman silently went into the bedroom of their home on Jewell Street; then, placing his hand over her mouth, he plunged a hunting knife three times into his sleeping wife's chest.

We would be right to ask ourselves: why didn't he kill his father and be done with it – get rid of this bullying, wife-beating patriarch problem once and for all? Why murder the two people he said he loved desperately, not the father he hated? Then, perhaps, he should have written a suicide note and shot himself to save a lot of terrible suffering to so many innocent lives. As a former US Marine, that might have been the honourable thing to do, yet he chose to commit suicide by cop, in which a suicidal individual deliberately behaves in a threatening manner with intent to provoke a lethal response from law enforcement.

We will return to that question, and come to Whitman's own death, soon enough. But Houston McCoy, one of the two police officers who shot and killed him, believed that

Whitman could have easily shot him and his fellow cop Ramiro Martinez, but that 'he was waiting for us and wanted to be shot'.

At this juncture, I think it's worth considering the cases of two other ex-US servicemen–cum–mass/spree killers who committed suicide by cop:: Mark James Robert Essex (1949–73) and Gavin Eugene Long (1987–2016).

In two attacks in New Orleans, Louisiana, on Sunday, 31 December 1972 and Sunday, 7 January 1973, Mark Essex killed nine people, including five police officers, and wounded thirteen others. His weapons were a Ruger Model 44 .44-calibre Magnum carbine and a .38-calibre Colt revolver.

Essex had been discharged from the US Navy in February 1971 as unsuitable for service because of 'character and behaviour disorders'. He had joined up as a dental technician in 1969, but went AWOL for nearly a month in the autumn of 1970; he was later to claim that he had been subjected to a couple of years of constant racial abuse while serving in San Diego, California. Thereafter, he had joined some of San Francisco's black radical groups, and is said to have subsequently fallen in with the Black Panthers in New York. By late 1972, however, he was in New Orleans. He claimed that while training to repair vending machines, in November 1972, he had been unsettled and enraged by the punishment meted out by police officers to student civil rights protesters (two of whom were shot dead by cops) at Southern University in the state capital, Baton Rouge, which historically has had high numbers of African-American students.

Essex was finally gunned down on the roof of a Howard Johnson's hotel as he picked off strangers on the streets below. As sharpshooters finally cornered him and a helicopter clattered overhead, he put up something like a General Custer's Last Stand in a concrete blockhouse on the roof, but died in a hail of bullets that left him riddled with 200 gunshot wounds.

On Sunday, 17 July 2016, military veteran Gavin Long – who, like Essex, had also been stationed in San Diego – shot six Baton Rouge police officers in response to the highly controversial killing of thirty-seven-year-old Alton Sterling. Sterling had been shot dead at close range on Tuesday, 5 July 2016 on 2112 North Foster Drive, by two of the city's white cops. Long's firearms were a 5.56-calibre IWI Tavor-21 SAR rifle and a 9mm Springfield XD semi-automatic pistol. The IWI Tavor-21 is an Israeli 'bullpup' assault rifle chambered in 5.56x45mm NATO calibre, with an effective firing range of 500 m.

Four people died in Long's final shootout – including Long himself – and three were injured. Videos of his ambush, and slaying, of Baton Rouge police can be found online, but this is to entirely miss the point. Which is: why on earth was Mr Long allowed to own such a lethal military-grade firearm in the first place?

Now take a look at the YouTube video entitled 'IWI TVOR SAR' – it's the 3.47-minute one. The guy showing us his 'first-hand experience' with this weapon is almost breathless– compulsory viewing for all US gun nuts. Even better is the video 'Tavor x 95: The "FUTURE" Rifle?' Haven't these enthusiasts ever seen what such a weapon can do to living, breathing innocent people? I can tell you this much: show these videos to any special forces guys, be they

SAS, SBS or US Navy SEALS, and they would doubtless want to stick these enthusiasts into a real-life battle situation and watch their reaction.

So let's get back to Charles Whitman. During his initial eighteen-month service between 1959 and 1960, he'd earned the Marine Corps Expeditionary Medal and a sharpshooter's badge. He was a crack shot, achieving 215 of 250 possible points on marksmanship tests, doing well also when firing rapidly over long distances and at moving targets. This man was trained to use a firearm with unerring accuracy, and he was just about to this again – this time from his eagle's nest atop the University of Texas Tower.

At 9am that August morning, Whitman drove to a store where he bought a secondhand bolt-action Remington 700 ADL 6mm with telescopic sight, after which he visited Chuck's Gun Shop, where he bought hundreds of rounds of ammunition. Next he was in a local branch of Sears Roebuck, purchasing on credit a slide-action Remington Model 141 .35-cal and a Sears-branded Model 60 12-gauge semi-automatic shotgun. Finally, he went to a tool supply store where he rented a foldaway three-wheeled trolley before returning home to ready himself for his 'mission'. His other long arm was a Universal M1 .30-cal semi-automatic carbine. His sidearms: a Smith & Wesson Model 19 .357 Magnum revolver, a 9mm Luger P08 and a .25-calibre Italian Galesi-Brescia, the two last both being semi-automatics. He also had three hunting knives.

Note a total absence of any computerised, centralised state or federal gun purchasing register that would have immediately red-flagged to any other gun stores that Whitman was suddenly buying a small arsenal of firearms and ammo. Buy a television in the UK and the TV licensing authority know about it in milliseconds, yet in the USA Whitman bought enough weapons within an hour to commit mass murder and no one gave a fiddle.

> Ye shall know the truth and the truth shall make you free.
>> John 8:32: inscription in massive block letters at the entrance of the University of Texas Tower

Whether or not this former US Marine marksman thought he was a Rambo-type we will never know, but he had packed enough supplies to withstand a siege. Zipping a pair of grey nylon overalls over his blue jeans and white shirt, Whitman loaded the locker into the trunk of his Chevrolet Impala, and drove to the 307-ft-high white granite tower housing the University of Texas administration offices, soaring high above the surrounding buildings to command views all over the city. This sort of sniper vantage point has an advantage, but signally also a terminal disadvantage: it's an ideal location for a coward to rain down gunfire on unarmed people but one is up shit creek when trying to get back down alive when armed opposition turn up en masse.

To give you a cinematic example of the perils of a high shooting position, I refer you to the 1970 movie *Kelly's Heroes*, starring Clint Eastwood. Upon arriving at the town of Clermont, one of Private Kelly's men climbs a church tower to take up a sniper position and spot German troops. All good so far, but then a Panzer tank swivels its turret, elevates its gun, and BANG! It's the end of the soldier, the top of the tower, bell and all.

But I have digressed.

Using a lift, then lugging his stuff up four flights of stairs, Whitman arrived at the twenty-seventh floor, which opens onto the public observation platform, and here at the reception desk sat fifty-one-year-old Edna Townsley. A widow with two teenage sons, her suspicions must have been aroused when this out-of-breath, sweating stranger, pulling a three-wheel trolley loaded up with so much kit suddenly appeared. Indeed, I would have imagined that she questioned him along the lines of: 'Good morning, sir, and the rifles are going to be used for... what?'

To avoid any fuss, Whitman mercilessly clubbed Edna unconscious with a rifle butt, then dragged her behind a sofa. At this very moment, a young couple came in from the observation deck. The girl sheepishly smiled at Whitman, who grinned back, then discreetly steered her boyfriend around a large puddled bloodstain on the carpet in front of Mrs Townsley's desk, to make a judicious exit down the stairs, passing a family who were on their way up.

M.J. Gabour owned a gas station in Texarkana, Arkansas. He had brought his wife, Mary Francis, and teenage sons Mark and Mike, to Austin to visit his sister, forty-five-year-old Marguerite and her husband William Lamport. As the group climbed the stairs, Whitman stepped out and fired three rapid shotgun blasts. The boys and the women spilled back down the stairs. Sixteen-year-old Mark was killed. Mike Gabour and his mother were seriously injured. Mary would be paralysed from the neck down for the rest of her life. Mike, a cadet at the US Air Force Academy, would live, but his legs were horribly damaged from the shotgun blasts

Whitman then barricaded the door and finished off Mrs Townsley with a shot to the head, and now he was alone, protected by a chest-high limestone parapet 18 inches thick. Below him, the campus spread serenely in the sunshine, the handsome white buildings with their red-tiled roofs separated by lush green lawns and malls. It was 11.45am. There were not many people about; morning classes would not end until 12.20pm, following Whitman's ninety-six minutes of destruction.

He selected his bolt-action .35-calibre Remington rifle with the telescopic sight. This firearm has a muzzle velocity very much the same as the aforementioned 7.62mm L1A1 SLR: with a bullet energy of circa 1,920 ft-lbf (foot-pound), it packs a deadly wallop and has a realistically maximum 'effective' range of 200 yards (183m), although that's still 100 yards less than the average battle range of the SLR. Depending on the load, 150 yards may be a better estimate for the Remington, so Whitman was firing at the rifle's maximum effective range, but he was a trained marksman and he was using a scope, not firing over iron sights.

He put his head over the parapet. He squinted, selected a target, held his breath and gently squeezed the trigger. BANG!

His first bullet went low, ripping through the leg of seventeen-year-old Aleck Hernandez, who was cycling around the campus delivering newspapers. Whitman made a sighting adjustment then three students fell in quick succession and the shooting continued as the cops arrived.

McCoy was a true Texas hero. He was an extraordinary man, quiet and a great police officer.

> Officer Jerry Day: on his colleague,
> Houston McCoy

With bullets flying everywhere and people dropping left, right and centre, three Austin PD officers – Ramiro 'Ray' Martinez, Houston McCoy and Jerry Day – managed to zigzag across the open plaza around the tower to get inside. Here, they met a plainclothes APD officer called Dub Cowan along with Allen Crum – a university bookstore employee who had just completed twenty-years' service in the USAF.

> You are not going by yourself.
> Allen Crum: to Martinez and McCoy

'Are we doing this for keeps?' asked Crum, while insisting on accompanying the cops. 'You're damn right,' replied Martinez, so Crum was given a rifle and deputised on the spot.

The four men rode the lift to the twenty-sixth floor to where Mrs Lamport and the Gabours lay. Mr Gabour attempted to wrest a gun from the officers, so Officer Day took the man downstairs to safety. The other three men inched their way 'service style' up to the reception area, where they slowly pushed aside the barricade. Using an overturned desk as a shield, they crawled out onto the observation gallery on their hands and knees.

Martinez, who had a .38-calibre sidearm, and McCoy, armed with a 12-gauge shotgun, went one way, Crum the other.

Unit 34 (Harold Moe) to Headquarters. We have got
that man. Martinez got him.

Call # 15 AR.2000.002 Box 5: dispatch recording

As Crum approached the western corner, he heard the
sniper's pattering footsteps coming towards him, so he loosed
off a rifle shot, which smacked into the parapet, tearing away
a chunk of stone.

Whitman ran back the way he had come and, as he
rounded a corner into Martinez's line of sight, the officer
fired. Whitman whipped round and fired one wild shot from
his semi-automatic rifle. Martinez, who had never fired a gun
in anger before, emptied his pistol into the crazed Whitman,
who went down, still clutching his weapon. As he thrashed
around on the stone floor, McCoy fired at him twice with
the shotgun. But as Whitman was still moving, still holding
on to his weapon, Martinez grabbed the shotgun from his
colleague, stepped forward and allegedly fired point-blank at
the mass-killer's head to finish him off like the mad dog that
he was. I say 'allegedly' having read the medical examiner's
report, because the post-mortem photos of Whitman's head
do not show the trauma one might expect to see when a
shotgun is discharged at pretty much point-blank range.

REPORT MADE BY OFFICER LIGON
REGARDING CONTENTS OF TRUNK (AS LISTED)
AND GUNS FOUND SCATTERED AROUND
OBSERVATION DECK:

1. Channel Master 14 Transistor AM-FM radio
   (portable) brown case

2. Robinson Reminder (note book, no writing)
3. White 3½ gallon plastic water jug (full water)
4. Red 3½ gallon plastic gas jug (full gas)
5. Sales slip from Davis Hardware for August 1, 1966
6. 4 'C' cell flashlight battery
7. Several lengths of cotton and nylon ropes (different lengths)
8. One plastic compass ('Wonda-scope')
9. One paper mate ball point (black)
10. One Gun Tector, green rifle scabbard
11. Hatchet
12. (Nesco) Machette [sic] with green scabbard
13. (Hercules) hammer
14. Green ammunition box with gun cleaning equipment
15. Alarm Clock, 'Gene' brand
16. Cigarette lighter
17. Canteen with water
18. Rifle Scabbard, green, 'Sears'
19. Hunting knife (Camallus) with brown scabbard and whitt stone [i.e. a whetstone]
20. Large knife (Randall) with bone handle name of <u>CHARLES J. WHITMAN</u> on blade with brown scabbard with whitt stone
21. Large pocket knife (wooden handle) lock blade
22. Pipe wrench (10").
23. Pair eye glasses, brown frame and brown case
24. Box of kitchen matches.
25. 12 Assorted cans of food and two cans Sego, jar honey

26. One can charcoal starter
27. White and green 6-volt flashlight
28. One set ear plugs
29. Two rolls tape (white adhesive)
30. Approximately one foot long solid steel bar
31. Army green rubber [duffle] bag
32. Green extension cord
33. Lengths of clothes line wire and yellow electric wire
34. Bread – sweet rolls
35. Gray gloves
36. Deer bag (same bag)
37. 6mm Remington, (full 20 box) shells – ammunition
38. 35 Remington (full box) shells
39. 35 Remington (full box) shells – 'Peters'
40. 35 Remington (full box) shells
41. 357 Mag (Peters 50 rounds) full box
42. 357 Mag Western (full box)
43. 357 Mag Western (7 shells)
44. 30 caliber 'Peters' (2 full boxes).
45. Box Western 25 caliber auto. (approximately 40 in box)
46. Box Remington 9mm Luger (full box)
47. Box 35 Western two shells

Guns found around body:

1. Remington Model 700 – 6mm, Bolt action #149035 with Leupold four power – M8-4X scope, cheek stock (serial #61384) and leather strap
2. Sears 12-gauge 2-3/4 chamber automatic shotgun, barrel and stock, both sawed off

3. Remington 35 caliber model 141 pump #1859 rifle
4. US carbine 30 caliber M-1 Universal #69799 with Webb sling
5. 357 Mag Smith and Weston [sic] 4 ½ barrel, chrome, Model 19 #K391583
6. 9mm Luger #2010
7. 6.35mm Caliber Automatic pistol – Galesi-brescia #366869

I keep returning to that observation made by Mike Malchik: 'So what if a killer had a disturbed mind?' Do the victims' families really care a jot what is going through these monsters' heads? However, something did spring into my mind while researching Whitman, for his autopsy had revealed a small tumour, about the size of a walnut, in the area at the back of his brain associated with emotional responses.

Interestingly, none of the medical authorities could agree on the physical or psychological effects that this tumour might have had on Whitman's state of mind. Some thought it could have produced headaches, others that it would have significantly affected his fragile emotional stability. The state pathologist (see above) was adamant, however, insisting that it was benign and could not have caused pain; that said, he does not seem to have addressed the issue of whether or not this would have affected Whitman psychologically. Another report commissioned by the Governor of Texas, said it was malignant and would have killed Whitman within a year, and that it could have contributed to a loss of control. All of which proves one thing: that no medical person back then, and none of them today, possesses a single clue as to what turned Charles Whitman into a mass murderer, More to the point, even if we did know what went wrong with his head, it still changes nothing, does it?

As Professor Elliott Leyton succinctly points out in his book *Hunting Humans*, and I paraphrase here: 'Often the police are regarded as stupid and brutal, yet it is obvious that they appear to possess more intelligence and insight into the killers than do the professionals.' And, this is further endorsed by the distinguished American psychiatrist William Gaylin – someone who does know what he's talking about – who freely admits: 'Most of us are aware how trivial, ephemeral, descriptive, and meaningless are psychiatric diagnoses.' In my own experience, I have witnessed time and again the way that many of Gaylin's colleagues are unaware of this problem yet willingly allow themselves to be used, in the crassest possible way, by any legal team that hires them.

> The guy's the fuckin' Devil. They should have fried him years ago, period, an' they would have queued up to pull the switch. When he was dead, they should have driven a stake through his heart and buried him, digging him a week later to ram another stake in, just to make sure he was fuckin' dead.
>
> Detective Russell J. Kruger: Chief Investigator, Minneapolis PD, on Harvey Carignan, to the author at interview, 1996

As a slight digression, I recall the 1975 trials of sado-sexual serial killer, Harvey 'Harvey the Hammer' Louis Carignan (b.1927), whom I later interviewed at the Minnesota

Correctional Facility (MCF), Stillwater. My book *Talking with Serial Killers* contains many of his conversations with me, and there no prizes to you, the reader, for guessing correctly that his two trials revolved around lengthy psychiatric debate.

For the defence, the late and highly regarded Dr Hector Zeller argued that Carignan was a paranoid schizophrenic who hated his mother because she had rejected him, but he did not want to kill her because God would not approve. 'He believes that he is an ambassador of God and that his mission was to kill certain women,' Zeller propounded. Whether Zeller actually believed this seems unlikely, because after Carignan was found guilty his co-counsel, Joseph Friedberg, told him: 'I would not advise you to dress in a white robe and wear leather sandals at your next trial. God didn't help you this time so I doubt he will ever help you again!'

In any case, isn't being an ambassador of God a nonsensical claim to have from the mind of a homicidal sexual psychopath – especially from one who hadn't been inside a place of holy worship in his entire life? Even more stupid because we only have Carignan's word for this, as unfortunately God was unable to back him up – at least as far as I am aware, God's name didn't appear in any witness list. And if it had He certainly didn't appear throughout the proceedings. Yet we have to doff our cap to the Mexican-born Dr Zeller, for he was one of a rare breed of psychiatrists who would willingly mitigate in favour of killer's state of mind, at once recommending to any court that the man should be locked up.

One day... just *one day*... we might be able to find
just two psychiatrists who can agree with each other.

> Prosecution psychiatrist Dr Dennis A. Philander:
> throwing his hands in the air following
> Harvey Carignan's first trial

Who cares if Harvey is a fruitcake? I tell you this,
those psychiatrists are as mad as he is.

> Robert Nelson, MPD: one of the two
> arresting officers [Robert Thompson] to the
> author during an interview

Carignan used to type many lengthy letters to me every
week – and I mean very long, rambling letters in which he
went on and on about not much at all. Then, his typewriter,
which he named 'Clyde', broke and the prison refused to
pay to have it repaired. According to one of the guards, this
was the first time a typewriter had ever become airborne as
Harvey slung it out of a window. Thereafter, he was reduced
to writing in longhand, in a style suggesting an inebriated
spider having crawled out a bottle of ink and staggering
across the paper. Can you imagine receiving four voluminous
letters written like that every week? Never mind Charles
Whitman's headaches, what about my own?

The lesson is that human behaviour is complex, and a
brain lesion is neither necessary nor sufficient as an excuse
for criminal conduct. There are nearly 700,000 people living
in the US with brain tumours, and approximately 800,000
US citizens have strokes every year, but the known cases
leading to criminality number in their dozens.

Another theory as to why Whitman flipped is put forward by Gary Lavergne. In his biography of the murderer, *A Sniper in the Tower*, Lavergne suggests Whitman was aware of the international infamy achieved by the murderers at the heart of Truman Capote's 1966 novel-based-on-fact *In Cold Blood*, and that just seven months later, Whitman was seeking the same sort of lasting, true-crime notoriety. 'He climbed the Tower because he wanted to die in a big way,' Lavergne wrote, and one might suppose that he succeeded, because five decades later, Whitman's name is still synonymous with US mass killings. However, I am not sure that I can agree with Lavergne's theory that Capote's *In Cold Blood* was a contributing factor to the Texas Tower massacre. In fact, I don't buy into it one bit.

In Cold Blood has sold millions of copies and has been translated into thirty languages. It was initially made into a black-and-white movie of the same name in 1967, then a TV mini-series in 1996. But are we to accept that it was only Whitman who became so deeply 'impressed' with the plot that it formed a seed in his mind from which his murderous intentions grew, when the USA, has a long and bloody history of mass murders dating back more than a century? I think not.

Probing a little deeper, it seems that Whitman had become clinically depressed to the degree that no matter how hard he struggled to succeed in life, he reasoned that the odds were always stacked against him. He was under a great deal of stress. Headaches and migraines are more likely to occur when one is subject to great emotional tension, which, along with other triggers, can make the suffering even worse to the degree that some say it feels like a clamp squeezing the skull.

The other point worth raising is this: I have never come across an emerging serial murderer or spree killer who, knowing that he is about to embark on multiple homicide, starts advising his friends then consults a psychiatrist of his murderous intentions beforehand. In fact, aside from Whitman, I cannot find a reference to any other mass murderer ever doing so, either. I mean, what would be the point?

Without implying any mitigation whatsoever, it seems clear to me that Whitman had psychologically reached the end of his life's journey. He was at his wits' end. Having emotionally arrived at the end of the line, and planning suicide, in his fragile mental state he first decided to kill his mother and wife to save both the ignominy and mass of public attention that would inevitably be generated and surely heaped upon them after his deadly 'mission' was completed.

> Revenge is barren of itself: it is the dreadful food it feeds on; its delight is murder, and its end is despair.
> Johann Christoph Friedrich von Schiller:
> writer and philosopher

To return to a question I raised earlier: why did Charles Whitman not kill his father, whom he hated with a passion? It occurs to me that in not doing so, Whitman was actually punishing his father big time, in that he would have to live with the shame of his son's actions for the remainder of his days. Revenge is a dish best served cold, they say. And why did Whitman specifically choose the University of Texas tower as his sniper's nest? The answer to that stares us straight in the face. His *raison d'être*, I suggest, is that aside from his father he also harboured a deep-seated grudge against the US Marine Corps for summarily discharging him – albeit honourably – for his illegal loan-sharking activities. I have no doubt in my mind that this was a grudge he dwelt upon, one that festered in his mind. Every time he failed after that he would be pathologically transferring the blame for his problems onto the Marines, most certainly not on his own shortcomings.

He had earned a sharpshooter ranking at boot camp in South Carolina. He served at Cuba's Guantanamo navy base for more than a year. The US Marines had taught him to become a crack shot, so he would show the corps precisely what he could do: pick off people reduced by distance almost the size of ants from several hundred yards away.

Whitman's Texas Tower killings certainly have inspired others – all of whom it appears sought and will seek the infamy that he achieved post-mortem: the copycat killers. We might well say that Whitman's legacy has encouraged others.

* * *

According to recent figures from the Centers for Disease Control and Prevention, 39,773 Americans were killed in shootings during 2017 amid a growing number of suicides involving guns, marking the onward march of firearm fatalities in a country renowned for its lax approach to gun controls. And one of these suicides was Hunter Stockton Thompson, who is quoted in the epigraph at the beginning of the Introduction to this book. Big time into shooters, booze and drugs, he shot himself in the head at his home, Owl Farm, near Woody Creek in Colorado, at 5.42pm on Sunday, 20 February 2005. Johnny Depp made a 1998 movie of his best-known book, *Fear and Loathing in Las Vegas,* and seven years later Depp would finance Thompson's dying wish: for his remains to be shot out of a cannon at his funeral – way to go, bro!

Writing in *The Guardian* on Thursday, 13 December 2018, Ed Pilkington noted of those 39,773 fatalities: 'When adjusted for age fluctuations, that figure represents a total of 12 [firearm-related] deaths per 100,000 people – up from 10.1 in 2010 and the highest rate since 1996.' He continues: 'What that bare statistic represents in terms of human tragedy is most starkly reflected when set alongside those of other countries.

'According to a recent study from the Jama Network, it compares with rates of 0.2 deaths per 100,000 people in Japan, 0.3 in the UK, 0.9 in Germany and 2.1 in Canada.' The US's gun-crime rate per capita may be below those of Brazil, Mexico, Colombia, Venezuela and Guatemala, but all six taken together are responsible for more than half of all 250,000 annual domestic gun deaths around the globe.

At the time of writing, much public attention is on the intense tragedies of gun massacres in the USA. In fact, most suffering takes place in isolated and lonely incidents that receive scant media coverage. That said, the year 2017 saw the deadliest mass shooting by an individual to take place in the country in modern history when fifty-eight people died in a rampage on the Las Vegas Strip on Sunday, 1 October.

THE UNIVERSITY OF TEXAS TOWER MASSACRE

He's a sick man, a demented man. A lot of problems, I guess. We are looking at him very seriously. But we are dealing with a very sick individual.

> US President Donald Trump: on mass
> murderer Stephen Paddock and offering
> no condolences to the victims, while boarding
> Marine One, 3 October 2017.

On the day in question, Stephen Craig Paddock (1953–2017) opened fire into a crowd of approximately 22,000 concertgoers attending the Route 91 Harvest Country Music Festival on the Las Vegas Strip. As I write, this incident is the deadliest mass shooting by a lone gunman in US history, with 59 fatalities (including Paddock himself) and 851 injuries (422 by gunfire).

This sixty-four-year-old retired accountant, real-estate investor, property manager, amateur pilot and keen poker player committed suicide in the Mandalay Bay Hotel and Casino hotel room with a self-inflicted gunshot to his head. His weapons included no fewer than fourteen .223-calibre AR-15- type automatic rifles, eight .308 calibre AR-10-type rifles, a .308-calibre Ruger American bolt-action rifle and a .38-calibre Smith & Wesson 342 revolver. His arsenal also included a large quantity of ammunition in special high-capacity magazines, holding anywhere from seventy-five to one hundred cartridges each. Some of the rifles were resting on tripods, and were equipped with high-tech telescopic sights. All fourteen rifles were outfitted with 'bump fire stocks' that allow semi-automatic rifles to fire rapidly – simulating fully automatic gunfire.

This mass shooting once again reignited the controversy over gun-ownership laws, but the people who Trump said were 'looking into [Paddock] very closely' – i.e. the White House and Republicans – brushed aside any attempts to discuss firearm policy. To add insult to injury for the souls who lost their lives or were wounded, some maimed for life, when asked whether the Las Vegas shooting would prompt him to take up gun control, Trump responded:

> Look, we have a tragedy. What happened is, in many ways, a miracle. The police department, they've done an incredible job, and we'll be talking about gun laws as time goes by. But I do have to say how quickly the police department was able to get in was really very much a miracle. They've done an amazing job.

To return briefly to the case of Charles Whitman. His personal effects, including his firearms, remained in police custody until 1972 when they were auctioned off to augment the fund set up to help the victims of his crimes. In the UK, these lethal weapons would rightly have been destroyed. Nevertheless, the firearms once used by this mass murderer to cause seventeen deaths, including that of an unborn baby, and wound thirty-one, fetched $1,500 from a dealer in Kansas. One might wonder in whose hands these guns are now.

What macabre, morbid, twisted logic is there to be had in successfully bidding for such sick trophies to help support fund-raising for the victims' next-of-kin? After all, their loved ones were shot to death by the very same firearms. In fact,

I have met a lot of these 'morbidity collectors' during my road trips around the USA, and you will find the sellers and buyers of such trash online, too. From the clown portraits painted by the sado-sexual bisexual serial killer John Wayne Gacy (1942–94) to the recently worn panties belonging to deadly femme fatales and 'Black Widows', you can find much of this disgusting stuff on the internet – if one has the warped inclination to do so. Indeed, there is a big market for the alleged drawings of serial murderers, even though only the signature is real because the artwork is nearly always by another inmate.

It doesn't stretch even my imagination too far to imagine some overweight redneck loser paying around £1,000 to hang the Whitman guns in his 'den'; to show them off to his equally moronic buddies. Then on Sundays, after church, instead of going to the mall they load up into a battered pick-up truck and drive down to the range to let loose with the actual weapons, 'as used by Charles Joseph Whitman'.

Having got all of that off my chest, I leave this chapter on a mute note. Let's return to David Krajicek and the theory put forth in his book, to which I referred earlier, that when suspicions arise that someone is becoming unstable, and is sending out increasingly evident signals that they are about to explode, then intervention is advised.

Whitman told several of his friends *and* a psychiatrist that he intended to kill a lot of people; so where was the 'intervention' there? But then, in his foreword to Krajicek's book, the writer, journalist and former *Newsweek* editor Bruce Porter makes a very valid point, one that I agree with one hundred per cent:

Too often, reporters searching for answers come back with a list of childhood traumas and adolescent personality traits that, as a way of explaining the roots of the latest bit of horror, seem deeply unfulfilling.

They endured abuse from their fathers or schoolyard bullies, they played too much Dungeons and Dragons in the attic, they suffered from low birth weight, or had a brain tumour. Excuse me, but individuals possessing these same characteristics end up far more often leading perfectly normal lives rather than going out and shooting a lot of people.

That passage has nailed it in one. The comment echoes the sentiments of Professor Elliott Leyton, the Canadian social anthropologist, educator who is amongst the most widely consulted experts on serial homicide worldwide. In a letter Elliott wrote to me over a decade ago, he said much the same thing as does David Krajicek. To paraphrase him: 'Millions of kids have dysfunctional childhoods and are raised by dysfunctional parents, but they don't turn out to become serial killers or mass murderers, do they?'

8

Reloading with 'Precipitating Psychosocial Stressors'

'*What we've got here is failure to communicate. Some men you just can't reach. So you get what we had here last week, which is the way he* [Luke Jackson, played by Paul Newman] *wants it… well he gets it.*'

THE CAPTAIN (THE LATE STROTHER MARTIN): ADDRESSING

THE CONVICTS ON HIS PRISON FARM IN THE MOVIE

COOL HAND LUKE (1967)

The previous chapters have brought us neatly to the subject of this chapter. For as we blindly struggle in our attempts to understand the growing pandemic of mass murder (which the facts prove is just that – a pandemic, of sorts) and the twisted minds of those who are driven to kill our innocent loved ones in numbers – our children, even those still in their mothers' wombs – at least we must recognise, and accept, that easy access to firearms is a prime facilitator. For had Charles Whitman, and scores of other mass murderers not been able to arm themselves to the teeth, those killings would not have happened.

We have also noted along our Mass Murder Road trip that many psychiatrists have no definitive answers as to what goes on inside the heads of mass murderers or spree killers. Therefore, it occurs to me that perhaps we have been using the wrong optics when trying to understand their motivations: it is if we might be studying them through the wrong end of the telescope. Peering through my own virtual telescope, what do I observe? Abject losers; non-achievers; individuals apt to be society censorious, impulsive and possessing mediocre, desponding natures brimming with delusions. So I would like to think that the 'responsible gun owners' and members of the NRA in the USA would endorse my sentiments to the hilt. If they did, that would be as good as getting some 5.5 million men and women onside.

And, here, I sense a childlike, chuck-one's-toys-out-of-one's-cot anger-management problem coming into our road trip.

The most commonly used psychiatric diagnosis for sudden aggressive, angry or violent behaviour in adults is termed an 'Intermittent Explosive Disorder' – when one flips, big time. It's characterised further by repeated failure to resist aggressive impulses that can result in serious assaultive acts, or destruction of property. And I will extend this to the extreme of committing mass homicide, as was the case with Whitman and others of his ilk.

Of all the DSM-IV-TR diagnoses, it seems to me that these characteristics– without even a hint of psychobabble whitewashing – come closest to accurately describing the escalating explosions of domestic violence many societies are witnessing today. It follows that those who commit mass murder are non-achievers with a classic anger disorder, as in *ballistically extremis*.

We're all familiar with 'road rage', a psychological disorder in which motorists experience sudden heightened levels of stress, anxiety or hostility because of their driving environment. The man who flips the finger at another driver, who in turn, loses the plot going on to inflict serious injury, or even kill in a road-rage event, is but one almost example of someone acting grossly out of proportion to the provocation. Or, as the shrinks might say – if they are not bickering amongst themselves – 'suffering from precipitating psychosocial stressors'.

There will not be many British true-crime readers who have not heard of Kenneth Noye (b.1947), so I won't trouble you with a lengthy account of this man's life of crime. So let's cut to Sunday, 19 May 1996: while on release from prison on licence, forty-nine-year-old Noye, driving a dark-green Land Rover Discovery, was on a slip road of the M25 motorway, near Swanley in Kent. Here, he got into an argument with another motorist, twenty-one-year-old Stephen Cameron. Noye stabbed the younger man to death.

In the US, 37 per cent of aggressive driving incidents involve a firearm. In the UK, the motoring organisation the RAC reported in December 2018 that almost half (43 per cent) of UK drivers have been the victims of road rage, with more female motorists (49 per cent) targeted by an angry motorist than male drivers (at 37 per cent). I hope the reader is following me here because I am about to make another strong point about firearms. There are over 38.6

million vehicle licence holders registered on the UK roads. And 66 per cent of traffic fatalities are believed to be due to aggressive driving. Imagine if the Brits had as many guns per capita as they do in the USA, with all these precipitating psychosocial stressors on our roads...

That said, can you see the problem here with 'precipitating psychosocial stressors'? Can you imagine us lay people sitting as a jury and hearing a defence attorney pleading like this:

'My young God fearing-raised client, born and lovingly nurtured in the Land of the Free, was suffering from a precipitating psychosocial stressor when he failed his social sciences exam. So he stormed off home, picked up his dad's military assault rifle and a .357-cal Magnum revolver and put on body armour, before returning to class and shooting dead everyone sitting at their desks and a bunch of teachers, too.' Adding: 'I have gotten to know Richard over many months now. He would be welcome in my home at any time after you, members of the jury, find him innocent of all charges.'

This sort of crime and defence happens all too often. Please take my word for it.

I don't like Mondays – this livens up the day!
Brenda Ann Spencer, aged sixteen: following her mass murder attempt outside the Grover Cleveland Elementary School, San Diego, California, on Monday, 29 January 1979.

If we are to believe it, red-haired sixteen-year-old Spencer was suffering from a 'precipitating psychosocial stressor' caused by the fact that she lived opposite the Cleveland Elementary School on Lake Atlin Avenue, San Diego. As she later explained to police, she hated the noise the excited children made when they returned for classes after the weekends.

Her back history is of some interest to us, if only to prove a point: how on earth did this teenager get hold of a lethal firearm? So, before I explain, you might like to pour yourself a stiff drink and settle back.

In a nutshell, Brenda's parents, Dorothy 'Dot' and Wallace 'Wally' Spencer, had separated and the young girl lived in poverty with her father. They slept on a single mattress on the living room floor, and it was reported that police found empty liquor bottles and other types of detritus one would expect to find with folk living under such squalid conditions. After her arrest following the school shooting, police learned from some of Brenda's friends that she often expressed hostility towards policemen; she had spoken about shooting one and had talked about doing something big to get on television.

She has, indeed, gained a degree of 'fame', if one can call it that. Bob Geldof, then the lead singer of Irish band The Boomtown Rats, read about the shooting. He was particularly struck by Miss Spencer's claim that she did it because she did not like the start of the week; so, along with keyboard player Johnnie Fingers, Geldof wrote the 1979 hit song bearing the title 'I Don't Like Mondays'. And although Spencer didn't quite make it to the silver screen, *I Don't Like Mondays* was the title of a 2006 TV documentary about this sickening event.

Young Spencer had shown exceptional ability as a photographer – ironically, winning first prize in a Humane Society competition – but was also a truant, often fell asleep during classes and was exhibiting suicidal tendencies. She was known to hunt birds in the neighbourhood, was arrested for shooting out the windows of Grover Cleveland Elementary School with a BB gun, and for burglary.

In December 1978, her behaviour became so unruly that a psychiatric evaluation arranged by her probation officer recommended that she be admitted to a mental hospital for depression – so there was *an attempt* at intervention here. But Mr Spencer refused to give his permission. And wait till you hear this – that Christmas, Brenda had asked her father for a radio; instead, this moronic man, this 'Wally', gave his out-of-control sixteen-year-old daughter a Ruger 10/22 semi-automatic .22-calibre rifle with a telescopic sight and 500 rounds of rimfire ammunition.

This particular rifle has a maximum 'flat' range of about 125 yards (114m), so one doesn't need a scope for that distance. However, Brenda's stocking fillers *did* include a telescopic sight that enhanced her shooting abilities even more. When we refer to the 'flat' range of circa 125 yards, the NRA puts the maximum range of a standard .22 long rifle (LR) at 1,588 yards (1,452m), so a .22 LR round will easily travel about a mile or more when fired in an arc through the air.

At a distance of just 50 yards (47m), on the morning of Monday, 29 January, Miss Spencer started shooting at children waiting for fifty-three-year-old Principal Burton Wragg to open the school gates. They made for easy targets. Wragg fell dead first as he tried to get the kids into cover. Then she aimed at fifty-six-year-old school janitor Mike Suchar, as he attempted to pull a student to safety; he too was shot to death. In all, she fired thirty rounds – eight children and a police officer were injured, after which she barricaded herself inside her home for several hours. Ultimately, she surrendered.

Spencer, Brenda, CDRC #W14944, is presently housed at the California Institution for Women on Chino-Corona Road, Corona, CA 92880, where she still hates Mondays and every other day of the week. Well, there is no pleasing some people, is there?

Coincidentally, on Tuesday, 17 January 1989, almost a decade after the Spencer shooting, there was another event at another school also named Cleveland Elementary, this one being situated at 20 East Fulton Street, in Stockton, California. Also known as the 'Stockton Schoolyard Shooting', it saw Patrick Purdy (1964–89), who had an extensive criminal history, run riot. Five students were killed and thirty wounded before he shot himself in the head. His motive remains unknown.

An unemployed former welder and drifter, Purdy had armed himself with a Norinco 56S type of Chinese-made AK-47 semi-automatic rifle and a Taurus PT92 pistol. With a long list of criminal antecedents stretching way back to his teens, he was duly imprisoned for being an accomplice in armed robbery and for unlawful possession of firearms. He descended into drug abuse, and after two suicide attempts 1988 found him living with an aunt in Sandy, Oregon. It was here that he obtained the AK-47 at the Sandy Trading Post. On Wednesday, 28 December, he purchased the Taurus pistol at the Hunter Loan and Jewelry Company in Stockton. As in the aftermaths of all such tragic events, the mass murder at Stockton received national news coverage and again spurred calls for regulation of semi-automatic weapons, with *Time* magazine asking the most obvious question: 'Why could Purdy, an alcoholic who had been arrested for such offences as selling weapons and attempted robbery, walk into a gun shop in Sandy, Oregon, and leave with an AK-47 under his arm?' Reflecting precisely the theme of this book, *Time* magazine continued: 'The easy availability of weapons like this, which have no purpose other than killing human beings, can all too readily turn the delusions of sick gunmen into tragic nightmares.' I award another prize, this time to *Time* magazine for simple common sense.

It is fair to say that, following the Stockton schoolyard shooting in California, some well-intended measures were taken to define, then ban assault rifle-type firearms, resulting in the Roberti-Roos Assault Weapons Control Act of 1989 (AWCA). This state law was wide-sweeping, for it made illegal the ownership and transfer of over fifty specific brands and models of semi-automatic firearms classified as assault weapons; most were rifles, but some were pistols and shotguns. The law was then improved and amended to restrict the acquisition and transfer of magazines that could hold more than ten rounds of ammunition. But what about the firearms and magazines that were already legally owned when this law was passed? In effect, the weapons were 'grandfathered' – passed from father to son – if the receiver had no criminal record and was registered with the California Department of Justice.

On the federal level, and as might be expected, Congressional legislators bickered and argued as they struggled to find a means of banning weapons such as military-style rifles without banning sporting-type rifles, too. This in itself is a bit of a puzzle, for why would anyone need an AK-47, or an AR-15, or an M16A4 5.56x45mm NATO rifle to go shooting deer or rabbits? One would have thought that applying some logical thinking to differentiate between the two categories would have been as easy as shelling peas, but not Stateside. Instead, they settled for a halfway house when, in 1989, Alcohol Tobacco and Firearms (ATF) issued a rule citing the lack of 'sporting purpose' to ban the importation of assault weapons.

It really was that easy because in July 1989, the G.H.W. Bush administration made the import ban permanent. The Federal Assault Weapons Ban was enacted in 1994. It expired in 2004. President Bill Clinton then signed another executive order that banned importation of most firearms and ammunition from China.

At the time of writing, estimates vary as to how many rifles are owned in the USA. The National Shooting Sports Foundation has estimated that approximately 5–10 million AR-15-style rifles are in private hands within the broader total of 310 million firearms owned by Americans. And these are the legally owned weapons. In an effort to break this down, I have come up with: 114 million handguns; 110 million rifles of all types and 86 million shotguns. However, even the official US figures are all over the place because as far as assault rifles and fully automatic weapons such as the Uzi submachine gun are concerned, there are gaping holes in government record-keeping.

This entire period brought with it numerous instances of mass murder perpetrated by pathologically angry individuals with 'precipitating psychosocial stressors', usually males. They included the Columbine High School shootings and attempted bombing that took place on Tuesday, 20 April 1999. Twelve Colorado students and one teacher were killed, with twenty-four other people wounded – twenty-one by gunfire.

The mind-numbing array of weapons used at Columbine were: a 9mm Hi-Point 995 carbine with 13 10-round magazines; a Savage-Springfield 67H pump-action shotgun; a cheap 9x19mm Intratec TEC-9 semi-automatic handgun with one 52-, one 32- and one 28-round magazine; a Stevens 311D double-barrelled shotgun, sawn off to about 23 inches, 99 explosives and 4 knives. The perpetrators were two twelfth-grade students – eighteen-year-olds Dylan Bennet Klebold and Eric David Harris (both 1981–99) – both of whom committed suicide at the scene.

> He had a rage. It would just explode over everything. He would be good and then something would just set him off [...] he was extremely possessive, he drank to excess and he had a violent temper.
>
> Margaret Neal: mother of Wanda Stewart, wife of mass murderer Robert Stewart

If anyone should never have been allowed within a mile of any firearms, Robert Kenneth Wayne Stewart (b.1963) was a prime candidate. In North Carolina, on Sunday, 29 March 2009, he opened fire with a 12-gauge Winchester 1300 shotgun, a .357 Magnum revolver and a .22 Magnum semi-automatic pistol at the 120-bed Carthage nursing home, killing seven elderly residents and a nurse. One other person was wounded. Police speculated that the forty-five-year-old killer – who did not commit suicide by cop, as Charles Whitman had – targeted the facility because 'his estranged wife, Wanda Neal, worked there'.

Sentenced to 179 years 4 months, prisoner #1142611 Stewart is presently incarcerated at the medium security Caswell Correctional Center, 444 County Home Road, Blanch, North Carolina. Actually, he's got it cushy, as he can be assigned to work on road squads, help out in the kitchen and generally keeping the prison clean and in repair. Let's hope that unlike the serial killer Arthur Shawcross (1945–2008, whom I twice interviewed in prison), Mr Stewart isn't maintaining and repairing the prison's locks, as Art did.

In so many ways, the case of Robert Stewart – in whom festered vicious feelings that then exploded into mass murder – is replicated precisely with so many other US mass shootings, up to the present day and beyond.

I might add that many spree or mass murderers reportedly have no prior history of aggressive episodes. Typically the perpetrator is described by friends, family and co-workers as passive, polite and quiet. But then he is triggered by some insult, rejection or stressful event to embark on a vengeful rampage to restore honour or repay some supposed injury to his fragile ego. Others cynically and nihilistically seek recognition, attention and infamy all culminating in a gross overreaction to something almost too trivial to bother about, to then unleash an almost devastating mental nuclear detonation of pent-up aggression and rage.

Maybe we are witnessing a similar pattern in most of the other diagnoses traditionally applied to such angry, aggressive and violent individuals, among them 'conduct disorder' and 'oppositional defiant disorder', which are manifestations of underlying rage. The depressed, irritable mood and often furiously manic behaviour of a few individuals who suffer from bipolar disorder have deep-seated roots in unconscious anger and resentment, as do the hostility, temper tantrums, rage and aggressive acting out in antisocial personality disorder.

'Blowing one's top'? A simple analogy, one I have previously used in trying to understand this sudden, emotional release of fury, is to imagine a steam boiler with a jammed pressure valve. The compression builds up until it can no longer be contained and there is a massive explosion – one that not only wrecks the boiler but also kills or maims anyone unfortunate enough to be standing close by – which is precisely what happened to the great Isambard Kingdom Brunel's pride and joy, the SS *Great Eastern*, in September 1859. An explosion on the ship's maiden voyage destroyed the forward funnel and filled the boiler room with scalding steam. Five stokers were killed and many others injured. It's not too far-fetched to see a parallel here with the human mind when placed under pressure: the precipitating psychosocial stressors build up, which is why we witness so many people being killed in mass shootings and bombings while others close by get injured – the wounds often later proving fatal.

Anger disorders describe pathologically aggressive, violent

or self-destructive behaviours symptomatic of, and driven by, an underlying and chronically repressed rage. They result primarily from the long-term mismanagement of anger, a process in which ordinary, existential irritation grows insidiously over time into resentment, bitterness, hatred and destructive rage. It goes without saying that such disorders may also be caused or exacerbated by neurological impairment and substance abuse, both of which may inhibit a person's ability to resist aggressive angry or violent impulses, but further research into such behaviour is needed.

Let's not suggest for a moment, however, that there are any mitigating circumstances to be found here, nor could this be whitewashed over by arguing that the perpetrator was insane (or barking mad) when the mass killing was carried out. As we know, insanity is a mental illness of such a severe nature that a person cannot distinguish fantasy from reality, or right from wrong. Such individuals cannot conduct their affairs owing to psychosis, or are subject to uncontrollable impulsive behaviour. As Ryan Howes PhD, ABPP, suggests on the website Psychology Today: 'To be clear, insanity is a legal term pertaining to a defendant's ability to determine right from wrong when a crime is committed.' Therefore, for the most part, anger disorders cannot be blamed on bad neurology, genes or biochemistry. They arise from a failure to recognise and consciously address anger as it arises, and before it becomes pathological and dangerous. So, really it comes down to 'keeping a lid' on one's emotions and dealing with the knocks when they come.

'The red mist'. Let's move slightly off-road on our imaginary trip for a moment and park up to partake of refreshments and mull things over British killer Tracie Andrews (b.1969) was twenty-seven when she stabbed her fiancé, twenty-five-year-old Lee Raymond Dean Harvey, no fewer than forty-two times in an explosion of hell-bent homicidal rage.

Using a penknife, Andrews flipped after it had got to the point where Lee couldn't take any more. They were frequently arguing and the obvious outcome was looming: he was threatening to leave her. After an evening out, during the early hours of Sunday, 1 December 1996, they fought again while driving in their Ford Fiesta. On their way home, Lee stopped the car in The Becks, Alvechurch in Worcestershire, whereupon Tracie attacked him with a blitz of stabs. Initially, this pathological liar claimed that Lee was murdered in a road rage incident with a 'fat man'; but she was found guilty of murder with a recommendation that she serve at least fourteen years. She was released from prison in July 2011. But the good news is; in a low-key £3,500 ceremony on Friday, 25 August 2017, Andrews married bouncer Phil Goldsworthy, whom she had met in a pub. Wearing a traditional white gown and veil on the day, her once blonde hair now dyed jet black, she was snapped puffing away on a cigarette, as you do, outside Penventon Park Hotel, in Redruth, Cornwall.

Mr Goldsworthy was dubbed 'Britain's Bravest Groom' by journalist Stephen Moyes in *The Sun* of 25 August 2017. Mrs Goldsworthy does have a daughter who was born in the early 1990s, so if I were being a fair man, I'd hope it all works out just fine.

Lee Raymond Dean Harvey is buried at St Nicolas Churchyard in King's Norton, West Midlands.

Left: Charles J. Whitman (back row) with his father, mother and younger brothers. His mother was his first victim, followed by his wife. *(© Getty Images)*

Right: A woman takes cover from Whitman's fire, with the body of a wounded man lying at left. *(© Getty Images)*

Below left: The Texas University Tower in Austin. Whitman fired from behind the parapet that runs round the tower beneath the clock. *(© PA Images)*

Right: Some of the weapons and equipment used by Whitman for his shooting spree, including three rifles and a sawn-off pump-action shotgun. *(© Getty Images)*

Left: The body of Mark Essex lies on the roof of the New Orleans hotel from which he had shot and killed 9 people, including 5 police officers, and wounded 13, 31 December 1972 and 7 January 1973.

(© Getty Images)

Right: 'I don't like Mondays' – Brenda Spencer, the sixteen-year-old schoolgirl who killed 2 adults and wounded 8 children and a police officer when she opened fire on the Grover Cleveland Elementary School, San Diego, on 29 January 1979. Her father had given her a semi-automatic .22 rifle and 500 rounds of ammunition for Christmas.

(© Getty Images)

Left: Three bodies lie on the sidewalk of the McDonald's in San Ysidro, California, after James Huberty entered the restaurant and opened fire, killing 21 people, 18 July 1984. *(© Getty Images)*

Left: 19 August 1987: residents of Hungerford run past the house of Michael Ryan's, mother, whom he had murdered before setting off on his shooting spree in the town; he also set fire to the house.

(© Getty Images)

Below: A police marksman kneels in a Hungerford street to pick up one of Ryan's spent cartridges.

(© PA Images)

Left: Two of the rifles used by Ryan on his rampage in Hungerford. On the right is an AK-47-type assault rifle; the other weapon is an M1 semi-automatic carbine. *(© PA Images)*

Left: Robert Sartin, who ran amok with a shotgun in Monkseaton, near Whitley Bay, North Tyneside, 30 April 1989. He shot 17 people, although only one died, before he was tackled and arrested by an unarmed police constable. *(© Getty Images)*

Right: A car spattered with pellets from Sartin's shotgun during his murderous attack.
(© Getty Images)

Left: Port Arthur, Tasmania: a police officer peers through the shattered window of a vehicle abandoned by a gunman Martin Bryant, who had shot and killed 35 people and wounded another 23, 28–9 April 1996. *(© Getty Images)*

Left: Gwen Mayor with her Primary 1 class at Dunblane Primary School, near Stirling in Scotland. She and sixteen children were shot and killed by Thomas Hamilton before he turned the gun on himself, 13 March 1996. *(© Getty Images)*

Right: The Queen, attended by Princess Anne, arrives at Dunblane Primary School to lay a wreath in memory of Hamilton's victims, 17 March 1996. *(© Getty Images)*

Left: A police officer stands guard outside the classroom where Hamilton opened fire. A bullet hole can be seen in each of the two windows to the officer's right. *(© PA Images)*

Above: The Columbine High School killers Eric Harris (left) and Dylan Klebold trying out some of the weapons they had illegally acquired; Klebold is wearing one of their trademark black dusters. *(both © Getty Images)*

Left: A still from a CCTV tape showing Harris (left) and Klebold in the Columbine cafeteria during their shooting rampage. Klebold is holding the 9mm Tec-9 semi-automatic loaded with one of the high-capacity magazines he had acquired.

(© Getty Images)

Right: Two of the weapons used in the attack: Harris's 9mm Hi-Point 995 semi-automatic carbine and, nearest the camera, his sawn-off 12-gauge Stevens double-barrelled shotgun.

(© Getty Images)

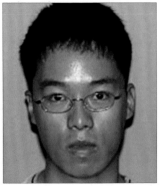

Above left: Pekka-Eric Auvinen, who referred to himself as 'Sturmgeist89' ('Storm Spirit') on YouTube. An admirer of the Columbine killers, he murdered 8 people at Jokela High School, Tuulusa, Finland, before killing himself, 7 November 2007.

(© DB Youtube/picture-alliance/dpa/AP Images)

Above right: Seung-Hui Cho, the twenty-three-year-old South Korean student at Virginia Tech in Blacksburg, VA, who shot and killed 32 people and then himself in a rampage at the university, 16 April 2007. *(© Getty Images)*

Left: Derrick Bird, the fifty-two-year-old taxi driver who went on a killing spree in Cumbria that left 13 dead, including himself, 2 June 2010. *(© Getty Images)*

Right: An officer of Cumbria Police stands guard over the bodies of two of Bird's victims, lying where they were shot outside the village of Seascale.

(© Getty Images)

Left and below: Anders Breivik as he saw himself (left), and as most of the world first saw him, in the back of a Norwegian police vehicle. .

(© Getty Images, left, and PA Images, below)

Below: The bodies of participants at a summer camp litter the shoreline of Utøya island, Norway, after Breivik's murderous spree, 22 July 2011. Earlier that day he had detonated a bomb in the capital, Oslo, killing 8; 69 died on Utøya.

(© Getty Images)

Left: An anxious woman talks to a state trooper outside Sandy Hook Elementary School, Newtown, Connecticut, 14 December 2012. Adam Lanza first killed his mother and then 26 others in the school, including 20 first-grade schoolchildren, before shooting himself.

(© Getty Images)

9

Massacre or
Mass Killing?

According to the FBI, the term 'mass murder' has been
defined generally as a multiple homicide incident in which
four or more victims are murdered, within one event, and in
one or more locations in close geographical proximity.
WILLIAM J. KROUSE AND DANIEL J. RICHARDSON,
MASS MURDER WITH FIREARMS: INCIDENTS
AND VICTIMS, 1999–2013, WASHINGTON DC,
CONGRESSIONAL RESEARCH SERVICE, 2015

Although British history offers a list of what are officially
called 'massacres', most of these events were politically and/
or religiously motivated (sometimes a confusing mix of the
two). And we can blame the Romans for the first recorded
massacre on British soil, dating back as far as the first century
AD. The event was, as we all know, the Roman Conquest of
Anglesey and the suppression of the druid religion.

Although the body count of that mass killing is unknown,

we do know is that circa AD 60, Boudica, Queen of the Iceni – a Brittonic tribe whose territory included present-day Norfolk and parts of Suffolk and Cambridgeshire – decided it was payback time for the Roman invaders.

She went forth on a revengeful road trip of her own design. The itinerary included attacking the Roman cities at Camulodunum (Colchester) – then a settlement for discharged Roman soldiers. Having settled a score there, she marched her army onwards to Londinium (London), which was pretty much burned to the ground. Finally, she set her sights on Verulamium (St Albans). More to the point of this book, Boudica was not too picky whom she had tortured and slaughtered. Britons as well as Romans were fair game. Some 75,000 Romans and Britons were killed by Boudica and her followers.

This orgy of killing across approximately two hundred miles so upset the Emperor Nero that he was considering withdrawing his forces. Then the Roman governor of Britain regrouped his army and the Romans started a massacre of their own. Boudica then either killed herself to avoid capture or died of an illness. One Roman historian, Tacitus, who tended to like a good story better than the truth, wrote that she deliberately took poison; another, Cassius Dio, wrote that she fell ill and died.

While it is fair to say that I have given the USA a hard time in the previous chapter, it seems that the early Brits had worked out the idea of massacres, as had their Roman enemies, and notably with their suppression of the druids, which culminated with a massacre of these spiritual leaders and the Welsh tribespeople who supported them on the island of Ynys Môn (Anglesey) circa AD 57. Centuries later, in what was then an American colony, the settlers finally got their own acts together and cottoned on how to get rid of a lot of people they didn't like in one fell swoop. The first example came on 19 May 1676, during King Philip's War (1675–8) when one Captain William Turner commanding 160 mounted, semi-literate militia volunteers enthusiastically attacked an Indian fishing encampment at the present-day Turners Falls, a village near the town of Montague in Franklin County, Massachusetts. In brief, about 150 innocent, sleeping, peace-loving women, children and elderly tribespeople were killed in this 'Mother of all Massachusetts Massacres'. This was the first real massacre in North American history, the like of which has not been since witnessed, or at least not in the 'Bay State' – with a proviso: there is always room for improvement in today's political climate for something more extreme, as the massacre at Waco would later prove. It is not as though the tribespeople were making a nuisance of themselves, either. They were, in fact, fishing peacefully and generally minding their own business on common land. However, the reader will be delighted to learn that Captain Turner and his butchering militia didn't have it all their own way at the Battle of Turner's Falls, aka the Peskeompscut Massacre. Once the Native Americans had woken up to what was actually happening, a two-hour battle ensued. With Turner's forces now outnumbered, a bugler was summoned and without further prompting sucked in a lot of smoke-filled air then sounded the retreat.

At least forty volunteers were killed as they scarpered. Some became separated from what remained of the main body of Turner's force and had to find their way home alone, bless them. A few were successful while others never returned at all, amongst them a fallen Captain Turner, whose head was also separated from his main body. His scattered remains were found about a month later and were buried on a bluff west of where he fell. To this very day a tablet marks the spot where he (at least, some of him) remains. This location and the nearby waterfall were named Turners Falls.

Oh, I almost forgot to mention the Great Falls Discovery Center in Turners Falls. A small museum in a mill, it declares, perhaps ironically, that it 'highlights the impact humans have had on the Connecticut River watershed'.

And, at this juncture I have spotted a problem: what is the difference between a 'massacre' and 'mass murder'? Before we start on what might seem to be another minor quibble, various dictionaries describe the noun 'massacre' along the lines of 'the killing of a large number of people, especially people who are not involved in any fighting or have no way of defending themselves'. Yes, I know that I am nitpicking here, but this sort of rules out the massacre at Turners Falls, because when the tribespeople cottoned on to what was happening they certainly defended themselves, if belatedly, didn't they?

The *Collins Dictionary* defines 'massacre' as: 'the killing of a large number of people at the same time in a violent and cruel way', which certainly fits with the Battle of Turner's Falls, at least in its initial phase. Massacres may result in fatalities ranging upwards from five to the tens of thousands, and include multiple massacres. Consider the Holocaust: mass murder in gas chambers committed by the Nazis in World War II; in more recent times such slaughter is gruesomely toe-tagged 'ethnic cleansing', such as took place in the 1992–5 Bosnian War.

The online *Cambridge Dictionary* likes to keep things short and simple, with: 'the act of killing a lot of people'. It gives the exact same definition for 'mass murder'. For 'spree killing', the *Oxford English Dictionary* offers 'an instance of random, multiple murder, usually confined to one time and location, as carried out by a spree killer', defining a spree killer as 'a person who kills in a frenzied, random, apparently unpremeditated manner with no obvious motive; specifically one who kills a number of people at one particular time and location in this manner'. In my view, however, the FBI has hit the nail on the head with its definition: 'the act of murdering a number of people, typically simultaneously or over a relatively short period of time and in close geographical proximity'; furthermore, mass murder is defined as: 'murdering four or more people during an event with no "cooling-off period" between the murders. A mass murder typically occurs in a single location where one or more people kill several others.'

Of course, we are not discussing terrorism or genocide in this book, nor refer to genuine politically or religiously motivated mass murder or massacres. But we must ask: were Native Americans committing mass murder or massacres or genocide or ethnic cleansing when they attacked other tribes? Was the US Cavalry committing mass murder or domestic ethic cleansing on 29 December 1890 at the Battle of Wounded Knee? Nearly three hundred Lakota Indians living near Wounded Knee Creek on the Lakota's Pine Ridge Indian Reservation in South Dakota were killed on that day following a botched attempt to disarm them. Almost two-thirds of them were women and children. This sounds very similar to the Waco Massacre, if you care to ask me. And as with all of these US outrages where soldiers have run amok and wiped out vast numbers of tribespeople, there has to be a monument of sorts, the Battle of Wounded Knee being no exception. But was it truly a 'battle' in the true sense? Commanded by Colonel James William Forsyth, the 7th US Cavalry had circa 460 troops including 22 artillerymen with a quartet of 1.65-inch Hotchkiss mountain guns. Led by one 'Spotted Elk', the Lakota had a fighting strength of 120, and although many of them had already been disarmed without too much fuss, the US Army began indiscriminately firing. Twenty-five soldiers died, most in blue-on-blue shootings, thirty-nine were wounded – of which six later died from their wounds. And, in the true US tradition, twenty soldiers were awarded the Medal of Honor for being mass killers at this shocking event, with the Lakota getting nothing at all except extremely belated condolences from Congress which, in 1990, expressed 'Deep regret for the massacre'.

And consider the Sandy Hook school shootings. Do they represent mass murder or a massacre? With the confusion over how to define mass murder and who may be classed as a victim of such an event, even though some were killed and others wounded at exactly the same place at the same time, our American cousins really ought to get their act together stop the interagency and politically partisan bickering, and define a mass murder as their own premier law enforcement agency, the FBI, defines it, because the FBI have got the definition spot on.

MASSACRE OR MASS KILLING?

Oops, I almost forgot that the FBI now mix mass murder, serial homicide and spree killing together within the same nomenclature – a variable noun, plus two nouns, all tucked up nice and warm in the same criminological basket. And even the Feds don't know why this is.

10

Dunblane

*We knew the guy, we went to his kids club, he had
been in our car, we had driven and dropped him off at
a train station and things.*
TENNIS CHAMPION ANDY MURRAY: ON THOMAS WATT
HAMILTON, THE DUNBLANE SCHOOL MASS MURDERER,
THE SUN, 26 NOVEMBER 2019

Andy Murray was just nine years old when, on Wednesday,
13 March 1996, forty-four-year-old Thomas Watt Hamilton
(1952–96) stormed into his school – Dunblane Primary
near Stirling in central Scotland. (The future Wimbledon
champion was there that day – as was his older brother,
Jamie – but hid away in a classroom.) Firing two 9mm
Browning HP pistols and two Smith & Wesson M19 .357
Magnum revolvers, Hamilton shot to death sixteen children
and a teacher, before turning a gun on himself; fifteen others
were injured.

This event was, by my definition and in its execution, a mass killing: a mass-murder event committed by one man at a single location and in close proximity with no cooling-off period between the shots fired. It was a 'continuum' of trigger pulling; of discharging bullets, often at point-blank range, into terrified little children, totally unable to defend themselves, many screaming for help and begging for their mums and dads to help them as they saw their classmates' heads being blown apart, their bodies ripped to pieces. So I would call this mass murder – not a massacre in the true sense at all. On this difference you pays your money and you takes your choice.

Turning to ballistics. I could spend the next three pages detailing the destructive power of any .357 Magnum firearm. But a video paints a million words, so please go to Google and check out 'Coonan 357 Magnum Semi-Auto pistol! (4K)'. My publisher's lawyers will crucify me if I put into print precisely what I think about Jerry – the guy presenting this video – although the word 'dickhead' is sleeping somewhere in my mind.

For millions of US gun aficionados, this video is amongst thousands of other similar ones to be found online by the neurotic losers who are able get hold of small arsenals (legally or illegally) even today.

So I beg you to watch this video. Listen to every word macho Jerry says. Hey, if you take up his offer even you could win all he wants to 'give away': including a JMA shotgun, a 'Vortex Razor' telescopic sight and the must-have red-dot telescopic sighting system. Watch our Jerry demonstrate the horrific power of a .357 Magnum 'down at the range', exactly the same calibre, perhaps even the same cartridge load, as used by Thomas Hamilton, who fired not at steel plate targets some distance away, but close up into precious kiddies and a protective teacher at Dunblane.

So who was Thomas Watt Hamilton? Undoubtedly 'his resentment burned for a quarter of a century. Then something made him explode,' as Nick Cohen wrote in *The Independent* on Sunday, 17 March 1996. I'm struggling to avoid penning a whole string of richly illuminated expletives in trying to describe this monster, We know that Hamilton had a death wish: he committed suicide by shooting himself in the head. And, although this will seem a highly unprofessional, borderline crass thing for me to say, in dispatching himself he removed from the bereaved families the lengthy trauma and heartbreak of his going to trial. Thenceforth to spend the rest of his days in some cushy jail or mental asylum where he would be waited upon hand and foot and given free first-rate medical care, to include free dental work at the taxpayers' expense till the end of his days, and even then he would have enjoyed a free funeral service, coffin and all. Fortunately, he ended his own life with one bullet paid for by him; a quick and perhaps painless death for him, to leave a monstrous legacy to the devastated parents and loved ones. And this mental trauma will remain with them for the rest of their lives. As tennis star Andy Murray told film-maker Olivia Cappuccini: 'You asked me a while ago why tennis was important to me. Obviously I had the thing that happened at Dunblane. When I was around nine... I am sure for all the kids there it would be difficult for different reasons.'

Another question: could the Dunblane School shootings have been prevented? The answer is yes and no.

'No' because, as we have seen in the previous chapter, sometimes someone determined to commit mass murder simply emerges out of nowhere. As if out of the blue, he executes his plan, then either kills himself, is shot dead by law enforcement, or is detained, tried and sentenced to life in jail – or condemned to death, as is often the outcome in the USA. Now, if you are morally inclined to forgive a man who has blown one's precious child's head apart, then so be it. But do not count on me enjoying the same sentiments.

It follows that mass murderers *are* completely unpredictable. As we will continue to see throughout this book, most of these people appear to live normal lives, although the majority are loners; holding down menial jobs, they have a deep sense of low self-esteem, are easily offended, prone to outbursts of anger at the drop of a hat and on the whole socially disinclined. Most of them have large chips on their shoulders, likely harbouring a particular hatred for people of certain ages, religions, castes, colours or creeds. Others have no particular, fussy pre-selection or preferred victimology: they simply go for a homicidal pick 'n' mix, killing anyone and everyone who comes into their sights.

But 'yes' also, because of course the Dunblane shootings could have been prevented; for that matter, so could most of the subsequent mass shootings in the USA, simply by banning the general public from purchasing such lethal firearms, lock, stock and barrel! Had not Hamilton been able to possess his 'Dirty Harry'-style guns by holding a police-issued licence, then all of those children and the teacher would still be alive today.

The flip side of this argument is: God forbid we are obliged to live in a 'nanny state', with, in the US, the NRA stressing that if 'responsible citizens' wish to carry and bear arms, why prevent them from doing just that? And these firearm owners do have a reasonable argument, *inter alia* why should the relatively few men who commit mass murder using guns spoil the fun of the millions of people who use them for their hobby, or for self-protection. I merely pose this open question; it is for the reader to decide.

Now stay with me, please, because there is a point to all this. Of course, the reader might already know that the NRA pumped $30 million into Trump's 2016 election campaign, with NRA chief Wayne LaPierre lobbying Trump six times against proposing new gun control measures. The problem is further exacerbated by the fact that not all members of the NRA, or anyone else who has been able to buy or trade these lethal instruments, are 'responsible' by any stretch of the imagination. Yes, some vetting is of would-be purchasers is carried out to see whether they have had prior criminal activities (to which a blind eye may even be turned in exchange for a backhander), but that's about it. At the time of writing, there is certainly no national register, one that would flag up how many firearms a buyer already owns, or what his purchasing intentions are for the future – a sporting goods/arsenal seller would need a crystal ball for the latter. The very fact that Charles Whitman was able to buy several high-powered weapons from different stores within the space of an hour or so proves my point ... and he was going around telling all and sundry that he was going shoot dead a lot of people, too, so what was that all about?

If the issue were not so deadly serious, it could almost be described as farcical. Take the time that Donald Trump gave his words of wisdom – some of the most incoherent responses to any questions about gun control– in the wake of mass shootings in Texas and Ohio. In August 2019, Trump spouted, while vainly struggling with the English language and losing the battle: 'I don't want people to forget that this is a mental health problem. I don't want them to forget that, because it is. It's a mental health problem.' He went on in equally woolly terms, to state that congressional committees were 'working on background checks and various other things [...] It's the people that pull the trigger, it's not the gun that pulls the trigger.'

Ducking any further meaningful questions about firearms from reporters, instead the Commander-in-Chief ranted on and on about the closure of hospitals for the mentally ill: 'You have to remember, also, it's a big mental – I was talking about mental institutions. They closed so many, like ninety-two per cent, of the mental institutions around this country over the years, for budgetary reasons.'

Quite where Trump obtained his figure of ninety-two per cent from is not clear. But his inference was clear: that if there were more mental institutions, more 'mad' people would be locked away after committing mass murder, because one cannot lock someone up just for *thinking* about committing a crime. Furthermore, it is unlawful for any US gun dealer to poke his nose into the mental health of a potential buyer.

Finally, after another rant about voter fraud, when asked by a reporter, 'Sir, what does that have to do with guns?' the President instead chose to answer a question about golf.

With all of that said, there is also something eerily similar between mass-murderer Thomas Hamilton and the serial killer John Reginald Halliday Christie (1899–1953), notwithstanding the excellent fact that they are now both dead, and aside from their faces, thinning hair, high foreheads, almost identical spectacles and beady eyes. I devoted a chapter to Christie in my book *Talking with Psychopaths and Savages: Beyond Evil*, wherein I peeled away the fake mask that Christie wore to fool everyone who met him, to expose a cunningly devious, self-opinionated 'little man' and control freak. I also revealed the 'waypoints' in his life, where he changed directions to plunge further in his downward trajectory towards sado-sexual homicide. Although Christie and Hamilton killed with different motives in mind – their targets and modus operandi being totally unalike – they appear to me to have very similar psychopathologies, which makes Hamilton (and so many more like him, as we will soon discover) even more chilling.

Indeed, it *is* chilling, almost icy-wintry-day chilling, when one starts to wear away at the façade that Hamilton presented to the outside world, to find a man with several personalities, a Dr Jekyll and Mr Hyde type. It's almost too terrifying to learn that both Hamilton and Christie were akin to two mentally decaying peas from the same pod. So, could this uncanny 'psychopathological resemblance' hold some of the clues that make so many mass murderers do what they do? The answer, I believe, is a resounding, yes.

Once he was dead, everyone knew how to sum up Thomas Hamilton. He was a lone madman in the

Lee Harvey Oswald mould; an obsessive misfit who bottled up his paranoid resentment until he was ready to write himself into the national consciousness with other people's blood.

Journalist Nick Cohen, *The Independent on Sunday*, 17 March 1996: using more than a touch of hyperbole to condense Hamilton's warped personality into just a few lines

It is Cohen's first sentence that attracted my attention. How right he is when he says: 'Once he was dead, everyone knew how to sum up Thomas Hamilton,' for it tells us everything. Despite many perhaps well-founded suspicions that people may have had about Hamilton's seemingly unhealthy behaviour, many refused to believe, or could not believe, or dared not even consider that such an insignificant little man (and this applies to Christie too) could metamorphose into a monster. Well, as *Talking with Psychopaths and Savages: Beyond Evil* proves beyond any doubt, these monsters are living and breathing amongst us right now. And one could be living next door to you!

Let's not beat about the bush here. We must also reflect upon the words of US serial killer Ted Bundy, for what he says about serial killers equally applies to mass murderers and spree killers, too:

Society wants to believe it can identify evil people, or bad or harmful people, but it's not practical. There are no stereotypes.

We serial killers are your sons, we are your husbands,

122

we are everywhere, and there will be more of your
children dead tomorrow.

As the grim annals of crime tragically show, everyone thinks
they know the man before he commits his terrible crimes
but they do not *really know* him until after the murderous
deeds have been done. To put this another way: in any part
of the world, we might see a neat-looking home in some
quite urban cul-de-sac, its garden carefully groomed. Yet it's
all a front, for what dread secrets might lie within? Time
and again police find torture chambers and corpses rotting
under floorboards or in some dark, dank cellar. We can use
this analogy to describe the 'outer person' because we cannot
yet see any monster behind the pleasant façade.

It all comes down to the mask of normality these serial
killers, spree killers or mass murderers wear. It is their social
camouflage that enables them to mix so easily within society.
And when cracks appear in their masks and suspicions *are*
raised, accompanied by the inevitable curtain twitching
and over-the-garden-fence gossip, these psychopaths apply
some social make-up and the cracks disappear. It is back to
the doffing of a cap, a good turn for an elderly neighbour,
who tells everyone, '... but he is such a nice man. Always
so considerate, too.' The rumours slowly cease, life returns
to normal... well, almost normal. Gosh, didn't all of British
serial killer Dr Harold Shipman's patients say that he was the
nicest doctor one could have?

So let's do some reverse-engineered offender profiling of
our own here. Let us see where it takes us on our journey into
the dark mind of the late, mass-murdering Mr Hamilton. It's

an academic exercise, of course, because the 'art' of offender profiling is used by forensic psychologists and police when trying to predict who a serial killer might be *before* he kills again – not *after* he has been arrested or is deceased.

At the time of the shootings, Hamilton lived in Kent Road, Stirling. While occasionally looking through the windows – as some neighbours have a wont to do – more than a few residents noticed dubious, though not hard-core, pictures of semi-naked boys in swimming trunks on his front living room walls. So, what might that tell you and me, if we were being nosy? Of course, I am not suggesting for a millisecond that any of my readers have a habit of peering through a neighbour's window – nor do I, come to that. I mean, all of my readers are truly wonderful, God-fearing folk, are we not? But let's imagine, as another academic exercise, that one by happenstance glimpsed the rather odd wall coverings that Mr Hamilton obviously enjoyed gloating over – so much that he didn't care two hoots if any passer-by spotted his taste in soft porn.

At this point, I know that a number of psychiatrists, psychologists and cops will come down on me like a ton of bricks, with: 'Hey, Mr Berry-Dee, there is nothing illegal in that.' Well, at the outset of this book I stressed that I always say it as it is. As we start looking behind Hamilton's screen of normalcy and peer through his front window, I not only see soft porn; I see a householder who has what one might term an 'unhealthy interest in young boys'. He would be single (because hopefully no right-minded wife or female partner would tolerate such behaviour). Consciously, the man is also sticking two fingers up to his neighbours –

deep down he doesn't give a damn what they think of him. Thus, he will be self-centred, inconsiderate and arrogant to a fault, moreover a complete failure when it comes to any form of successful relationship with one of the opposite sex – or his own gender, either. My female readers might like to look up Hamilton's photo on the internet… not exactly the catch of *any* century, you might agree? I can see the attraction in one of the former 'Chippendale' strippers or a sand-kicking beach hunk from *Baywatch*, but not Mr Hamilton, surely?

According to journalist Nick Cohen, only one person appeared to have become friendly with Hamilton: a pensioner called Cathleen Kerr who lived opposite him in Kent Road. She seems to have been the nearest person he had to a friend in the entire neighbourhood – and it's a big neighbourhood, I can tell you that much.

Cathleen recalled that Hamilton sometimes called round to her place for coffee. Important note: he never reciprocated and invited her to his place for a cup of instant coffee and biccies and to sit comfortably in his front room. Can you imagine the result – her shock as he proudly pointed out his numerous pictures of nubile young boys in wet swimming trunks, perhaps suggesting: 'Cathy, I have lots and lots more photos and some videos you can watch if you like. I filmed them at my boys club, and at my outings with lots of other schoolboys. The cheeky little rascals call me, "Mr Creepy"… Would you like to see my guns? I clean them every day.' And the thing is that Hamilton really was labelled, 'Mr Creepy' by lots of the schoolboys who knew him. With his podgy face, his insinuating voice and Dr Crippen-style spectacles, he made their flesh crawl. Yet, Mrs Kerr only really got to know all about Hamilton after the mass murder.

Reflecting on Hamilton, she noted that he'd always asked after her husband, Peter, who was poorly. And that he was 'quietly spoken, well dressed and placed'. Yes, he wore an anorak, but with a collar and tie beneath it.

Oh bless. But a nerdy anorak with a collar and tie underneath... oh, no! Not exactly the height of sartorial elegance, is it? Imagine Hamilton wandering around town, head down, hands shoved deep into his pockets, his persuasive manner and unctuous charm oozing from this oily little man. In so many ways I see him standing on a plinth in the Chamber of Horrors at Madame Tussauds, and right next to John Reginald Christie – two murderous individuals who in real life so perfectly multi-masked that although they might seem a bit odd at times, in general one would not have noticed that they existed at all, they were so inconsequential.

With that said, we should once again refer back to that first line by Nick Cohen, because by now you will be starting to see Hamilton as he really was. It is not exactly social rocket science to begin to figure him out, is it? For in putting up his soft porn wall décor for any passer-by to view, Hamilton was allowing us to take a look into his own twisted morality. It was as if he were consciously inviting anyone strolling past to take a glimpse into his warped psychopathology. I do not think one needs a degree in forensic psychology or psychiatry to figure this out either.

Are you enjoying your Mass Murder Road trip now? I hope so, because things might get a tad bumpier as we go along our way.

Various media articles suggest that Hamilton's problems began to manifest themselves at around the age of twenty-two. Reportedly, the incident that did profound damage – that he would carry with him for the remainder of his days – was that he was chucked out of the 4/6 Stirling District Scouts on the grounds that, 'he was not suitable to be a troop leader'. Perhaps someone saw something in the young man that raised a red flag. But so what if he was asked to pack his rucksack and clear off? Millions of young men around the world suffer setbacks like this. They don't go on in later life to become mass murderers, do they? They just get over it, full stop.

This might take some further unpacking. There were also reports in the media to the effect that Hamilton became convinced that others regarded him as a pervert, so perhaps those who effectively fired Hamilton had good reason to, for there is always smoke around a Scouts' campfire. The authorities, in their wise judgement – and with the pack's overall welfare at heart – knew that Hamilton was not a healthy influence on his charges. Whether it was thoughtlessness, or that he was a complete muddle, Hamilton was patently a rotten apple in a basket of perfectly happy and considerate youngsters. He was a bad influence, so he had to go.

For reasons only known to him, Hamilton fought a running battle with officialdom for the next two decades. To put it succinctly, he became a pain in the ass, an obsequious social misfit who easily manipulated and saw off any forces of authority with whom he came into conflict. We have all met one of these obnoxious 'little men' at some time or another: the barrack-room lawyer-cum-troublemaker, always moaning and making utterly damned nuisances of themselves. Think 'antisocial', 'narcissistic personality', 'borderline sociopath', 'a controlling man' and perhaps you can now see a little further into Hamilton's mind. Years previously, someone at his Scout troop had raised a red flag; now it was being hoisted even further up the slippery pole.

True, the social services were on to him. In the early eighties, following complaints from some Dunblane parents, Central Regional Council made a gallant effort to close down the boys' club meetings Hamilton held in Dunblane High School; but he was a litigious man and outwitted them. Further, it is known that there were a dozen complaints or accusations made against Hamilton, by concerned parents of young boys. And over the course of those complaints, *four* Scottish police forces were involved in investigations , but despite the scrutiny, police consistently failed to find enough solid evidence against him to charge him with any offence. In the light of all this, it is difficult not to sense a revenge scenario in the making.

The duplicitous 'Teflon Hamilton' was not only lucky to escape prosecution because the allegations didn't stick. He was also crafty enough to garner support from any and all corners, as well as from owners of gun clubs and gun shops; he even sought the support of the police officers who had approved his firearm certificates, and from the local government ombudsman for Scotland. A retired local councillor who knew Hamilton told *The Independent*:

I saw him in the street about once a month for ten years and he was always complaining. I never got the impression that he was concealing misconduct. He did have an ingratiating, almost oily manner but I put that down to the buffetings he had received.

Retired councillor Francis Saunders:
on Hamilton

Further, many parents even came to his aid – some from Stirling, Dunblane and other localities where he ran boys' clubs – honestly believing that the rumours about him were malicious tongue-wagging. Others thought differently...

Various sources suggest that Hamilton may have been obsessed with real or imagined enemies, but that he was not frightened of them. This is an oversimplification: I would say that he was becoming more paranoid as each week passed him by. He was losing control. Most people with nothing to hide in a similar situation would ignore any genuinely false accusations; rather than making a song and dance about the issues, they'd get on with their lives, letting the tittle-tattle fade away. Hamilton, however, must have had a guilty conscience preying upon him. To paper over the cracks in the fake mask he presented to everyone, this overt 'support seeking' mechanism was also an effort to conceal his oversized, self-opinionated ego – one that was slowly starting to deflate.

We might also see something of a 'mind-split' here. One part of his mental processing system was telling him that everyone was conspiring and out to get him; to compensate, the other half of his mind was saying that he was innocent of any wrongdoing. However, it would be only a matter of time before one side would win. Then all of his fuses would blow – rather like the steam boiler analogy I used earlier. Sooner or later, if a mechanical or a psychological release valve sticks shut, the pressure builds up until there is a cataclysmic explosion.

As far as Hamilton not being frightened is concerned, with this one might also fundamentally disagree. Of course he was frightened. He'd experienced the police knocking on his door before and had gotten away with anything he *might have done* through lack of evidence, yet people like Hamilton always live in perennial fear of a parental complaint – one that finally does stick. I dare say that every time he saw a police car pull up near his house his blood pressure went through the roof. Ask any criminal who has committed a crime and thought they were home free the same question. To see a bobbie beneath a tall helmet walking their way will be the best laxative they will ever have. It has been this way since Sir Robert 'Bobby' Peel founded the Metropolitan Police Service (then known as the 'Peelers') during the early nineteenth century – hence also the nickname 'bobbies'. Incidentally, 'cop' comes from 'copper', used from 1704 in Britain to mean: 'someone who captures', derived from the Old French *caper*, in turn from Latin *capere*, 'to capture '.

What's more, in Hamilton we find an extreme narcissist. These sorts are bullies, control freaks. They will use anyone, or any organisation, to favour them, support them, comfort them, all of which re-establishes any faith that they still have in their crumbling egos. But take away this support mechanism and the ego is damaged even more. Finally, the person has to face up to reality, to look at him- or herself in the mirror, physical, psychological warts and all. And he, or she, will be not be happy one bit with what they see.

Women who suffer abusive relationships with overbearing, spiteful, self-obsessed male partners will fully understand what I am referring to here. However, once the woman rebels, reveals her inner strength and leaves him, the man has lost control and is quick to write contrite love letters, make promises that he will never keep, and pester her on the phone, ever-so desperate to win her back. It works the same way with any type of relationship – gay ones too.

In a nutshell, narcissists are pathetically weak to their very core. As psychoanalyst Dr Alice Miller so beautifully puts it, and I paraphrase: 'The fragile ego is like a balloon floating high on very thin string. There is a final puff of wind, the string suddenly snaps and the ego bursts without warning sometimes with devastating outcomes.' For my part, I have seen this 'ego popping' numerous times in the back histories (or narratives) of many of the serial killers and psychopaths I have interviewed over the years. Most of them have very fragile egos indeed. We can see the same trait in the narcissistic British serial killer Doctor Harold Shipman (1946–2004). Once he had been locked up for life, his ego and self-esteem collapsed. Stripped of all the adulation he had enjoyed as a once-respected GP, he was forced to face what he truly was. Now, a mere prison number in system jam-packed with the ilk whom he despised, and being ordered to do this and that by upstart prison officers still wet behind their ears whom he disliked in equal measure, he lost control. He was ruined, so he hanged himself inside his prison cell.

Another example. On a number of occasions when the sado-sexual serial murderer Kenneth the 'Hillside Strangler' Bianchi (b.1951) was jilted by girlfriends, and once even by his common-law wife, Kellie Boyd, he took out his revenge by torturing and killing other women and even little girls. Indeed, if one watches the acclaimed Netflix FBI drama series, *Mindhunter*, one will get this 100 per cent.

> The grandiose person is never really free, first, because he is excessively dependent on admiration from the object, and second, because his self-respect is dependent on qualities, functions, and achievements that can suddenly fail.
>
> Dr Alice Miller: *The Drama of the Gifted Child*

> It seems that every time Ken had problems with a woman or they left him, he went out and killed someone.
>
> Frances Piccione, Kenneth Bianchi's adoptive mother, to the author, 2001

In many respects why should mass murderers or spree killers be any different? This is why many of them have a death wish. So the conclusion I have come to – and I stand to be corrected – is that narcissistic Thomas Hamilton had for too long suppressed his festering anger-management problem, which was exacerbated by a guilt complex that metamorphosed into a paranoid state of mind housing a fragile ego and a sense of low self-esteem. Subconsciously he knew he was a drowning man and all of his attempts to garner assistance to keep him afloat were to no avail. This self-esteem and faux grandiosity – his entire psychological infrastructure – were crumbling away like weathered cement.

He had exhausted all of the social make-up he'd applied to keep himself looking respectable and above reproach. Sooner or later he had to explode, for what anger management he once had in place finally deserted him. It would take just one more adverse influence to knock his house down.

The really big problem was that this human time bomb owned lethal firearms and he knew how to use them.

No guns, no revenge exacted with the Dunblane Primary School mass-murder tragedy. And you will not a find a single law-enforcement officer or serving soldier across the world who would disagree with me.

Could anyone even imagine revering Hamilton to the degree that they, themselves, see him as akin to an inspirational, mass-murdering latter-day saint? Well, maybe yes. We will meet nineteen-year-old Martin Bryant later, and he sought in some ways to emulate Hamilton and even surpass him. Bryant had the IQ of an eleven-year-old, so make of that what you will.

> ... as an ook cometh of a litel spyr [... mighty oaks from little acorns grow]
> Geoffrey Chaucer, *Troilus and Criseyde*
> (circa mid–1380s)

Our journey along Mass Murder Road has brought us to a crossroads where we have to make a decision about which path to take next. At this juncture, do we leave the Dunblane school shootings with an ever-so sad list of the deceased, as we have done previously? Should we do what I had initially proposed at the start of this book: leave out the offenders' back history, their narrative, altogether? For who really cares how his early life may have affected Thomas Hamilton? We know quite a bit about him already, so why trouble ourselves further. Nothing can change things now – what's been done cannot be undone. And I doubt very much if the bereaved parents, and those who survived his killing, care two hoots about what made Hamilton what he was, anyway. My heart goes out to them all.

In *Talking with Psychopaths and Savages: Beyond Evil*, I discuss the formative years, the 'waypoints' and the murderous directions that some of the most notorious serial murderers have taken, for *every* killer has arrived at a crossroads, a dread place where a life is extinguished while the other life changes forever. In Hamilton's case, eighteen lives were extinguished almost in a heartbeat, including his own.

Now, fellow travellers, I hesitate in getting academic here, and it rather sticks in my throat to change our pre-planned route, but I will do so for what I believe to be a worthwhile reason: because perhaps, just *perhaps*, Hamilton's early life may give us an insight into what makes so many other mass murderers tick. Moreover, like the neighbours who peeped through his front window, perhaps we can metaphorically look through the windows in the minds of other mass killers and try and see what was, and is, inside their heads too.

Complex? Not at all, so stick with me here. Furthermore, I categorically say that there is no mitigation to be found for what this scumbag Hamilton did to the pupils and a teacher at Dunblane. And adding to that death toll, the lifelong trauma that the next of kin and survivors suffer continues even to this day.

Unreservedly to reinforce these sentiments, may I remind you of the words of Russell J. Kruger, chief investigator in the case of sado-sexual killer Harvey Louis Carignan, from earlier in this book: '*The guy's the fuckin' Devil. They should have fried him years ago, period.*'

That's not 'Leftie speak', that's 'hard-nosed cop speak'. No diplomatic PC stuff either from my old pal, Irish-born, hard-as-masonry-nails, built-like-a-brick-shithouse Russ Kruger. And, along with most of my readers, I like this straight talking, I like it *very* much indeed − so much so that I will apply exactly the same approach to Thomas Watt Hamilton. Hey, 'Tommy,' burn in Hell! And this is my own brilliant, utterly non-professional opinion.

Now, there will be readers who say that I am being a tad harsh on the late Mr Hamilton − formerly of the Church of Scotland's Presbytery of Stirling. And there is no doubt that he did some good, healthy work with young lads, as one can see when one looks him up on *Wikipedia* or elsewhere, because there are fuller accounts on him available online, though sadly no room for them here, owing to the word count restrictions, for this book. There can be no denying that many serial killers and mass murderers are also involved in good community service: often they're overt Bible-thumpers, highly regarded by their friends, neighbours and colleagues as upstanding citizens. But, as we have already seen, this is all part and parcel of their fake personas: they are the consummate wolves in sheep's clothing, but far deadlier.

Some have been politicians, mayors, councillors. God knows how many doctors and priests have been amongst them, too. It seems that to many people Mr Hamilton *was* trustworthy, even a borderline saint, therefore, criticise them not. Perhaps we can understand the well-meaning faith these decent folk placed in his character – collar and tie under his anorak thrown in for good measure. And it goes without saying that Hamilton's past supporters were not by any means naïve. It's a case of: if you cannot trust a guy who gives up his free spare time to help young lads better themselves, who can you trust?

Dr Harold Shipman was a well-respected country GP. Over two hundred of his elderly patients trusted him with their lives – now they are all dead. He murdered them.

11

'Alienated Young Men'

*There's nothing that links him [Pekka-Eric Auvinen]
with the victims except that they attended the same
school … But the explanation can be found mainly in
his Web writings and his social behaviour.*
DETECTIVE SUPERINTENDENT TERO HAAPALA, FINNISH
POLICE: TO THE ASSOCIATED PRESS

The mass murder of school children is not exactly a recent
phenomenon. We can date one such event back as far as
Friday, 20 June 1913, at St Mary's Catholic School (St-
Marien-Schule) in Walle, a quarter of Bremen in Germany.
The killer was Heinz Jakob Friedrich Ernst Schmidt (1883–
1932), then aged twenty-nine, who was rapidly going
insane. He had been a teacher in Prussia before losing his
job due to his mental unsuitably in 1912 but after treatment
in a mental asylum he was declared 'cured'. He wasn't.

Further reading would be required elsewhere to fully

137

understand this man's narrative and it all makes for fascinating stuff. But to cut to the chase: while energetically blaming the unseen hand of Jesuits, in the spring of 1913 Schmidt bought six to ten handguns. The bulk purchases and his oddball behaviour prompted two separate gun shops to file reports with the police, but after having been given the once-over, Schmidt received the all-clear. So there was a form of 'intervention' to be found here but the cops 'uninterventioned' it, if there is such a word. Soon after, he indiscriminately shot at students and teachers at the aforementioned school, killing five girls and wounding more than twenty other people before being subdued by school staff, one of whom was armed with a pitchfork. Diagnosed as being as mad as the proverbial hatter, Schmidt was never tried for his crimes He died, aged forty-nine, in an asylum.

Still in Germany but decades later, nineteen-year-old expelled student Robert Steinhauser (1983–2002) carried out a mass killing in Erfurt, on Saturday, 26 April 2002. He shot and killed sixteen people, including thirteen staff members, two students and a police officer, before committing suicide at the Gutenberg-Gymnasium, his former secondary school, in the Thuringia state capital. His weapons were a Glock 17C semi-automatic pistol and a Mossberg 590 Mariner 12-gauge pump-action shotgun.

Another mass school shooting of note took place in the German town of Emsdetten on Monday, 20 November 2006. Eighteen-year-old ex-student Sebastian Bosse (1988–2006) shot five people, wounding but not killing them, and set off some smoke bombs; he then killed himself. His weapons were a sawn-off Burgo .22-calibre bold-action air rifle, a sawn-off Ardesa percussion rifle, a pistol, an Ardesa 'Patriot' caplock pistol, an assortment of home-made bombs, a knife and a machete.

As we are now beginning to see, mass school murders seem to be more of a German phenomenon than anything comparable in the USA, or, indeed, almost elsewhere around the world. However, it is worth noting that the two infamous Columbine killers, Klebold and Harris, inspired Bosse who, just like Harris, was a Nazi fanatic who idolised Adolf Hitler.

Writing in the *New York Daily News* on 21 April 2019, David Krajicek noted: 'If mass murder committed by alienated young men is a contagion, as many experts believe, then Eric David Harris is the Typhoid Mary of this particular disease.' He adds, 'The journal and videos left behind [by Harris] created a mass killing glossary for sociopathic fanboys around the globe. His phrases – the Eric Harris brand – frequently turn up in the notes of copycats: *Trenchcoat Mafia. Ich bin Gott. Natural Selection. Kick-start a revolution. Natural Born Killer. Wrath, I'm full of hate and I love it.*' Indeed, in his own journal (which can be found online), Sebastian Bosse wrote: 'ERIC HARRIS IS GOD!' before attacking the Geschwister-Scholl Schule.

Baby-faced, spectacled, bookish-looking Tim Kretschmer (1991–2009) was just seventeen when, dressed in black combat fatigues, on Wednesday, 11 March 2009, he attacked his former secondary school, the Albertville-Realschule, in Winnenden, Baden-Württemberg, in south-western Germany. Copycatting his fellow German mass killer Steinhauser, Kretschmer went from classroom to classroom brandishing a 9mm Beretta 92FS semi-automatic pistol. At one point, he cruelly taunted students hiding beneath their desks, singing: 'Are you not all dead yet?' In the first classroom he cold-bloodedly shot five students dead. In the second classroom, he killed two more. Nine others were wounded; of those, two later died on the way to hospital.

Needing to reload his pistol, Kretschmer left the room, upon which a teacher locked the door. His attempts to re-enter frustrated, Kretschmer then moved on to the chemistry lab, where he shot the teacher there dead. With deadly purpose and firing sixty rounds, he had killed nine students – eight female and one male, all between fourteen and sixteen years old – and a female teacher. As police arrived, he fled the scene and carried on with his rampage until officers shot him in both legs and he committed suicide.

Kretschmer came from a wealthy family and had never been in trouble with the police, it was reported in *The Times* on 11 March 2009 that in 2008, the lad had received treatment as an in-patient at the Weissenhoff Psychiatric Clinic, near the town of Heilbronn. It is also reported that after being discharged, he was supposed to continue his psychiatric management as an outpatient in Winnenden, but he ended his treatment. According to police and clinical staff, he had been treated repeatedly for clinical depression on an outpatient basis in 2008. His parents, through their lawyer, rejected these claims, maintaining that he had never received any psychiatric treatment whatsoever. This somewhat flies in the face of a psychiatric report prepared for the prosecutor's office, which determined that Kretschmer had met five times with a therapist and talked about his growing anger and violent urges, and that the therapist *had* informed the parents of this.

This is all supported by the fact that he was a very poor student at school and was a 'lonely and frustrated person who felt rejected by society' according to one of his peers.

Here, we see echoes of Michael Ryan's early narrative. Kretschmer was a youth who had temper tantrums when he lost during his tennis-table training, yelling and throwing his racket down. His coach, Marko Habijanec, said that Kretschmer had a very high opinion of his own abilities and was quick to denigrate his teammates. When Herr Habijanec discussed the lad's attitude with Frau Kretschmer, he discovered that she fully sided with her son. In simple terms: he was a rich kid with an overinflated ego.

In Kretschmer we also see a withdrawal into a fantasy world, all too common with emerging mass murderers and spree killers. He had profiles at MyVideo.de, Kwick.de and other websites. When police examined his computers, they found he was interested in sado-masochistic scenes where a man is bound and humiliated by women. He viewed one of these films the evening before his attacks.

Herr Kretschmer Sr legally owned fifteen guns. He was a member of a local marksmen club, 'Schutzenverein' ('Protecting Association'), and when police raided the family home at around 11am on the morning of the shooting, one 9mm Beretta handgun was found to be missing, along with several hundred rounds of ammunition. Herr Kretschmer had kept fourteen weapons in a gun safe, while he had left the Beretta lying around in the master bedroom. Police confiscated the fourteen remaining guns.

On Thursday, 10 February 2011, the state court in Stuttgart found the patriarch guilty of involuntary manslaughter in fifteen cases. He received a suspended sentence of one year and nine months. He appealed the verdict, which was later reduced to a suspended sentence of one year and six months in 2013. On Sunday, 18 May 2014, *Die Welt* reported that Kretschmer's parents had since changed their name and moved to a different city – and perhaps none too soon, one might add.

Chancellor Angela Merkel described the shootings as 'incomprehensible', adding, 'It is unimaginable that in just seconds, pupils and teachers were killed – it is an appalling crime,' she told reporters. 'This is day of mourning for the whole of Germany.' And there were the usual condolences to the victims, students and families, with the European Parliament holding a minute's silence to honour the dead.

In the days following the tragedy, some German politicians called for legal consequences, including a total prohibition of all shooting video games, a better monitoring of gun club members (and a provision to have them store their weapons at the club house) and a directive to have all ammunition deposited with police. As might have been expected, others dismissed such demands as mere placebos. However, Germany has since taken large steps to tighten up gun control, something for which they should be applauded, while the USA has done hardly anything at all. And a certain David Ali Sonboly thought that Tim Kretschmer was the bee's knees.

Newspaper boy and student Sonboly (1998–2016) was of dual Iranian-German nationality. He had a clean rap sheet: neighbours described him as 'a quiet boy'. Not unlike Kretschmer, Sonboly had undergone psychiatric treatment for depression, anxiety and post-traumatic stress disorder. In 2015, he had been treated for two months as an inpatient in a mental-care facility, and it is known that he was largely isolated from his peers and suffered years of bullying by classmates, which included physical abuse. All of which ended when, during the evening of Wednesday, 22 July 2016, he opened fire at a McDonald's restaurant near the Olympia shopping mall in the Moosach district of Munich. During his spree, he shouted 'I have been bullied for seven years'; brandishing a Glock 17 semi-automatic pistol, he shot dead nine people and wounded another thirty-six, before shooting himself in the head.

His motive was established as one of revenge for bullying, so his narrative is of great interest to us here. A former classmate even admitted that, 'We always mobbed him in school, and he always told us that he would kill us.' In fact, Sonboly grew to hate those of a similar age and background to those who bullied him, mainly Turks and Albanians. He is said to have developed an 'irrational worldview' in which he believed that the people he hated were infected with a virus and must be exterminated.

For some time before the shootings, Sonboly had retreated into the world of online material concerning mass killings. He had compiled a scrapbook of news clippings of shootings and had bought several books on the subject, including a copy of Peter F. Langman's book *Why Kids Kill: Inside the Minds of School Shooters*. He was particularly impressed with Tim Kretschmer and bizarrely took a 300-mile round trip from his home in Munich to visit the Albertville-Realschule where Kretschmer had killed so many students. Sonboly was also in awe of the Norwegian killer Anders Behring Breivik (b.1979) – indeed Sonboly's attack was carried out on the fifth anniversary of the Breivik killings.

Following this terrible incident there was the usual amount of handwringing and well-meant condolences from all and sundry, with equal amounts of post-mortem psychiatric evaluations and attempts to finger-point blame all over the place. Sonboly's school firmly maintained that bullying could not have been the reason why their former student had murderously flipped.

* * *

Born in Tuusula, Finland, Pekka-Eric Auvinen (1989–2007) had no prior criminal record. He was just eighteen years old and had been a registered member of the Helsinki Shooting Club since Friday, 31 August 2007. On Friday, 2 November that year, he bought a SIG Sauer Mosquito .22-calibre blowback operated semi-automatic pistol and 500 rounds of .22-calibre long rifle (LR) rimfire ammunition.

Somewhat remarkably at the time, the Finnish police required a shooting hobby to start with a 'low-risk' .22-calibre firearm. In the case of 'relatively low-risk' weapons, the police could not mandate that sports shooting should take place in a club, or even in any kind of company. Furthermore, the permit decisions were based entirely on information provided by the applicant. 'Low risk' indeed, for this extremely accurate pistol, with its 10-shot magazine, a muzzle velocity of 1,255fps. In any sane person's book this is a lethal firearm, and one shudders at the thought of it being fired at anyone's head at point-blank range.

So, here we have a Finnish youth, at about the age when he's just old enough to pass a driving test, giving police any information he sought fit to, to be able to obtain a highly lethal firearm and go and shoot it anywhere he so chose. And the police already knew that Auvinen had previously attempted to obtain a licence to purchase a 9mm Beretta pistol that was *refused* because this gun was considered too high powered.

And what about Auvinen's state of mind, we might rightly ask. To be as concise as possible, between December 2005 and January 2007 his parents, Ismo Auvinen and Mikaela Vuorio, tried to get him referred to a psychiatric outpatient clinic for his depression and anxiety, but the request was refused, apparently due to what was perceived as his mild symptoms. Instead, psychiatrists recommended treatment with antidepressants before there were any attempts to hospitalise him. Added to this was the fact that he was allegedly bullied at school, and so worried were other students they reported changes in his behaviour to a youth worker, explaining that he was acting threateningly and had remarked that they would die in 'a white revolution'. Obviously, by now the worm had turned.

As is pretty much always the case with young emerging mass shooters, Auvinen had a few online accounts, including two with YouTube under the aliases of 'Sturmgeist89' ('Storm Spirit') and 'NaturalSelector89' – the '89' being, of course, his year of birth; the firstname was infamously used by mass killer Eric Harris. A fascination with anti-Semitism and Nazism began to emerge in his schoolwork. He uploaded morbid videos about school shootings and violent incidents, including anything he could find on the Columbine High School killings, the Waco siege, the Tokyo subway Sarin attack and bombings during the Iraq invasion – and we have to remember that he was merely an adolescent at the time. Shortly before his attack, he posted his last video: 'Jokela High School Massacre – 11/7/2007', depicting blood-red-filtered photos of him proudly holding his pistol along with, in the background, his intended target – the Jokela High School in Tuusula.

The writing was all over the walls soon to be drenched with blood, yet no one, not even his own parents, knew what this young lad was about to do. Or did they? Several months before Auvinen's attack, an American YouTube vlogger, Thomas James Kirk III (aka T.J. Kirk), called for authorities to investigate accounts with content on school shootings, including one used by Auvinen. In response, a Ms 'Robin McVeigh' later organised the small but vociferous community of online individuals into offering 'emotional support' to Auvinen.

In an article by Wif Stenger in the *Sunday Times*, 11 November 2007, it was reported that 'Robin McVeigh' portrays herself on the internet as a 'willowy blonde, atheist immortalist' who numbers *Natural Born Killers* and *Kill Bill* among her favourite films. Acknowledging that her other online name is Tana Scheel, she admitted she had been Pekka-Eric Auvinen's girlfriend, but rejected claims that the recent ending of their relationship may have sparked off his rampage.

It is at this insidious point that the inability of these online forums in dealing promptly with these issues of incitement to commit mass homicide is laid bare. A spokesman for the Helsinki Cyber Crime Department has stated: 'It is highly probable that there was some form of contact between Pekka-Eric Auvinen and Dillon Cossey' – the latter a fifteen-year-old boy arrested in October for planning an attack on his school in a suburb of Philadelphia.

The apparent link between the two was a female YouTuber whose username was 'Robin McVeigh', in reference to the US domestic terrorist Timothy McVeigh, whom she idolised, as she did Eric Harris and Dylan Klebold, as well as other well-known school killers. She would regularly attack those who disagreed with murder, and she threatened to kill several YouTube users. She was also electronically traced to the second 'YouTube Killer' Dillon Cossey.

Auvinen's shooting spree occurred on Wednesday, 7 November 2007, at Jokela High School. He entered the school that morning and between 11.42am and 12.04am, he shot dead eight people and wounded another person before shooting himself in the head; flying glass injured twelve others. Yet this was not the end of Auvinen's homicidal legacy.

Two days later, on 9 November, Finnish police rushed to three other schools, prompted by threats posted on the internet. They were Hyrla High School in Tuusula, and two other institutions in Kirkkonummi and at Maaninka. A sixteen-year-old boy who posted a video entitled: 'Maaninka Massacre' on YouTube was arrested on 11 November. He stated that that his video was a 'joke'.

On Tuesday, 23 September 2008, there was another school shooting, this time at the Seinäjoki University of Applied Sciences in Kauhajoki, western Finland. Wearing an Eric Harris-branded T-shirt with the logo 'Humanity is Overrated' and armed with a semi-automatic pistol, twenty-two-year-old student Matti Juhani Saari (1986–2008) killed ten people, before turning the gun on himself. A few days later, in neighbouring Sweden, two boys, aged sixteen and seventeen, were arrested in Stockholm for conspiring to murder their school's principal and a janitor. They had spoken about and glorified the Columbine event and what had previously happened in Finland.

The Finland Ministry of Justice later released a 147-page report covering the Auvinen case. In part it says:

> The perpetrator admired the USA's Columbine school killings of 1999 and tried to copy several of the details [...] The material he wrote in his manifesto and diary was largely copied from the writings of previous school killers. He was well informed on school killings. At the time of the Columbine shooting, he was only nine years old, which suggests that his interest and expertise in the subject clearly originated from a later period. Another school killing that interested the perpetrator occurred at Virginia Tech, again in the USA, in April 2007. By this time, he had already written his first diary entries concerning his plan. The perpetrator familiarised himself with school killings mainly via the internet, where it was easy for him to see that they had attracted a lot of publicity in traditional media as well.

Here endeth the lesson.

12

Hunting Humans

I am going hunting humans today.
JAMES HUBERTY: TO HIS WIFE AFTER TAKING
HIS FAMILY TO THE SAN DIEGO ZOO

Before we refer to Hungerford and other British mass murders and spree killings, as some back history it is widely reported that Charles Whitman was the first of modern-day mass murderers who went berserk. This may or may not be true, but it is of interest to learn that the word 'berserker' was originally applied to a type of Viking shock trooper, distinguished by his wearing a bearskin (from which the word derives). Berserkers eschewed armour, often fighting naked, and hurling themselves into battle with deadly fury, seemingly oblivious to any threat to their own lives. Some authorities believe they took hallucinogenic drugs – interestingly, many of today's mass murderers and spree killers are often as high as kites when they commit their crimes, during which they, too, go crazy.

The berserker, therefore, is someone who sets out to kill as many people as possible in a sudden explosion of violence. This is not such a rare phenomenon as it once was and again, for the most part, a killer's rampage ends with their own death. Killers such as Whitman are shot down by police, while others, such as Michael Ryan, turn their guns on themselves. Nevertheless, contemporary domestic berserkers tend to be isolated, lonely men with a puritanical streak, who find the mass of humanity disgusting. They have rigid, extremely controlled personalities. Most have real or fantasised military experience, and a love of weapons – the wannabe soldier suffering from 'Little Man Syndrome'.

So we see definite parallels between mass murderers, spree killers and berserkers – in a way they are so closely entwined that, like mixed paint, it is pretty much impossible to label them as different types. As we will later see, Michael Ryan was a member of gun clubs and an aficionado of military and survival magazines. Mark Essex, the young black radical who killed nine people in New Orleans in 1973 by sniping from the top of a seventeen-storey hotel, had learned to hate whites in the US Navy. Murderer James Huberty, who we'll meet again shortly, was a keen game hunter and Nazi sympathiser.

Yet, can the term 'going berserk' really be applied to the likes of Whitman and so many other mass murderers and spree killers? Maybe not. So often, these killers are not erupting in a furious rage, neither are they crazily violent, indeed, in scores of instances, witnesses who survive these murderous attacks report that the killer seemed calm, organized and so cold-blooded that no emotion was exhibited whatsoever.

Some criminologists might call Howard Barton Unruh (1921–2009) the 'quintessential' berserker. He had an unhappy childhood in Camden, New Jersey. During World War II, he fought as a machine-gunner in the Italian campaign, keeping a detailed diary recording the exact times of all enemy deaths for which he was responsible. He was a gallant soldier, but his bravery had a sinister aspect – he really enjoyed killing.

Honourably discharged at the end of the war, he returned to his boyhood home, where he began a weapons collection and enrolled at university to become a pharmacist, but he became more bitter and reclusive. He was subject to paranoia. He filled diaries with records of his neighbours' real or imagined sleights. He even persuaded his parents to build a high fence at the rear of the house, and constructed a huge gate to keep the world (the self-perceived enemy) at bay – all reflecting his pathological siege mentality.

So, if you were a fly on his wall, and just as we did with Hamilton, can you visualise Unruh now? Can you see his flight from reality and into fantasy assuming a dissociative quality as his defensive solution (the high fence he erects around his garden being a physical defence) as he loses hope in object relations. For he is entering a dangerous enclave in which he ends up enclosing himself, experiencing an illusory self-sufficiency, the pathological dynamics of which may seem very complex but are not so difficult to understand when we learn that Unruh was in an ongoing feud with the Cohens who lived next door. They owned the drugstore below the apartment he shared with his mother. Indeed he had, for some time, contemplated killing several of his Cramer Hill neighbours over petty squabbles and name-calling, all of which fed into his psychosis – a similar derangement to that of Hamilton.

Unruh's countdown to murder started on Labor Day 1949, when he decided to go to the movies, so he left his apartment and headed to the Family Theater in downtown Philadelphia. On the bill that night was a double-crossing gangster movie, *I Cheated the Law,* and another called *The Lady Gambles* – in which Barbara Stanwyck played a poker-and-dice game addict. Unruh was gay and wasn't so much interested in the cinema itself; a bit of nocturnal bonking was in his mind, for he was supposed to meet a man with whom he had been having a week-long affair. Sadly for twenty-eight-year-old Unruh, he was held up in traffic and by the time he reached the picture house – a well-known gay pick-up joint on Market Street – his hot date was gone, most probably picked up by another man.

Now sexually frustrated and fuming, Unruh sat in the darkened cinema until 2.20am, bitterly stewing through multiple onscreen repeats of the movies. Then, when he arrived home, he found that pranksters had stolen the gate and messed about with the fence. He felt that this was the final insult.

Unable to sleep, he made yet another mental list of his intended targets: a group of local shopkeepers; a druggist; a shoemaker; a tailor and a restaurant owner. Then he dozed off. On the following morning, Tuesday, 6 September, Unruh armed himself with two pistols and embarked on his 'Walk of Death'. In the space of just twenty minutes (some say twelve minutes) he shot dead thirteen people and wounded three others with a 9mm semi-automatic Parabellum pistol of the type designed by Georg Luger and named after him. (Unruh had purchased the Luger at a sporting goods store for $37.50, and secured it with two clips containing thirty-three loose cartridges.) The streets emptied and he strolled calmly back home to barricade himself in his room. The house was surrounded by police who attacked with tear gas. Unruh surrendered, with his hands reaching for the sky.

Some twenty psychiatrists agreed that Unruh was unfit to plead, so he was confined to a mental hospital where he told one of the examining psychiatrists, 'I'd have killed a thousand if I'd had bullets enough.' On Monday, 19 October 2009, he died at the ripe old age of eighty-eight, at the New Jersey State Hospital in Trenton, New Jersey. His 'Walk of Death' was to foreshadow an era in which such tragedies would become all too common.

* * *

On Wednesday, 18 July 1984, the name of James Oliver Huberty (1942–84) entered the record books when he killed twenty-one people – predominately Mexican and Mexican-American – in a McDonald's in San Ysidro, California. This was a single incident in a single location – it was mass murder, *not* a spree killing.

Forty-one-year-old Huberty's weapons were a 9mm Browning Hi-Power semi-automatic handgun, a 9mm Uzi semi-automatic and a Winchester Model 1200 pump-action 12-gauge shotgun. He was fatally shot dead by a SWAT team:

a single sniper on the roof of the post office across the street had a clear view of him and fired a single round, dropping the killer stone dead in his tracks.

> To those who oppose the death penalty – in my particular case, anything short of death would be cruel and unusual punishment.
>
> Ronald 'Gene' Simmons

Having been jilted by a girlfriend, between Tuesday, 22 and Monday, 28 December 1987, heavily bearded, fifty-year-old former USAF Master Sergeant Ronald 'Gene' Simmons (1940–90) killed sixteen people in Pope County, Arkansas. Fourteen of the victims were his own family, including a daughter whom he had sexually abused. This was spree killing – with 'familicide' thrown in to please the criminology-inclined purists.

Simmons's weapons included: a crowbar; some rope for restraints; a Ruger Single-Six .22-calibre revolver, and an H&R Model 929 .22-calibre 9-shot revolver; one US gun reviewer describes the latter as: 'A hearty gun with a lot of character'. Of some interest is the fact that Simmons had previously been awarded the Bronze Star Medal, the Republic of Vietnam Gallantry Cross, and a USAF Ribbon for Excellent Marksmanship – and that is about as good as he gets.

> Hoka hey, it's a good day to die. Let the torture and suffering in me end.
>
> Ronald 'Gene' Simmons: last words

Simmons surrendered shortly after the killings in the city of Russellville, the county seat of Pope County, Arkansas. He was executed by lethal injection on Monday, 25 June 1990. No one would claim Simmons's body, so it was buried in a 'potter's field' – meaning a paupers' place for the burial of the unknown, unclaimed or indigent.

> There didn't appear to be any struggle. The whole incident probably occurred within a period of fifteen to thirty seconds.
>
> Ron Makin, Iowa Division of Criminal Investigation, on Robert Dreesman

On Wednesday, 30 December 1987, and just a few days after Simmons ran amok, copycat killer and forty-year-old loner Robert John Dreesman (1947–87) shot dead six members of his own family with 'hunting weapons' as they were dining at their upscale two-storey home in a small town in Iowa, before shooting himself. This would also be called 'familicide', much in the same way that Ronald DeFeo shot dead his family of six in Long Island – the difference being that 'Butch' DeFeo is now in prison and Dreesman isn't.

Dreesman's victims were his father John, seventy-nine, mother Agnes, seventy-four, his widowed sister, Marilyn Chuang, forty-seven, and her three children, Jason, twelve, Jennifer, eleven, and Joshua, aged eight. He then killed himself – and did find a grave and a headstone too, at East Lawn Cemetery in Algona, Kossuth County, Iowa.

Dreesman's killings marked the state's worst mass murder since thirty-year-old Elsie Marie Joens Nollen (1906–37) of Denison County, Iowa, asphyxiated her six children and herself by running a hose from a car exhaust into her home in 1937. This case is a real tearjerker, so a box of tissues at the ready, please.

> I have tried and tried to live a decent life, and raise my kids up right so they would be decent.
>
> But they have a father that does not care for them or either me. He don't know any better. Albert was awfully good to me when he wasn't drinking. I couldn't ask for a better husband. But, oh, he sure was awful when he got drunk.
>
> He has beat me up lots of times and I always forgot about that just because I loved him and wanted to live with him [...]
>
> Now today he got drunk. I never said much to him because I knew it would just be a fight again. Oh, my, such a life.
>
> I'm doing this because I can see that this family is not going to be raised up right and I think it is a shame to let them grow up and life such a life [...]..
>
> I've always said if I couldn't live with him I didn't want to live, because there isn't any other beside Albert [...] But I getting [sic] tired. I hope Albert will be happier when he is rid of us.
>
> Elsie Nollen: from a fifteen-page, pencil-written suicide note

Elsie died with her youngest child, Viola, aged two, in her arms. At her feet were Orvin (eleven, Wilber (ten), Pauline (seven), Earl (six), and four-year-old Leona, who had died as they left their upstairs bedroom and staggered towards their mother's room. For this terribly tragic and broken-hearted mum, the final straw had come when her husband had gone out on the booze and to meet another woman. When Elsie asked where he was going, he told her that it was none of her business.

Elsie is buried at the Zion Lutheran Cemetery in Crawford County, Iowa.

Technically, this was 'filicide' – the word being derived from the Latin words *filius* and *filia* (son and daughter, respectively) and the suffix '-cide', meaning to murder, or cause death, but I have included this case because a mass murder could be filicide as could familicide. And that's why, up until that date, the single worst mass murder case in Iowa history occurred on Monday, 10 June 1912, when Mr and Mrs Joe Moore, their four children with two of their children's friends – the oldest of the six children was only twelve –were killed with an axe at the Moore's home near Villisca. This case has never been solved, and at the time of writing police are *still* looking for a man carrying a bloodstained axe.

Of course, these types of explosive mass murders and spree rampages – there are countless more – are not confined the United States of America – far from it. Step forward mass murderers from 'Down Under'.

> Pain and suffering are always inevitable for a large intelligence and a deep heart. The really great men must, I think, have great sadness on earth.

MASS MURDERERS AND SPREE KILLERS

> What is hell? I maintain that it is the suffering of
> being unable to love.
>
> Fyodor Mikhailovich Dostoevsky: *Crime and
> Punishment* (1866)

At about 3.30pm, on Saturday, 17 August 1991, a thirty-three-year-old man went berserk in a Sydney shopping plaza armed with a rifle and a machete, in what has become known as the Strathfield Plaza Massacre. Wade John Frankum (1958–91) was tooled up with a Norinco SKS semi-automatic rifle. He left seven dead and six wounded before he turned the gun on himself as police arrived on scene.

The Norinco SKS is not strictly an assault rifle, despite being cloned from the Russian type SKS-45 (which was succeeded by the fully automatic AK-47) manufactured in China. Nevertheless, it has a maximum effcetive range of 460 m and a 10-round magazine. Once again, in Frankum we find a fantasy-driven loner. He possessed a large collection of violent literature and videos of violent films. One of his books was a well-thumbed copy of *American Psycho*. He had also read Fyodor Dostoevsky's *Crime and Punishment*.

* * *

Undoubtedly the Hungerford spree killer, Michael Ryan, shared characteristics with so many other mass murderers and spree killers, being a white, lower middle-class male. Many of these perpetrators also tend to be fairly well off and live in affluent suburbs or the countryside. There are exceptions but generally they are not married; they are usually single, often living with a parent or close relative, or divorced and have no children. They have extremely fragile egos, are not good with women and subconsciously see themselves as failures.

More often than not they have a disturbed relationship with one or both parents. George Jo Hennard, whose bloody acts we'll cover shortly, had a mother who was highly strung and domineering he had often talked about killing her. According to a friend, he compared her to a snake, picturing her head on a rattlesnake's body. After the carnage he wreaked, his mother talked of a tragedy and the death of 'my beautiful son' – yes, well, what more can one say?

Mass murderers and spree killers live fantasy lives in worlds where lead balls bounce, elephants fly and fairies reign supreme. As loners, they have no outlet for their rage. They resort to television, violent films, videos, guns and survival magazines. These merely serve to fuel their extreme fantasies, promising relief pouring from the muzzle of a gun. And, as their world becomes distorted by their murderous delusions, they begin searching for scapegoats. Some blame their teachers – others, such as David Burke, blame their bosses. We'll move on to him next.

> Hi Ray. I think it's sort of ironical that we end up like this. I asked for some leniency for my family. Remember? Well, I got none and you'll get likewise.
>
> David Burke: suicide note to his former boss, Ray Thomson, written on an aircraft sick bag before shooting him

In a mass murder/suicide event, aircraft cleaner David Augustus Burke (1952–87) shot the pilot of a four-engine BAE 146-200A aircraft flying a scheduled flight from Los Angeles to San Francisco at 22,000 ft over California. His reason: he had been sacked after stealing $69 from his employers. His weapon was a Smith & Wesson Model 29 .44-calibre revolver, borrowed from a colleague. The date was Monday, 7 December 1987. With its pilot dead, Pacific Southwest Airlines Flight 1771, 'The Smile of Stockton', spun out of control then crashed, killing all forty-three passengers, including Burke himself, the five crew members, James Sylla, President of Chevron USA, three of Chevron's public affairs executives and three Pacific Bell representatives.

Burke had 'history'. While employed at USAir in Rochester, New York, he was suspected of belonging to a cocaine-smuggling ring that was shipping the drug in from Jamaica to Rochester. Although he was never charged, USAir terminated his employment, so he moved to Los Angeles. It seems that Burke had an anger-management problem, as some former girlfriends and police described him as prone to violence. We can add to this that he had fathered seven children, but remained unmarried. 'I'm The Problem/Pacific Southwest Airlines Flight 1771' makes for an interesting watch on YouTube. But this is sad and sickening stuff.

Even pilots can be mass murderers.

Co-pilot Andreas Lubitz (1987–2015) had been treated for suicidal tendencies and clinical depression, in his case a Major Depressive Disorder (MDD). What's more, he feared he was losing his eyesight. He had even been declared 'unfit for work' by his doctor, but the twenty-seven-year-old Lubitz kept this information from his employer, the Lufthansa-owned Germanwings airline.

On Tuesday, 24 March 2015, Germanwings Airbus A320-211, Flight 9525, took off at just after 10am from Barcelona-El Prat Airport, destination Dusseldorf. When the plane reached its assigned cruising altitude of 38,000 ft, and while the captain was out of the cockpit, Lubitz locked the door, then initiated a controlled nosedive. While the passengers screamed in abject terror, the plane hurtled towards the ground to impact at 430 mph on a French mountainside at 10.41am. All 144 passengers on board were killed, along with the 6 crew members. I direct those of you with a stomach for a gruesome watch to 'Murder In The Skies Germanwings Flight 9525' on YouTube.

Is it not conceivable that airline pilots – whom we trust with our own lives and those of our loved ones – could become so mentally pressurised that they, too, can blow up, sending hundreds of innocent passengers to their doom in a suicide event combined with mass murder? Is it beyond our imagination to think that this *may* have happened aboard Malaysia Airlines Flight MH370 on Saturday, 8 March 2014, when 239 people vanished without trace – in what became one of the world's most baffling aviation mysteries? There are an estimated 140,000 airline pilots internationally, around 70,000 of them in the US alone; troublingly, one in eight of all pilots worldwide showed signs of depression.

A 2016 study published in the journal *Environmental Health* was the first to examine the mental wellbeing of airline pilots outside the context of a crash investigation, regulator-mandated health exam or through identifiable self-reports. It is thought that pilots are extremely reluctant to seek mental-health treatment, given the stigma and professional implications of mental illness within the industry. They are often effectively placed between a rock and a hard place.

'Our results should not be surprising,' says the study's senior author, Joseph Allen, an assistant professor of exposure assessment at Harvard University. 'The idea that pilots can be susceptible to mental health issues just like the rest of us should not be shocking. Unlike the rest of us, though, not all pilots have the ability to seek treatment or counselling due to fear of repercussions.'

I have insisted throughout this book that a mass murder event is not the same as a 'massacre', despite some experts arguing otherwise. In the case of Lubitz, his actions were not a massacre because this was mass murder in anyone's book, and, by any true definition, it was neither a 'spree killing' nor 'serial homicide'. He committed mass murder using Flight 9525 as his weapon whichever way one cuts it, and his victims were helpless. And this brings me to the subject of suicide.

Of course, we can all empathise with a person who, for whatever reason, finds themselves at their wits' end. Usually they have a history of depression that has been noted by people close to them as well as the counsellors and doctors who prescribe medication in their efforts to reduce the symptoms. Intervention for these unfortunate souls is available – but whether they are able to accept it is another issue entirely.

If the final outcome for suicidal people becomes inevitable

for them, then most kill themselves without physically harming anyone else. This cannot be said for mass murderers such as Charles Whitman, who opted for suicide by cop, or Thomas Hamilton, who killed himself.

Undoubtedly, pilot Andreas Lubitz had suffered severe mental problems and had clinical depression. However, as I have noted time and time again in this book, psychologists and psychiatrists trying to mitigate a killer's actions along the lines of: 'Oh dear, bless the chap. He was depressed.' Well, how depressed and distressed were the passengers on Lubitz's flight, with a terrible death soon awaiting them all? How depressed and distressed have been the victims next of kin and those who loved them dearly? Ninety-five days after the crash, Lubitz was buried during a secret ceremony in Germany. His remains were interred at a graveyard in the southern town of Montabaur, with his girlfriend leaving a *message of love* at his graveside, over which was erected a plain wooden cross, with 'Here rests in God – Andy' on it. Amongst a large wreath and scores of cards from well-wishing mourners, on parchment wrapped around a bouquet of red roses, twenty-six-year-old teacher Kathrin Goldbach even wrote a note of farewell to a man whom she knew people the world over now despised.

Bearing in mind the terror that the passengers on that aircraft went through for the better part of twenty-minutes, with Captain Patrick Sondenheimer fighting to get back through the reinforced door and regain control of a lunatic and the plane – and that those same victims could only be identified through body-part DNA – any post-mortem mitigation that Lubitz was suffering from depression when

he plunged these people to their deaths cuts no ice with me.
'Here rests in God'... indeed. I bet he doesn't.

> The world has no room for cowards.
> Robert Louis Stevenson: writer

Some mass murderers blame women for their emotional
upheavals and George Jo Hennard (1956–91) was one of
them. In a letter to Jill Fritz and Jane Jernigan – two sisters
with whom he was obsessed – he refers to 'the abundance of
evil women' and 'female vipers' in Belton, Texas, where he
was living. Of the twenty-three victims he killed, fourteen
were women. Twenty-seven others were wounded. Hennard
shouted, 'You bitch' at one woman before pumping bullets
into her. And, if that is not a cowardly act and indicative of
a serious anger-management problem, I don't know what
is. However, he told another woman, Anica McNeil, with
her four-year-old daughter Lakeshia to 'Get your baby
out of here.' It was the only time he showed compassion.
Anica's own mother, Olga Taylor, who was lunching with
her daughter and granddaughter, was gunned down.

The massacre took place on Wednesday, 16 October 1991,
at Luby's Cafeteria in Killeen, Texas, after Hennard drove his
Ford Ranger pick-up truck through the front window of
the restaurant. His weapons: two semi-automatic pistols – a
Glock 17 and a Ruger P89 series.

When police arrived on the scene and ordered Hennard
to surrender, a short firefight ensued, after which he shot
himself dead. A pink granite memorial stands behind the
Killeen Community Center with the date of the event and

the names of those killed. As usual, a hue and cry was raised by irate citizens over gun control, with the Texas State Rifle Association and others arguing that Texas should allow its citizens to carry concealed weapons. But how could this limp-wristed idea resolve the problem? Because the *real issue* was that this awful man had been allowed to buy firearms in the first instance.

> He was as good as gold.[...] Wouldn't hurt a fly.
>> Marjorie Jackson: school caretaker,
>>> on Michael Ryan

We briefly met Michael Robert Ryan (1960–87) at the start of this book. This can only be speculation, but it has been said that he may have been driven to kill because of a pathological hatred of women. I cannot find any evidence of this at all; although his first murder was that of Mrs Susan Godfrey, there was no evidence that he had stalked her. Under similar circumstances his victim could as easily have been male.

Like Hennard, Ryan spared the children. However, next he tried to kill Mrs Kabaub Dean, a mother of three and petrol station attendant at the Golden Arrow service station in Froxfield. Mrs Dean knew Ryan, who often bought petrol for his Vauxhall car there. He always paid by credit card but he, and she, never passed the time of day. But today *was significantly* different, for Ryan was acting suspiciously. After filling a can with petrol, he pulled out a gun from the boot of his car and started shooting. The gas station window was shattered. Mrs Dean was showered with glass. She dived for cover.

But Ryan was not yet finished.

As Mrs Dean lay helpless under the counter, he loomed over her as she begged for her life. Coldly, he took careful aim. At point-blank range he pulled the trigger. 'Click' – the gun was out of ammunition. 'Click', 'Click', 'Click', 'Click'. Then Ryan walked off, got into his car and drove away. Can the reader even begin to imagine the terror Mrs Dean went through as the gun clicked five times?

Twenty minutes later, Ryan shot his own mother dead after riddling his car with bullets. She fell to the ground outside her house at 4 South View, Hungerford, which he then set ablaze. The fire quickly spread to the three adjoining houses in the terrace. It was these three initial shootings of females that have given rise to the theory that Ryan hated women.

Ryan had built up a fearsome arsenal. In a steel cabinet bolted to a wall in the house he kept at least one shotgun, two rifles, a 7.62mm Chinese Norinco 56S (a variant of the AK-47), three handguns, including a 9mm semi-automatic pistol, and an American-made M1 semi-automatic carbine. He also had 50 rounds of ammunition, which he had bought for £150 at the Wiltshire Shooting Centre just eight days before his rampage, having joined the club a month earlier.

Ryan was remembered as 'polite' and 'unremarkable'. Those who *did* get to know him better found him to be articulate, especially when talking about his favourite subject – firearms. He could reel off a detailed history of the M1 carbine and its use in World War II and the Korean War. He had been practising with the M1 on the club's shooting range on the day before he started his own private, one-sided war on society.

It would be redundant of me to further detail Ryan's killing spree – this is well covered elsewhere– but back then it was his easy access to firearms that enabled him to indiscriminately kill as he did. For this reason I can attempt to take us a little deeper into this man's warped psychopathology, before asking what in God's name were the authorities doing by allowing Ryan to obtain such a lethal collection of guns? Furthermore, one might ask, why were these firearms even being imported and sold in the UK in the first place.

The AK-47 rifle used by Ryan was designed by the Soviet Russian engineer and inventor Mikhail Kalashnikov, who used German firearms designers captured during World War II to produce a gun that fired 7.62mm ammunition, modelled on the 7.92mm German Sturmgewehr 44 assault rifle. Sacrificing range for rate of fire, the Avtomat (automatic) Kalashnikova, first manufactured in 1947, could pump out bullets at a rate of 600 rounds a minute. Reliable, accurate at close quarters, easy to clean, it became popular with guerrilla fighters. In Northern Ireland the gun was known as 'The Widow Maker'. AK-47s were produced throughout the Communist world – including Eastern Europe, North Korea and, like Ryan's weapon, China, although made to a far inferior standard to the original Russian specifications.

Ryan had been issued with a shotgun certificate in 1978. On Thursday, 11 December 1986, he was granted a firearms certificate covering the ownership of two pistols, plus the AK-47 and the M1 carbine. However, it was not until the shootings committed by Derrick Bird in Cumbria on Wednesday, 2 June 2010 – more of which anon – that Britain decided that enough was enough. At this point along our route I turn to Barry Kenneth Williams; we will return to Ryan soon enough.

> He was a quiet boy. We had no idea what he was going to do.
>
> Mr and Mrs Williams: on their
> spree-killer son, Barry

Foundry worker Barry Williams (1944–2014) lived with his parents, Horace and Hilda, at 14 Andrew Road, on the Bustleholme Mill estate in West Bromwich.

Williams held a valid firearms certificate allowing him to possess a single semi-automatic weapon, a 9mm Smith & Wesson pistol, which he used at approved gun clubs for sport shooting. But the writing was on the wall. To be frank, he was mentally off the wall, too. And how do we know this?

To start with, Williams was eccentric. He shot at moving dummy targets dressed in wigs and modified his bullets – dum-dum style – to make them more destructive on impact, which saw him banned from one club, in Telford, Shropshire, where he was nicknamed 'Cowboy'. Members of another club had complained that he stole bullets. All of which gives rise to an issue of not some insignificance, because, as the reader will know, Smith & Wesson pistols were designed to kill people – not to be used to fire at dummies dressed in wigs travelling along a steel wire in some gun club. I mean, only a living human dummy would do that, can we agree?

During the 1970s, Williams quarrelled on a number

of occasions with his neighbours, self-employed builder George and Iris Burkitt, their son Philip and daughter Jill, complaining that they played noisy music or had their television on too loud and were disturbing him and his parents. The arguments over the Burkitts' alleged noisy behaviour became a fixation with him to the point of paranoia, Williams believing they were mocking him, and on one occasion he said to twenty-year-old Philip, 'I'm going to exterminate you'. A week or so later, on the evening of Thursday, 26 October 1978, George Burkitt and Philip were working on the youth's Triumph Spitfire car in front of their house. At around 7pm, annoyed by the noise they were making, Williams, who had been cleaning his guns, marched out and shot both of them. George was hit in the left eye, chest and thigh; he died immediately. Philip was wounded. Terrified, he ran into his home. Williams followed him, shooting him with five rounds that slammed the lad through the front window, killing him. Williams then shot dead forty-eight-year-old Iris. Amidst a hail of lead, a bullet ripped through her heart. The Burkitts' daughter, Jill, was hit once in the chest, three times in the back, once in her right leg and once through her left arm. She collapsed in the hallway next to her mother. Miraculously, despite suffering these horrific wounds, she survived.

A neighbouring couple witnessed the shootings. The wife, Mrs Judith Chambers – Iris's cousin – opened her front door. She too was shot, but mercifully survived.

Having fired off twenty-three rounds, Williams drove off in his Ford Capri, firing six more shots from another .22-calibre pistol. He shot at but missed two boys aged ten and eleven, who were playing football, and a woman.. Driving on through the town of Wednesbury, he fired through the windows of a barber's shop and two houses, and tossed home-made bombs randomly. In one of the homes, flying glass hurt a nine-year-old girl. He eventually had to stop for petrol and then drove off without paying.

As in all such spree killings and mass murders, the outcome for the perpetrator is inevitable: he either is shot by police, commits suicide with a self-inflicted gunshot or is captured.

Shortly after 8pm, Williams pulled in to the Aubury Road Service Station at Stockingford, near Nuneaton, and fired at Michel and Lisa Di Maria, its managers. Lisa died instantly; Michel was to pass away in hospital.

With nowhere else to go that night, Williams slept in the woods. A high-speed, 30-mile police car chase, ensued the following morning. After his car was involved in a collision, Williams pulled a pistol and tried to commandeer one of the police vehicles that were pursuing him in Spring Gardens, Buxton. Brave, unarmed cops overwhelmed him, though. (He later confessed that he'd wanted to be gunned down.) Meanwhile, one hundred children were queuing up to watch the movie *Grease* outside a cinema nearby.

In his Capri, police found 147 9mm and 770 .22-calibre rounds, plus the .22-calibre pistol, still with a full clip of ammunition. The criminal charges brought against him included five counts of murder, possessing a prohibited firearm, putting a neighbour in fear of violence and making an improvised explosive device.

Now comes the really, *really* bad part. In 1979, Williams was convicted of manslaughter on the grounds of diminished responsibility, and duly detained at the high-security psychiatric hospitals Broadmoor in Crowthorne, Berkshire, and Ashworth in Parkbourn, Liverpool. In due course (yes, you've guessed right), psychiatrists declared him to 'have been a model patient who reacted well to treatment and counselling [He] has made a sound adjustment to the restrictions placed upon him while with us at Broadmoor and, collectively we believe that Mr Williams is now ready to be released back into society where, in our opinion, he will pose no threat to society again.' Mr Williams was conditionally released on licence and initially lived in a bail hostel six miles from his home, all of which resulted in complaints from the local MP Peter Snape to the Home Secretary.

Being forced to move on, Williams changed his name to 'Harry Street', relocated to North Wales and married in 1996; the couple had a child later that same year. In 2005, they moved to Hazlefield Road in Hall Green, Birmingham, where he began harassing another neighbour. Once again he began to threaten extreme violence, so the West Midlands Police were called to investigate. At first, they had no idea who Harry Street was. There was no notification of him changing his name anywhere. However, one astute officer soon learned of Harry Street's criminal antecedents: that he was the infamous Barry Williams – and that he was out on a life licence that could be revoked at any time.

Now get this, for Williams was found to be in possession of an improvised bomb, fifty home-made bullets, a revolver and two other pistols. He was immediately arrested then convicted of further firearms offences, and was ordered once again to be detained in a secure mental institution. He returned to Ashford Hospital, with little likelihood of him ever being freed.

Williams, who oddly enough bore a striking resemblance to the ageing Ronnie Kray (whom I once interviewed at Broadmoor), died from a suspected heart attack at Ashford Hospital on Christmas Eve 2014, aged seventy.

> See that man over there sweeping up the leaves? He is a psychiatrist and he spies on me. At night, he turns into a fly and watches me in my room. What time is it now? I want to hit him over the head with a spade.
>
> Paul Beecham: to the author as we walked around the gardens at Broadmoor Hospital

Several times I interviewed the murderer Paul Beecham (1943/4–98) at Broadmoor. He had been sent there in 1969 for shooting his mother, father and grandfather dead. On the recommendations of the Broadmoor psychiatrists, Beecham was discharged as posing no threat to society. He was under supervision for three years until he was completely discharged in 1985.

But then, years later, in 1998, he killed fifty-one-year-old Rita Riddlesworth, a former Broadmoor patients' social care visitor, with a single blow to the head and buried her under the patio of their garden of their Bracknell home. He and Rita had lived together happily as man and wife for some sixteen years, remembered fondly by her sons who had lived with them. Two weeks later, he shot himself dead. He was fifty-five years old.

Here is my point. If convicted mass murderers or spree

killers have been placed into 'secure hospitals', to be supervised day in, day out for several decades by allegedly the best medical people on Planet Earth, then are eventually regarded as being 'of sound mind' and released, only to kill again and again, how can we trust the profession, who are paid for at mega expense by the taxpayers, to try to mitigate a dead mass murderer's actions by striving to explain how the killer's state of mind became so wrongly wired up, and then form *guesswork* conclusions as to what might have gone wrong inside a brain which, post-mortem, no longer exists?

C'mon guys and gals, are we being taken for mugs here? 'The Deadly Dr Harold Shipman' worked with psychiatrists year after year, and not one of them suspected that he was a serial killer, did they?

13

Derrick Bird – Anatomy of a Spree Killing

We are utterly devastated over the death of our father Derrick
Bird. To us, he was the nicest man you could ever meet.
He was a loving dad and recently became a grandfather.
We would like to say that we do not know why our dad
committed these horrific crimes. We are both mortified by these
sad events […] We would also like to send our condolences
to all the other families and people involved in this tragic
incident. Our thoughts are with them.

STATEMENT OF DERRICK BIRD'S FAMILY: READ OUT BY THE
REV. JIM MARSHALL, AT THE MASS FUNERAL OF THE VICTIMS,
FRIDAY, 18 JUNE 2010

The Cumbria shootings were a spree-killing event that occurred on Tuesday, 2 June 2010. Lone gunman Derrick Bird killed 12 people and shot at another 25, with 11 of them suffering injuries, before he turned a gun on himself. The question is: how did Bird manage to commit a three-hour shooting spree in three separate towns and why didn't the police catch him more quickly? Along with the 1996 Dunblane School mass killing, the 1987 Hungerford killing and the 1989 Monkseaton shootings, this Cumbria case counts amongst the worst criminal acts involving firearms in British history. So let's meet the perpetrator.

Derrick Bird had lived all of his fifty-two years in West Cumbria. Leaving school aged sixteen, he went to work as a joiner at the Sellafield Nuclear Plant (then called Windscale). He married and had two sons, but in the early 1990s his marriage broke up and he had to leave Sellafield after being accused of stealing wood. Thereafter, he lived alone and worked as a taxi driver.

> Derrick Bird was a quiet guy. He was a pleasant guy. He kept himself to himself, but he was a nice guy. He was not overly aggressive. He just plodded along and got on with it.
>
> Paul Wilson: former taxi driver colleague.

> He came from a decent family, from a decent, very beautiful neighbourhood. I was upset by the photographs put up on the television [...] He looked like a thug but he wasn't a thug. He was a reasonable lad who went about his business, apparently, in the right way.
>
> Nan Wilson: a former teacher of Derrick Bird.

So what drove this quiet, reasonable man, to turn on his own people in the towns and villages where he had always lived? Friends would later say that a critical event in 2007 would change Bird's life – an incident in Cleator Moor Road, Whitehaven, when some lads jumped out of his taxi and made off without paying the fare. He chased after them. Unfortunately he came off the worse, for they hit him in the face, some of his teeth were knocked out and when he fell down he smashed his skull on the pavement, leaving a big gash in the back of his head. After this incident, he started to go downhill and began drinking heavily.

John McDonald, a fellow taxi driver, explained:

> He didn't work on Fridays, so he went out and got so drunk he was bouncing off all the walls in the town, and that wasn't Derrick. There were guys on the rank winding him up and that. He didn't like it. Frankly, the guy could have done without it.

Derrick Bird, was licensed to own a George Fisher 12-gauge double-barrelled shotgun and a CZ 452-2E ZKM .22-calibre bolt-action rimfire repeating rifle. Manufactured in Czechoslovakia by Česká Zbrojovka Uherský Brod, the latter features a standard five-round detachable magazine and has an effective range of 200m. Bird's rifle had a scope and was fitted with a silencer – the correct name being a 'suppressor'. And it is true that Bird loved his guns – several times he visited Thailand and practised on shooting ranges.

As a side note: there are a couple myths surrounding these misnamed 'silencers' that I'd like to dispel. Firstly, they don't really silence much at all. Furthermore, James Bond stuff aside, the science of ballistics tells us that far from slowing a bullet down, an attached suppressor adds length to a gun barrel, all of which improves better accuracy over a *slightly longer* effective maximum range. As any military sniper will confirm, the use of a suppressor means just what it says: it 'suppresses' the muzzle flash. The makes the sniper feel that he or she is far less easily detectable by an enemy, whom the sniper's spotter watches as the target ends up in a 'pink splash'.

Technically, the .22-calibre was a hunting rifle, yet it and the shotgun would prove deadly enough for the carnage Bird intended to cause. It all started on the afternoon of Tuesday, 1 June 2010, while Bird was at the taxi rank on Duke Street in Whitehaven. He called over another cabbie called Darren Rewcastle. The two men had argued several times before, with Bird accusing Rewcastle – who was well thought of in the community – of queue jumping and poaching his fares. To make matters worse, Rewcastle had allegedly slashed the tyres on Bird's cab and gone around boasting about it. As Bird drove away he shouted out, 'There's going to be a rampage tomorrow,' then he went home, still fuming and worried about going to jail for not paying his taxes. To Bird, it must have seemed like it had all become too much. It was dark when he left his two-bedroomed, mid-terraced house at 26 Rowrah Road, Frizington, to drive three miles east to the scattered community and civil parish of Lamplugh, where his twin brother, David, lived at High Trees Farm. David owned the farmhouse and had also sold part of his land for the development of four detached homes. David had plenty of money. Derrick didn't.

Derrick Bird opened an unlocked back door to the house, crept up the stairs and shot the semi-naked David *eleven times* in the head and body in his bed. At first blush the motive seems to have been money. David had received not only a loan but also an inheritance from their late father, which was to be split between the two brothers but was still outstanding. Derrick believed that the family solicitor was conspiring with David to withhold his share of the money. However, if Derrick resented this, it wasn't apparent to other family members, although others say that the brothers had argued previously. It never behoves well to speak ill of the dead, yet there is never smoke without fire and perhaps Bird smelt a rat – believed that he was being conned out of money, and that his brother and the family lawyer, Kevin Commons, were conniving to have him arrested over tax issues. That said, David Bird's three daughters, Rachel (twenty-eight), Tracey (twenty-six), and Katie (nineteen), dismissed any suggestion that the brothers had been involved in a feud. In a joint statement, the three young women said: 'He was a loving husband and doting dad and granddad. [...] Our dad's only downfall was to try and help his brother [Derrick].' After killing his brother in cold blood, Derrick Bird returned home and started washing his car as if nothing untoward had happened at all.

Bird now held a deep-seated grudge against sixty-year-old Kevin Commons for what he saw as the lawyer's favouring of David in the matter of their inheritance. At 10.20am the following morning, Bird turned up at Commons's farmhouse, where he parked up in the road for some time. When the lawyer had got into his car to drive to work, Bird fired both barrels of his shotgun, hitting the terrified man once in the shoulder. Staggering out of his vehicle, Commons was killed by two rifle shots to the head. The gunshots were heard by a few local people, who reported them to the police, and as the cops responded they passed Bird's taxi going in the opposite direction. He was heading the five miles to Whitehaven and there is a strong suggestion that he was heading for Commons's legal firm, K.J. Commons & Co, of which sixty-six-year-old Marcus Nickson was Kevin's fellow director.

Years later, I happened upon the following information. As would be reported in *The Times* on 9 November 2018, Marcus Nickson eventually admitted swindling vulnerable clients, including the family of a brain-damaged baby and a twenty-two-year-old stroke victim out of £711,000, after acting for them in multimillion-pound claims against the NHS. Some time after Commons's death, Nickson had left the firm, allegedly because he was 'distressed' over the tragic loss of his partner, and a new solicitor, David Dawson, became head of the firm's Clinical Negligence and Personal Injury Department. When he took over the files, Nickson's scam was discovered and Dawson alerted the police.

> It is hard to imagine anything else other than a high degree of trust when the parent or parents of brain-damaged children seeking damages from the medical authorities place their trust in their legal advisers. It seems to be like the trust one would place in one's teacher, surgeon or priest.
>
> Judge Simon Newell: sentencing
> Marcus Nickson

Marcus Nickson pleaded guilty to two counts of fraud at Preston Crown Court on Wednesday, 7 November 2018.

The court heard that both offences contained an 'element of false accounting' after Nickson had charged huge legal fees to the families, having initially told them that the charges would be minimal.

One of Nickson's victims – a baby who was left with severe quadriplegic cerebral palsy after failings during her birth – was awarded £3.5 million in damages from the NHS after Nickson represented her in court. The youngster tragically died aged twelve, but in 2010, after securing the financial settlement for her and her family, the charlatan Nickson stole £104,688.87 from the trust fund that had been set up for her care.

Nickson's other victim, a twenty-two-year-old who had suffered a stroke that went undetected, was awarded more than £3 million in damages, He would need ongoing care for life, yet between 2007 and 2011 Nickson stole £606,193.36 from his settlement.

Things get even murkier when we learn that just a year before he was murdered by Derrick Bird, Kevin Commons and Marcus Nickson were boasting that they earned circa £250,000 a year each, with Nickson owning a top-of-the-range Mercedes; both men were charging clients up to £400 per hour. This once highly regarded firm's reputation was now in tatters. It folded in 2014, with the loss of all of its fifty-five jobs. On Monday, 17 December 2018, Nickson was sentenced to serve four years in prison – he's most likely a free man today. There is no evidence that Nickson's criminal activity was also directed at the Bird family or that Kevin Commons was in any way involved in Nickson's criminality.

He's probably about the single most generous person I've ever met. Just a really, really nice character.

Gerard Richard, friend of Kevin Commons
and local businessman

All the staff are deeply saddened [...] Kevin was a man committed to the service of the local community here in West Cumbria and beyond, and his passing will leave a massive void in the legal community as well as the local area in which he had made his home for many years.

Tim Frost, solicitor: speaking on behalf
of K.J. Commons & Co.

The second phase of Bird's shooting spree took place between 10.30am and 11.35am on 2 June. It started at the taxi rank, where he spotted fellow taxi driver Darren Rewcastle, who was holding a cup of coffee in one hand and a cigarette in the other. Bird called him over, produced his shotgun and fired both barrels, obliterating the man's face.

I was in the wrong place at the wrong time.

Donald Reid

Bird then shot Reid, another cabbie, in the back, drove off, circled the block and returned to the rank, firing twice more at Reid as the wounded man waited for the emergency services to arrive. Reid survived. Then Bird shot taxi driver Paul Wilson once in the right side of his face. At first Wilson thought it was a prank –that Bird was shooting blanks – until blood started to pour from his face. He too survived.

> I just seen the two barrels coming out the window,
> and I heard a bang. The glass on the passenger side
> door smashed in. Glass was everywhere. My taxi
> driver's blood and flesh were all over me.
>
> Emma Percival

By now the police were literally on this bird's tail as he drove through the streets, next firing his shotgun in Coach Road at a passing taxi driven by Terry Kennedy and containing a female passenger, Emma Percival. Both were wounded. Kennedy later had his right hand amputated, as he had put it up to his face to protect himself and had received horrific injuries.

An unarmed cop commandeered a car to pursue Bird while two other officers in a transit van closed in, placing their vehicle in between the gunman and Kennedy and Percival to shield them from further fire. Bird pointed his shotgun at the police; they ducked into cover and that gave this spree killer the chance to take flight. Thereafter, with the manhunt for him by now underway, he drove around to randomly wound and kill others.

Upon reaching a road junction, Bird drove towards a housing estate – the pursuing police took another direction and lost him. He was now on the B5345 road between Whitehaven and St Bees.

At 10.55, Jaqueline Williams was shot at while walking her dog. She survived.

> Susan was from the heart; not just in her work
> surroundings but in her family surroundings. She
> thought the world of her family. She would never say

a bad thing about anyone, or anything, to be honest. That void will never be filled.

Alan Hunter: friend of Susan Hughes

In the market town of Egremont, divorced Susan Hughes, a fifty-seven-year-old mother of two grown-up daughters – one of whom was wheelchair-bound – and who described her as 'irreplaceable', was hit in the chest and abdomen as she walked home carrying two bags of shopping. As she fought for her life, Bird shot her in the back of her head with the rifle.

Close by was Bridge End. Here, Bird discharged the shotgun at seventy-one-year-old Kenneth Fishburn, who suffered fatal wounds to the head. A retired security guard at Sellafield, he had served twenty-five years in the Durham Light Infantry and was a former United Nations peacekeeper. He was shot just yards from his home.

Bird drove off, then saw Leslie Hunter.

I was on the main road. A taxi pulled up. The driver said, 'Can I see you a minute, mate,' so I stepped off the kerb towards him and looked in the car and saw a shotgun lying on the passenger seat. I thought that was weird for a kick-off. Then, he started to lift the gun up, and I knew something was wrong then, so tried to get away as quickly as I could. He fired one shot. The heat went past me head and pellets hit me in the face. It was a loud bang. It nearly deafened me, and as I crouched down further, he fired another barrel, and right in the middle of me back. I've still

got the twenty-nine pellets in me back. I've never had
pain like that in me life – he was as calm as anything.

Leslie Hunter

Fourteen-year-old Ashley Glaister was out running an
errand. Here is her shocking near-death account:

> I was coming out of the shop and he was heading
> towards me. He pulled up beside me and said some-
> thing, so I went over to his car, and he said: 'Do you
> like something?' So I said, 'What do you mean?' He
> pointed a gun at me. I ducked down. The shot went
> past my head so I started running, and crying, so he
> shot at me again. As I was crying and running down
> the road to me sister's, I was thinking, why he was
> after me. Why is he shooting at me? Is he gonna kill
> me? I haven't done anything wrong.

It's now 11am. Five people are dead, many others are injured,
and Bird is heading for his next target just off the main road,
with armed police officers desperately trying to locate him.
He'd driven to the village of Wilton with the intent to shoot
Jason Carey – a deep-sea diving instructor at the club Bird
belonged to. On his way through the country lanes and
back roads to Wilton, Bird was spotted by farmer Norman
Sherman, who later told police:

> When I first seen him, a car came speeding round the
> corner [...] I identified it as a taxi and a very evil, sort
> of madman driving straight at me. Never forget his
> face [...] he came speeding right past me [...] looked

straight in my face and kept going. Thought that something had upset that guy [...] that he had been run off the road, or something like that. That he was in a foul mood.

A short distance away, a sixty-five-year-old mole-catcher, Isaac 'Spike' Dixon, was walking his dogs and going to look at his traps when Bird pulled up and shot him twice with the shotgun, killing him.

Spike wouldn't have harmed anybody. There wasn't a streak of badness in him. He was a guy I went to school with, grew up with [...] he was at my wedding, I was at his wedding [...] He died just two hundred yards up the road for no reason. No reason at all.

Norman Sherman

At around 11.05am Bird reached Wilton and the home of Jason Carey. He made a noise outside the house but no one came out because the family dog was barking loudly and needed calming down. Seemingly frustrated, Bird turned around and headed up the road where he spotted Mrs Jennifer Jackson and her husband, James.

Jimmy Jackson. A great, great guy. A witty fella. He was a guy who devoted his life to the ambulance service [...] spent a lifetime saving lives, and then he is shot by the roadside for no reason. An absolute waste of a great life.

Jennifer was a church-going lady. Just a lovely lady.

Norman Sherman

Jennifer was shot once in the chest with the shotgun then twice in the head with the rifle. Bird drove away, then almost immediately returned to kill her husband, James, with a single shotgun blast to the head, and to wound their neighbour Christine Hunter-Hall in her back – yet *still* he carried on with his murderous firing.

It was now about fifty-five minutes since the police first learned of the shootings, and the Cumbria Constabulary did not have the technical and policing resources enjoyed by many other agencies. Their communications were not up to scratch, which didn't help them when trying to liaise with other resources, and, of course, a manhunt such as this could never have been planned for in any event. So although by now several people had already been killed, the police still didn't know where the gunman was. In fact, so cash-strapped was the Cumbria Constabulary, it didn't have its own helicopter, so they had to call one in from neighbouring Lancashire. RAF Search and Rescue helicopters were also drafted into the area to assist in the massive search for the spree killer. However, by now, Bird was on the road speeding past his former workplace, Sellafield. The nuclear processing plant had been locked down because news had spread that the gunman, a former employee of course, was on the loose.

After failing to locate his diving instructor in Wilton, Derrick Bird seems to have had no clear sense of direction, so he headed towards the built-up area of Seascale. On the way he reached Gosforth, and, at about 11.20am, he saw thirty-one-year-old farmer and semi-professional rugby player Garry Purdham – who had played for the British Amateur Rugby League Association and toured Australia – trimming his hedge. Bird fired from his car, killing him. Fellow players recalled their friend:

> Garry played for us for a long time. He played over a hundred matches, and was really an exemplary player [...] everything about his character; his commitment, his discipline, was first class. He was always considered an automatic choice in the team when he was playing at his very best, and he was really an example to young rugby players, to young people and to the standards they need to meet [...] Garry was the best you could meet.
>
> Tim Knowles: Whitehaven RLFC,
> on Garry Purdham

> He was a man who you would respect. He had a wonderfully calm disposition. A wonderful temperament on and off of the pitch, and a wonderful sense of humour.
>
> Dave Bowden: Workington Town RLFC,
> on Garry Purdham

Described as a 'gentle giant', he left behind his wife, Ros, his sons, Cameron, aged eight, and Flynn, aged two. At the next Whitehaven home match, his widow, Ros, would release twelve white doves, each to signify the twelve people who died in Bird's killing spree.

Twenty-three-year-old estate agent, James 'Jamie' Clark died of a shotgun blast to the head as he drove along in his Smart car. It crashed and turned on its side in a ditch. He had recently moved to the area; his partner was a schoolteacher. After this kill, Bird drove along the B5344 into the seaside village of Seascale, where he came across a Land Rover driven by a local landlord, Harry Berger. Two shots were heard and local builder, William Hogg, came out of a house out to investigate the noise.

David Moore, a retained firefighter in Seascale, was pottering around in his greenhouse and heard a commotion down the road. There was a helicopter clattering overhead and as he was looking out towards the village he heard the two shots. Moments later, Moore's beeper alerted him and within minutes he would be at the scene of a shooting incident, for the gunshots shots had come from a railway bridge close to the seafront. Harry Berger had been hit in the shoulder. He was in his car, very badly injured but still alive. Harry had courteously given way to Bird, allowing him to drive through the narrow one-way passage underneath the bridge and onto South Parade. Bird repaid him with two shotgun blasts, causing severe injury to his right arm.

Three police armed-response vehicles – two Volvos and a 4x4 – were six minutes behind Bird, but Berger's Land Rover was blocking the road. The cops had to push it out of the way before they could resume the chase. Berger was soon airlifted to hospital and survived.

Twenty-six seconds later and a hundred yards south along the coast road, two more gunshots were heard. Bird had killed sixty-four-year-old cyclist Michael Pike, a former Liverpool shipbuilder who worked as a fitter and then a trainer at the Sellafield nuclear plant, where he became a trade union organiser.

He was a good fella. He was always happy. He's all around us. He built the walls in our garden. We have his railway in the garden. He had his way [...] his special spot to sit here every morning to drink his cup of tea, so he will always be here.

Jude Talbot: Michael Pike's daughter

Moments after shooting dead Michael Pike, Bird fatally shot sixty-six-year-old Jane Robinson in the neck and head with his shotgun. Jane was out delivering Betterware catalogues, and she was just yards away from the home she shared with her twin sister, Barrie. Jane was the last to die but several others were soon to be wounded.

Jane, and her sister, have lived here all of their lives. Ordinary people who just got on with their own lives and did their own thing [...] would never have done any harm to anybody. They were very much liked by many people. Now people have lost people who gave back to the community and that can never be replaced.

A former local postman

Every killing is a wasted life. The tributes paid to the victims of Derrick Bird serve only to reinforce the poignancy of that truth

* * *

After killing twelve people, Bird headed into the Lake District National Park, which was packed with holidaymakers in this half-term week. After firing at two cyclists and crashing past other cars, Bird finally crashed his silver Citroën Xsara

Picasso and burst a tyre close to the historic Doctor Bridge in the quaint village of Boot in Eskdale. He made off into nearby woodland, and it was only now that armed police with dogs could finally close in.

Police asked him to give himself up without any further problems, but at around 1.45pm, a muffled gunshot was heard. At 2pm, Deputy Chief Constable Stuart Hyde announced that Bird had been found dead. He had put the rifle muzzle to his forehead and fired.

So what turned Derrick Bird into such a terrible spree killer? Maybe we can we start to answer some of the questions here.

Perhaps psychologist Dr James Thompson makes a few revealing points, when he says: 'To the people that knew him superficially, they said that he [Bird] was absolutely usual [...] those who knew him well said that sometimes he did express a lot of anger.'

Muriel Gilpin, who worked in a local post office, said: 'Bird was very quiet. He would come in the shop. Buy milk, say "How do" and "See ya" [...] he didn't stand and chat, he was that quiet.'

Bird's next-door neighbour, Ryan Dempsey, spotted something was wrong. 'He would just stand there looking through people [...] several people said that he was not the sort of person they would associate with normally. He didn't say "hello" to anybody. He wasn't at all cheerful,' he said.

And, I rather think that Dr Thompson is telling us the facts when he says: 'The ability to judge a person's dangerousness is very, very limited. By all means, look at what the best screening techniques seem to be, but we do not yet know how to do that, particularly of course if someone is on their best behaviour.'

We like to assume that there is always a motive – a reason behind any type of criminal offence – yet many criminologists will say that there are crimes that appear motiveless. I believe that they are referring to the 'stranger killings' committed by serial murderers – homicides where there are no apparent links between offender and victim; however, I say that there is always a motivation present in all types of homicide although it may prove very difficult to determine. Now, as legal people and students of crime will know, proof of motive is never necessary in proof of the crime. Therefore, absence of any discoverable motive is of little consequence in deciding whether or not the prisoner committed the crime, for the most brilliant jury is helpless in deciding the 'mental processes' that 'actuate' the criminal. Where a motive *is* proved, however, it is at least a factor of importance to be taken into account.

Now, there is every possibility here that a reader with more legal expertise than I will ever enjoy might wish to debate 'motive' with me till the cows come home, so I will nip this in the bud. Let me refer to none other than Judge Travers Christmas Humphreys QC's *Seven Murders* (1931), a copy of which I have the pleasure of owning. I'm specifically interested in the foreword, written by Sir Archibald Bodkin, KCB, JP, Director of Public Prosecutions from 1920 to 1930, for it illustrates that when we look at the mental processes that actuate our mass murderers and spree killers, most of the commonest forms of motives fall into the following categories:

1. The desire of avenging some real or fanciful wrong.
2. The getting rid of a rival or obnoxious connection.
3. Of escaping from the pressure of pecuniary or other obligation.
4. Of preserving reputation, or of gratifying some malignant passion.

This is *not*, of course, legal rocket science. Yet I mention this because it is all too easy to start looking for wild and woolly psychopathological 'let's-bring-the-shrinks-in' cockamamie motives behind mass murderers and spree killings when, in truth, (1) through (4) are always staring at us straight in the face. Can the reader see some, or all of this, in our Mr Bird? I think the answer is a resounding 'Yes.'

And could Derrick Bird have committed his shootings had he not owned firearms? Obviously, the answer is 'No', and this applies in the cases of practically every shooting by a domestic mass murderer and spree killer past, present, and well into the future, for firearms are the facilitators.

Fortunately, unlike the USA the UK has never really had a 'gun culture', for most UK owned firearms are used for sport, game shooting and pest control. Nevertheless, at the time of writing there still around 1.3 million licensed shotguns in the UK, which equates to a bit less than one in every 64 people. Added to this, there are also 535,000 legally licensed firearms – basically, any other type of gun that's not a shotgun –in circulation. All hopefully owned by people who are responsible and of sound mind, too. Derrick Bird was neither of these; like all mass murderers and spree killers, he was a human time bomb psychologically primed to go off.

We also often label many of these awful killers as being 'mad' when they are not insane at all. They know *exactly* what they are doing is wrong; they are fully aware of the consequences of their actions. Prior to his shooting spree, it seems that Bird bumbled through life as best that he could. Like so many of his evil breed, to all those who knew him, either in passing or a little better, he came across as a quiet loner, sullen, a bit threatening and argumentative bordering on obnoxious. But there are millions of people who have the same psychological make-up and they don't turn into spree killers, do they?

Yes, Derrick Bird did have a fight with some youths who jumped his taxi without paying the fare and beat him up when he gave chase. A few years beforehand he'd been in another fight, this time outside a nightclub. But thousands of people across the world, physically and psychologically, suffer far worse than Bird ever did. Consider the unfortunate folk who are involved in serious car accidents and survivors who suffer the most terrible physical and mental trauma following bomb explosions. They do not turn into mass murderers or spree killers, do they? So I don't find *any* mitigation for Bird's atrocities in the fact that he came off the worse for wear after a short fight. What I think we might agree upon, however, is that Bird was becoming paranoid, if he hadn't become so already. He was exhibiting all of the symptoms of irrationality accompanied by persistent feelings that people were 'out to get him'.

The three main types of paranoia include: paranoid personality disorder, delusional (formerly paranoid) disorder and paranoid schizophrenia, but it is highly unusual for schizophrenia to be diagnosed after the age of forty-five – Bird was fifty-two. It is also worth noting that if there were any motive to be found for any of his shooting events, it might be related to his misguided belief that his brother, David, was financially ripping him off. Police found no evidence that he was.

It has been reported, however, that Bird's financial affairs had been in order. They were anything but: he made a point of telling a few people that he might go to prison because he owed money to HMRC. One cannot be put in prison for not being able to pay one's taxes unless one embarks on tax evasion, which carries a sentence of between one and three years. Any action taken to evade the assessment of tax, such as filing a fraudulent return, carries a stiffer sentence of up to five years, so this tells me that he'd been fiddling his books. He was under enormous pressure, and if the money that he'd hoped to receive from his brother and the family lawyer didn't arrive quickly, enabling him to pay his dues, he would go to prison, lose his livelihood and his home as well.

I ask myself what had David Bird to gain from ripping off his brother? Nothing, it seems to me. David had done very well for himself by selling off some of his land for the development of a few detached homes; he had a loving family, which Derrick Bird did not. And even if the family lawyer, Commons, had a totally corrupt business partner in Marcus Nickson, this would hardly matter too much in the general scheme of things, and surely would not offer Bird sufficient reason to fatally shoot and injure a lot of innocent people who had never crossed his path in their lifetimes.

Then we have the shooting death of Bird's cabbie

colleague Darren Rewcastle. Taxi drivers enjoy ribbing, or taking the Mickey out of each other – it comes with the job just as it does with any other trade or profession. Rewcastle's fellow cabbies said that Darren was a lively chap who enjoyed a joke. All of the drivers did, and some of them admit that they sometimes jumped to the front of the rank and poached a fare, just as a bigoted Bird had himself done. Maybe Rewcastle had slashed Bird's taxi tyres, maybe not, but surely this was not a reason for him to be shot to death, nor for Bird to start shooting at other taxi drivers too?

Why did he want to kill his diving instructor, Jason Carey? What had Carey done to deserve this? The police found absolutely no reason for it. The same applies to everyone else Bird shot at in his attempts to kill.

To sum this all up, do we not see psychopathological similarities between Bird and many other mass murders and spree killers referred to in this book? Brooding loners, inconsequential people who cannot face the fact that they *are* losers; pathological fantasy-driven grudge bearers.

CRIMES THAT SHOCKED TYNESIDE: ROBERT SARTIN'S MONKSEATON RAMPAGE

This twenty-minute spree on Sunday, 30 April 1989, at Monkseaton, North Tyneside, was committed by twenty-two-year-old Robert Sartin, a social security clerk. Using a 12-gauge double-barrelled shotgun, he killed one person and wounded fourteen others. This case was included in the CBS TV series *Murder by the Sea*, in which I appeared as an on-screen contributor.

Picking up his father's double-barrelled shotgun, and ammunition which he loaded into a cartridge belt around him, Sartin (a self-confessed Satanist) left the home he shared with his parents in Wentworth Gardens, Whitley Bay, to carry out another of the most horrific random shooting events in British criminal history. Thank goodness that he only had a shotgun and not an AK-47.

Mr Sartin Sr legally owned his 12-gauge shotgun and had a firearms certificate for its use. In his own hands this was quite acceptable. However, it was later determined that not only did his son have a grim obsession with 'Old Nick', but he had also been diagnosed as suffering from acute schizophrenia. Following his killing spree, Robert Sartin was declared insane, yet he had been thought sane enough to hold down a job as a clerk with a government department, I might add!

Sartin's parents and brother were so 'devastated' by the incidents that followed they left the region and changed their names. Nonetheless, the events of that horrifying day remains etched in many people's memories and will never be forgotten, especially with regard to the victims and their families.

At around 11.40am, on what was to become a Holy Day nightmare, Sartin left home for what his parents thought would be a morning stroll. Fifteen minutes later, he fired his first shot at Judith Rhodes as she sat in her car near Pykerley Road. The windscreen shattered but she ducked under the dashboard. Remaining as calm as she could, Judith attempted to drive away as he fired again. Luckily she made it to safety.

As families went out for their Sunday newspapers, chatting to neighbours, their children playing in the streets, Sartin calmly walked along, shooting indiscriminately. He spotted a father of two who had just left church. As he begged for his life before the killer fired from twenty yards, the last words ever heard by forty-one-year-old Kenneth Mackintosh, were: 'Now, it's your day to die.' The man was hit by two barrels that blasted lead shot into his chest – he was the only person to die that fateful day.

Sartin then got into his car, but PC Danny Herdman was in an unmarked police vehicle and had heard a radio call about the shootings. He spotted Sartin's car and followed. Reaching speeds up to 60mph, Sartin drove a short distance before parking in a Whitley Bay car park and climbed out. Although unarmed, PC Herdman pounced. He threw Sartin over the bonnet and handcuffed him, finally bringing the rampage to an end. In July 1990 PC Herdman was awarded the Queen's Commendation for Brave Conduct for, as the Supplement to the *London Gazette* of 26 July 1990 put it, 'services in single-handedly arresting an armed gunman, following a serious shooting incident in which a man was killed and several people were injured.'

As for Sartin – well, he will spend the remainder of his life in a secure mental institution and let's pray that no psychiatrist will ever allow him to be released.

14

The Monster Sleeping Within

He [Michael Ryan] was a very quiet person and seemed
to do his own sort of thing. He was very much alone …
A friend and myself was playing in a barn one day, the
next thing the door was being peppered with an air rifle.
After the firing stopped we came out with our hands
up, very frightened.

ANDY RICHENS: ATTENDED THE SAME SCHOOL
AS MICHAEL RYAN

With mass murderers and spree killers, pretty much anything
at all can spark the final murderous event: an outrageous
telephone bill; a snub from a girlfriend; a sidelong look in
a restaurant, or unexpected dismissal from a job. The killer
– specifically one who has reached a level of paranoid rage
– has often collected an armoury of weapons by this time,
the time when the sleeping monster within awakes. Then he
declares war on humanity.

This is *precisely* what Michael Ryan did. And just like all of the other spineless mass killers before him, since, and into the inevitably grim future of homicide en masse, he started his private war against innocent people who were completely unable to fight back.

'Michael Ryan rarely – if ever – had friends come round to visit him as a child,' Claire Carter wrote in the *Daily Mirror* on Saturday, 16 September 2017. He was a known loner; he struggled socially and had been bullied at school, singled out for being different, but at home his mother Dorothy lavished attention on her only child – even when he reacted to her with violence. In simple terms, I would call him a spoilt little brat.

Dorothy, aged thirty-four at the time of the killings and her husband, Alfred Henry Ryan, aged fifty-five, were polar opposites in the way they treated their son. Alfred and Michael were said to have had a 'distant relationship'. Mum, a lunchtime supervisor at a primary school, adored her son, and he developed a sense of superiority. According to some sources, Ryan had an early interest in Action Man figures that spiralled into a fascination with toy soldiers, a fervid interest in the military and eventually an obsession with guns.

Speaking on the CBS Reality programme *Murderers and their Mothers*, criminologist Dr Jane Monckton-Smith observed: 'She [Ryan's mother] would indulge him, and she would protect him and she wouldn't let anyone insult him [...] It seemed also that he was bullied. He was not only isolated, he was singled out as someone to pick on.'

At secondary school, the bullying continued. Ryan would later withdraw from college and gained no qualifications, making it difficult for him to get a job. This, it is claimed, made it a problem for him 'to join in with society'. Ah, do we hear a bit of limp-wristed 'mitigation' for his crimes creeping in here?

The young Ryan had now found solace retreating into a fantasy military world, one where he could turn the tables on the children who had 'betrayed' him by using them for target practice. He also practised using an air rifle, which his mother bought for him when he was thirteen. He used it to shoot at cows and other animals.

As Ryan grew older, his obsession with guns, aligned with his need to be in control, intensified. He is thought to have modelled himself on his father – a clerk of works, a traditionalist who valued authority, and whose values did not preclude violence towards his wife. Young Ryan started to hate his mother's weakness. He would scream and shout at her, even strike her, and eventually was to purchase an arsenal of lethal firearms.

On Tuesday, 14 July 1987, Ryan applied for an amendment to his firearms licence. This would enable him to add to his existing stash of guns: two shotguns, two pistols and a .30 semi-automatic rifle. Under the existing firearms laws there was no reason to decline any of Ryan's applications, therefore two weeks later PC Trevor Wainwright of Thames Valley Police approved this application. Ryan duly went shopping for a Kalashnikov and a Beretta pistol. Although no blame could ever be attributed to PC Wainwright, who was merely following the rulebook, the fault *can* be levelled elsewhere: an issue that we will look at shortly. Ryan, by now a twenty-seven-year-old handyman and 'antiques dealer', owned enough firepower to start a small war. On that point, however, Ryan's rampage killing led to a backlash over UK gun laws, and saw the introduction of the 1998 Firearms Act, which among other restrictions banned the use of shotguns with a capacity of three or more cartridges, while also proscribing ownership of semi-automatic centre-fire weapons. Better late than never.

Although the motive for Ryan's killings remains unknown, one psychologist has suggested that its origins may lie in the 'anger and contempt for the ordinary life around him, which he himself was not a tangible part of'. And further, although no firm diagnoses on Ryan's state of mind have been made by experts on mental health, more than one have suggested that he might have been either psychotic, or a schizophrenic. Among their number were John Higgins (at the time a consultant forensic psychiatrist at Merseyside Regional Health Authority) and John Hamilton (the then medical director of Broadmoor Hospital). Hamilton posited that: 'Ryan was most likely to have been suffering from acute schizophrenia. He might have had a reason for doing what he did, but it was likely to be bizarre and peculiar to him.'

Ryan, however, was sufficiently in control of his senses to find occasional work as a handyman, and an antique dealer of sorts to earn some money. And enough to know all about the histories of the firearms he owned and of which he professed great knowledge.

We cannot turn the clock back. But since the 1998 Firearms Act was enacted, domestic spree killings and mass-murder events using firearms in the UK have, I believe, almost, though not quite, ceased, in light of the 12 August

2021 Plymouth spree killings (ironically, that date being the start of the grouse-shooting season).

> It is a ghastly story of family dysfunction, professional and sexual failure, grotesque narcissism and the temptation of apocalyptic delusions.
>
> Ian Buruma: *The Guardian*, Thursday,
> 26 February 2015, on the Norwegian
> mass murderer Anders Breivik

'If the lone wolf suicide killer [...] the avenger of all the sleights and snubs from a hostile world, had a generic face, it might look like a bit like Anders Breivik's: pudgy, piggy-eyed, with thin blond sweaty hair and a sickly smile,' writes Ian Buruma in his review of Åsne Seierstad's book *One of Us: The Story of Anders Breivik and the Massacre in Norway*. We can therefore ascertain that, as with many of the murderers contained in these pages, Breivik perfectly fits into the mould of these cold-hearted killers who acted alone. He continues: 'Breivik is the perfect example of what the German writer Hans Magnus Enzensberger once called "the radical loser", the angry fantasist who wants to bring the world down with him.'

> If you drink much from a bottle marked 'poison', it is almost certain to disagree with you, sooner or later.
>
> Lewis Carroll (Charles Lutwidge Dodgson):
> *Alice in Wonderland* (1865)

Just like serial killers, mass murderers and spree killers let nothing show; they just wait and wait. They reveal nothing, concealing their intentions under the social camouflage they wear. They guard their delusions, and as we have already learned, we only come to know the true nature of the beast when he finally and violently reveals himself.

Now, at this point fellow travellers, put away your lunchboxes because you might instantly lose your appetite. I often use cinematic analogies to paint a more vivid picture of what I am getting at in my books. So now I turn to the 1979 science-fiction horror film *Alien*. Those of us who have watched Ridley Scott's scare-us-half-to-death nightmare inducer will remember the scene when 'foetus alien' incubates inside the chest of crewman Kurt (played by John Hurt) then explodes out, all bloody, umbilical-cord slippery and wet – ugh; then it grows into an even bigger alien and goes on to do some inside-a-spaceship-spree-killing of its own. There it was inside Kurt, and no one suspected anything. Then, when the time came for it to be hatched, it gave Kurt a serious bellyache and blasted out, a vision of horror. And this happened as the crew were eating a meal, for Christ's sake! I mean, give me a break... what happened to intergalactic table manners these days?

In a similar vein, all mass murderers and spree killers pathologically incubate, waiting patiently for their hour to come when they metamorphose into a monster. They save their energies before arriving at that dread moment when their emotions can be contained not a minute longer – then, they detonate, with the bloodbaths that inevitably follow. It's an totally off-the-wall analogy, to be sure, but one that I think fits quite well.

Here's another fascinating aspect common to serial killers, mass murderers and spree killers. Day-to-day, week-in, week-out, no one pays any mind to them, other than noticing that they might seem to act a bit odd or suspiciously sometimes. Otherwise they come across as just another face on the street, or 'Mr Joe Average' sitting behind you on a bus, or shopping in the store close to you. They are non-people and subconsciously they know it. Moreover, as with *all* of the killers I have studied and written about over several decades, and as Ted Bundy has rightly said (and he was, after all, 'the expert' on his given subject), when it comes to such figures there are no stereotypes.

No lone killer of any type will reveal himself until the time is right for them. They don't have to, for in their minds they are in control. Just like stalkers and terrorist 'sleepers' they are unobtrusive, silent: yet, inside they are smouldering, their emotions simmering away until, like human bombs, they detonate to cause carnage on scale almost inconceivable to the likes of you and me, and this is why they are so feared. But as we have no knowledge of who they are, or how, if and when they will strike, this imagined terror breeds a form of social neurosis which spreads exponentially, and this we see throughout the USA today, with firearm sales going ballistic, so to speak.

This is my .480 Ruger Super Redhawk six-shot revolver. Wisconsin is an open-carry state, so anyone eighteen or older can visibly carry weapons under state law. I'm gonna protect myself and my kids if and when the shooting starts.

Forty-something Milwaukee homemaker:
Channel 4 News, 26 October 2020

A Trump supporter, bless her. So, as I write, the November 2020 presidential elections are coming to an end and I am watching on TV the voters lining up in the 'battleground state' of Wisconsin, which has always been, to my knowledge, a Republican 'stronghold'. 'Battleground' and 'stronghold' kind of remind us of the Wild West, do they not? Can you imagine Devon becoming a 'battleground county' with Budleigh Salterton a 'stronghold'? Of course not, but that's the US of A for you.

Nevertheless, here in the 'Badger State' they are lining up in their thousands, waving placards – dyed-in-the-wool Republicans shouting abuse at the Democrats, and vice-versa. Many of these voters are openly carrying firearms and being marshalled by scores of right-wing civvies, some of them overweight, gum-chewing redneck types dressed like Rambo: Ray-Bans; full black combat kit; body armour; walkie-talkies; cargo pants stuffed full of ammo and spare batteries for their Maglites; carrying high-powered military-type firearms and with automatic pistols in holsters slung low from their waists. Just across the street, almost hidden from view, are the National Guard, called out in readiness for any trouble. There is a Boeing AH-64 Apache military helicopter buzzing around overhead, narrowly avoiding several media helicopters hoping to film a bloodbath.

What in creation is that all about? In the UK, we simply amble along to, let's say, the local school, say, 'Hello, nice day, isn't it?' to a long-retired, heavily moustached army major wearing a tweed jacket, cavalry twill trousers and spit-and-polished brown brogues; have our names ticked off a list and then enter a booth to mark an 'X' on a slip of paper, fold the paper and pop it in a box, then wander off to watch the TV and the riots and arson attacks that may be taking place in Milwaukee. Well, at least you might be able to see *some* of the footage once the tear gas and smoke clear away.

* * *

Long before (and ever since) the attack on the World Trade Center in New York on Tuesday, 11 September 2001, political scientists, sociologists and psychologists vainly searched for a reliable pattern; one common thread between all types of mass killers that may offer clues as to how give society an antidote to this evil living amongst us. However, there are too many imponderables, too many variable psychopathological matrixes to this homicidal Rubik's Cube; for unlike the German Enigma machine – a mechanical encryption device whose coding would eventually be cracked using *human* brain power – expecting the human mind to decrypt the thought processing systems of these killers who cannot even understand their own minds is, at least for now, impossible. So does this mean that those who try to find a 'cure' are on a losing wicket? Yes, perhaps they are.

Instead of looking into the faces of hundreds of spree killers and mass murderers, studying their crimes, their past ways of living (their narratives), their interpersonal domestic social and employment histories, going way back to their teens and formative years, sociologists stubbornly keep to their statistics, their 'median values', 'standard deviations' and 'normal distributions'. These represent well-intended attempts to find some kind of empirical magic bullet that will predict what an emerging monster *might* do before he, himself, has even considered what he may or not do if the right situation arises. It rarely occurs to these 'experts' that they might be on a losing team. What's the point, when in every single case the atrocious deed has already been done?

Thomas Hamilton subconsciously knew that his life had no real meaning, that it was futile to carry on pretending to himself that he was something other than what he was. The penny finally dropped and he understood that he was worthless. The egotistical Dr Shipman did a similar thing by hanging himself when he realised that he had become a 'nothing person'. However, people like Derrick Bird, Hamilton and countless others, including all the serial killers I have interviewed, feel that they are never to blame – it is always the fault of somebody else. So deep runs this twisted pathology that, bizarrely, they transfer any blame for their behaviour onto others, even society as a whole, when the truth is staring straight at them. It's the negative way the world treats them, they reason. For whatever purpose, society has been against them from the get-go; they were dealt a bad hand of cards and the odds have never existed in their favour. Let's face the facts here, and not dress them up. These people are sociopaths and/or psychopaths. The majority of them are forlorn, solitary, cold-shouldered and trapped in their own private worlds, their own pathologically warped island universes – and they know it, too. Their egocentric world becomes a vicious circle, an everlasting struggle that they cannot escape. Indeed, escape to what? These people think only of themselves without regard for the feelings or desires of others. Indeed, these antisocial individuals absolutely cannot re-enter a society as a social animal because this is the society that they 'perceive' has always been against them all along, so what would be the point?

They reach a stage where they become morbidly entrenched in self-pity. They realise that their own lives are now worthless. But then so are the lives of everyone else too, and the only way out of the dilemmas these weak people can find is to exact revenge. It is their way of saying: 'Well, you lot truly f*cked up my life and made me feel worthless, so now I am in control and I am going to stick it to you all good and proper. Hey, it's payback time.' Then they fuse destruction and self-destruction, aggression and auto-aggression into their own 'Big Bang'.

As German author Hans Magnus Enzensberger, says:

On the one hand, at the moment of his explosion, the loser for once experiences a feeling of true power. His act allows him to triumph over others by annihilating them. And on the other, he does justice to the reverse of this feeling of power, the suspicion that his own existence was worthless, by putting an end to it.

The time-worn phrase 'Revenge is a dish best served cold' encapsulates the sentiment that revenge delayed then executed well after the heat of anger has dissipated is more satisfying than retribution taken as an immediate (knee-jerk) act of rage. Can you now see this revenge (this curse) acted out in the killers we have met thus far? The waiting, the planning game, which is all part of their mission – to plot then execute and never mind the consequences to themselves and anyone else. Remember the Confucius proverb: 'Before you embark on a journey of revenge, dig two graves,' meaning one for you, because you might as well destroy yourself too.

* * *

I simulate various future scenarios relating to resistance efforts, confrontations with police, future interrogation scenarios, future court appearances, future media interviews, etc.

Anders Behring Breivik: from his
1,500-page manifesto written under the
pseudonym 'Andrew Berwick'

I will spare the reader the mental turmoil of reading pretty much anything about Breivik's manifesto in this book. All it amounts to is yet another of society's abject losers imagining that his words will be chiselled into stone and passed down for the benefit of the generations of other societal failures to come.

Born on Sunday, 13 February 1979, Breivik is a Norwegian far-right domestic terrorist who, on Sunday, 22 July 2011, dressed himself as a police officer and detonated a van bomb in Oslo near the prime minister's office, killing eight people. Having done so, he travelled to the lake island of Utøya, about twenty-five miles north-west of Oslo, where, still in police uniform, he shot dead sixty-nine participants at a Workers' Youth League summer camp. Most of his victims were aged fourteen to nineteen. When the police finally arrived, this self-proclaimed fascist, a Nazi, an Odinism practitioner who used counter-jihadist rhetoric to support ethno-nationalists, threw his hands up in the air to meekly give himself up. This lowlife didn't even have the guts to have a shootout with the cops.

Of some interest to us is that two teams of court-appointed forensic psychiatrists examined Breivik before his first trial in 2012, and diagnosed him as having 'paranoid schizophrenia'. Not surprisingly, this evaluation came under much criticism before a second evaluation concluded that he was not psychotic during his attacks, but that he did have a 'narcissistic personality disorder' and 'antisocial personality disorder'. Wow. It must have taken a lot of highly paid-for shrink brainpower to figure that out. And quite how two teams of court-appointed forensic psychiatrists arrived at the same conclusion of paranoid schizophrenia will forever remain a mystery.

Paranoid schizophrenia is characterised by predominantly positive symptoms of schizophrenia topped up with hallucinations. These 'debilitating' symptoms blur the line between what is real and what is not, making it difficult for the person to lead a 'typical' life. In Breivik's mind, he was indeed living the typical life... of an emerging mass murderer who was planning his own private war with almost military precision, while to everyone around him, although he seemed a bit odd at times he appeared absolutely normal. As for him having a 'narcissistic personality disorder' and 'antisocial personality disorder', do we need a team of overpaid consultant psychiatrists and psychologists to figure this out? Why not just look up what *Wikipedia* has to say about these conditions, for God's sake? by any legal definition Breivik was never insane; but he was, and he remains, distilled evil personified. Just take a look online at this man's smirking face: smug; self-opinionated; contemptuous; arrogant to a fault. Who would want to emulate him? Well, plenty of other like-minded deadbeats, that's for sure.

The maximum term the law allows for Breivik's crimes is twenty-one-years of cushy 'preventive detention' with all mod cons – the Norwegian equivalent of doing 'hard time'. It kicks off with a meagre ten years' incarceration and the possibility of one or more unspecified time extensions for as long as he is deemed a danger to society. Heavens above, let's pray that when he next comes up for parole the panel of shrinks who evaluate his state of mind do not tell us that Breivik is fully compos mentis, that he should be released without further ado, along with hand-wringing apologies for the justice system and medical profession having had the temerity to have detained the poor chap for so long. Indeed, if Breivik had any wits about him at all, he should zip up his loud mouth, put away his pen and paper, stop writing and whining to the European Court of Human Rights about his own human rights being violated. If he licked some correctional ass instead of kicking it, he could probably walk out of jail a free man much faster than he thought. Shhh. Mum's the word, so please don't write and tell him this or he'll reply with another turgid 1,000-page dissertation.

THE MONSTER SLEEPING WITHIN
* * *

I had it in mind to bring this chapter to a close at this point, yet I was reminded of the words of Ian Buruma in *The Guardian* (26 February 2015). He makes a telling point about pensmiths who write exhaustively on these mass killers, giving the oxygen of publicity to their loathsome actions and expanding their profile and importance. 'Worldwide publicity transforms these misfits into heroic or villainous representatives of global religions, political ideologies and even entire civilisations.'

So are we indeed doing everything to grant these killers' wishes? Is there any suggestion from Ian Buruma that Åsne Seierstad, Hans Magnus Enzensberger, the legions of journalists and TV presenters and the countless TV documentary makers who investigate these offenders are milking the loss of the innocents and transforming these 'misfits' into (in Buruma's words) 'heroic or villainous representatives of global religions, political ideologies and even entire civilisations'? Of course not.

* * *

In 2017, there were circa 7.53 billion of us living on Planet Earth. The USA has around 331.8 million citizens, with far too many guns amongst them. It has the third highest firearm mass-murder rate per capita in the world. Top of the world's population list is China, with nearly 1.4 billion citizens. But there, by contrast, mass killings are as rare as hen's teeth ... The same applies to North Vietnam, the Philippines and most other Far-Eastern countries.

Now my fellow travellers, we have arrived at another

truck stop. Time to disembark, and stretch your legs.

15

Copycat Killings

What is this – a country or a slaughterhouse? Mass
murder has become part of the American way of life [...]
It is a style, a vogue, we are forced to live with every day
[...] had I gone on much longer without a cigarette,
I might have become a mass murderer.

ANDREW F. TULLY: AMERICAN WAR REPORTER, WRITER
AND COLUMNIST

Much has been written about copycat killers – those who
hold their murderous predecessors in such high esteem that
they, whatever their own warped motives, try to emulate
those who have previously found a grim place in the annals
of criminal history, thereby gaining some 'fame'.

So do their motives, often all so carefully laid out
throughout inane rambling letters, lengthy manifestos and
YouTube videos, help us understand them any better? No,
they do not. They spew out self-serving bullshit, there is no

other word for it. In fact, after decades of studying these killers' so-called motivations, even today the work of the world's finest social scientists and psychologists has come to nothing, as in a fat zero. In countless magazine articles, TV programmes and during lectures, I have been put on the spot as to the motivational drivers that propel mass murderers and spree killers. Sexual serial killers are easy to figure out; mass murderers and spree killers are something else. I am very strong, as I must be, about the heartache and suffering these monsters cause; not so much on whether some killer had still been wetting his pants at the age of eighteen.

I will go even further by suggesting that intuition, or psychological crystal ball-gazing, plays no part in trying to predict what an evil person is thinking. Because we can only know the true nature of these beasts when they finally emerge and kill – sometimes on an almost industrial scale.

A number of mass killings may be deemed copycat killings – so many seem to involve educational establishments, for instance, even if each killer might have had a personal reason to target a school or university. Consider Australia's Martin John Bryant, a convicted mass murderer who shot dead thirty-five people and injured twenty-three others between 28 and 29 April 1996, in what is known as the Port Arthur massacre.

Born on Sunday, 7 May 1967, in Hobart, Tasmania, Bryant has a narrative as fascinating as it is bizarre, and well worth reading up on elsewhere. To say that he was mentally challenged almost from the start would be the psychiatric understatement of a lifetime. Not only did Martin, aged twenty-nine at the time of the shootings, have the IQ of an eleven-year-old boy – even to this very day he still doesn't know why he did what he did. He has plenty of time on his hands to ponder it, though: he's been locked up for life, to serve no less than 35 life sentences, plus 1,035 years, in Hobart's Risdon Prison.

If Bryant does not know why he did what he did, we most certainly know how he did it. For some obscure reason, after killing a number of people he parked up his yellow Volvo 244 at the Port Arthur ruins, entered the Broad Arrow Café carrying a large duffel bag, ate a meal, set up a video camera on an empty table, took out a Colt AR-15 SP1 carbine and, firing from the hip, began shooting at other diners and staff. According to the police report, within fifteen seconds, he had let loose seventeen shots, killing twelve people and wounding ten being the official account (but work the maths out for yourselves because that makes little sense to me). Then, he walked around to kill another eight people and wound two others. And then on and on and on. Sadly I have no room here for a fuller account, but to cut to the chase: as it had already been diagnosed that Martin was a complete crazy man, how on earth did he manage to legally purchase an semi-automatic military-grade rifle?

Totting up Martin Bryant's mental shortcomings, we know that at school he suffered from an 'intellectual disability' (mental retardation), and in 1983 when he finished what education that *did* manage to sink in, he left school with a disability pension. It was now obvious that he had a neurodevelopment disorder. The fact that he was a very dangerous kid to be around other children did not help matters, either; on one occasion he had pulled away another boy's snorkel as the lad was diving, and on another he hewed down trees on a neighbour's property. He smashed up his own toys, was disruptive and bullied by his older pupils, while he was happy to torment the younger ones. Added to which he enjoyed torturing animals and could neither read nor write.

While Bryant was awaiting trial, Ian Sale, a court-appointed psychiatrist, examined him and concluded that he 'could be regarded as having shown a mixture of conduct disorder, attention deficit hyperactivity and a condition known as Asperger syndrome'. Psychiatrist Paul Mullen, for Bryant's legal counsel, weighed in with the obvious observation that the defendant was impaired both socially and intellectually.

He also said that Bryant exhibited signs neither of schizophrenia nor of a mood disorder, finishing off with: 'Though Mr Bryant was clearly a distressed and disturbed young man, he was not mentally ill.' Of course, in itself Asperger syndrome is not a mental illness, but I would hope that any right-minded person would readily say that anyone with Bryant's history of mental history should never have been allowed near a firearm in the first instance.

Perhaps an even bigger question is: what or who inspired Bryant to commit mass murder on such an industrial scale? Well, here is the kicker. According to his psychiatrist, he was partially inspired by our own, homegrown Dunblane mass murderer, Thomas Watt Hamilton. Prior to reading about Dunblane, Bryant had intended to commit suicide. Then he changed his mind to something along the lines of, 'Nope! In fact, I'd be delighted to double the Scot's body count.'

In March 2012, the highly regarded, multiple-prize-winning Sydney visual artist Rodney Pople controversially won the $35,000 Glover Prize for his landscape painting depicting Port Arthur with Bryant in the foreground holding a firearm. Can the reader possibly imagine a British artist being awarded £17,600 after painting Thomas Hamilton holding his guns and standing in front of the gates of the Dunblane Primary School? I certainly hope not.

Returning to copycat killers, these include wannabe serial killers who aspire to scale the lofty homicidal limelit heights such as Ted Bundy, dear old one-eyed Henry Lee Lucas (1936–2001), or our mysterious, probably British, Victorian 'Jack the Ripper'. In deference to my American readers, I should add that Jack *could* have been a US doctor/quack called Francis Tumblety. Some of our Stateside cousins are adamant that Jack was one of them, which is not something one might wish to claim, especially as they have more than a fair stock of home-raised serial murderers, spree killers and mass murderers of their own. So why try and nick one of ours? It is certainly something they might want to distance themselves from, not brag about.

The reason I bring this up is because these days, and you are going to murder me for saying so, serial killers are the 'cool kids on the block'. Indeed, I have written a book called *Serial Killers at the Movies* about this very subject. To prove my point let us take a look at the mass killer Christopher Harper-Mercer (1989–2015), a twenty-six-year-old student who was enrolled at the Umpqua Community College near Roseburg, Oregon.

The day was Thursday, 1 October 2015. Harper-Mercer

had somehow got hold of a Smith & Wesson M99, a Taurus PT24/7 Hi-Point CF-380, a Glock 19, a Smith & Wesson M642-2 revolver *and* a Del-Ton DTI-15 semi-automatic rifle. Then he shot dead ten people, including himself, and injured eight others, If you have a mind to seek some form of extenuation for his crimes, you can read up on this killer's back history on the internet. It's worth noting, however, that prior to his attack, this man wrote a journal in which he placed himself in the 'elite' pantheon of mass killers – in his words, 'people who stand with the gods'. Indeed, he tried to rally other like-minded social losers to join in with a bloody continuum:

And just like me, there will be others, like Ted Bundy said, we are your sons, your brothers, we are everywhere. My advice to others like me is to buy a gun and start killing people. If you live in a country like Europe [*sic*] with strict gun laws, either pay the necessary fees/time to get a licence or become a serial killer. The world could always use an additional serial killer. Butcher them in their homes, in the street, wherever you find them [...] Human life means nothing, we are what matters. I hope to inspire the masses with this, at least enough to get their passions aroused. It is my hope that others will hear my call and act it out. I was once like you, a loser, rejected by society.

Christopher Harper-Mercer, journal

The upshot being that, unlike Theodore Robert Bundy, an archetypal monster who *did* make it to the silver screen more times than one can count, and in more movie modi operandi subtext plots than one can count too, Harper-Mercer got zilch, as in zero cinematic, put-bums-on-seats post-mortem acclaim.

Ah, I see that some of you travellers are getting a bit tired now. Don't worry, we'll be stopping at a motel soon. In the meantime, may I introduce you to Randy Stair (1992–2017)?

Stair was fed up with his worthless existence and his job as a fruit stacker at Weis Markets in Eaton Township, Ohio. Every morning when he looked into a mirror, he saw a twenty-four-year-old sap staring back at him. He was depressed and wanted out, so he prepared himself to go down in a blaze of glory. The reason for his 'depression' was that he appears to have been transgender, feeling 'trapped' as a woman inside a man's body. 'In this respect transgender people often encounter stigmatisation, oppression, and discrimination, which can all contribute towards mental heath problems,' writes Louise Morales-Brown in *Medical News Today*, 20 May 2021. And Stair was fascinated with the mass killing at Columbine High School in Colorado, too.

He lived and worked near Scranton, Pennsylvania – the state that birthed a famous rifle. He owned two pistol-gripped Mossberg 500 pump-action shotguns, which he loaded with 12-gauge shells with hardened 00 buckshot. Slightly modified for military use, the Mossberg was used very effectively for trench-clearing during World War I – and much later, in Vietnam, for close-quarter jungle warfare. The Royal Ulster Constabulary also used similar types during 'The Troubles'. The Mossberg is the bee's knees if one wants to blast a big hole in someone. Now imagine this ballistic lethality being used inside a shop where they sell fruit and veg, melons, grapes, carrots, peaches, marrows ...

For some seven months before he let loose, Stair did what so many others of his killer breed do: write. Then, as if his pathologically driven, handwritten 237-page journal (under the penname 'Andrew Blaze') weren't enough, he compiled videos – his self-described 'Suicide Tapes'. So can you now imagine this sap sitting alone, fantasising in his own antisocial bubble world of nihilistic rants? I can, that's for sure.

The time came for him to leave his mortal life, to carve out a niche of everlasting infamy for himself. In the early hours of Thursday, 8 June 2017, while his fellow workers were stacking fruit at that Weis Markets supermarket, Stair – who had never held down a plum job for long in his life – barricaded the exits of the store. Then he blasted his colleagues to death before killing himself.

Here is a short extract from Stair's journal.

What makes someone as innocent-looking as me want to cause mass devastation and manipulation?

I've hated humans my entire life. I hated making friends, 'socialising' amongst my classmates, and just overall being spoken to. Humans are <u>WORTHLESS.</u> We are living, breathing, moving trash. I don't care what you say; life is a never-ending simulation of hell.

So there you are, then. And if you have nothing more riveting to do, Stair's videos are something to behold. Moreover, they have received over 118,000 views over the years.

HATE! I'm full of hate and I Love it. I HATE PEOPLE and they better fucking fear me if they know whats good for em. yes I hate and I guess I want others to know it, yes I'm racist and I don't mind. Niggs and spics bring it on themselves, and another thing, I am very racist towards white trash p.o.s.s [...]

I love the nazis too... by the way, I fucking cant get enough of the swastika, the SS, and the iron cross. Hitler and his head boys fucked up a few times and it cost them the war, but I love their beliefs and who they were, what they did, and what they wanted..

[...] fuck fuck fuck it'll be very fucking hard to hold out until April. If people would give me more compliments all of this might still be avoidable... but probably not. Whatever I do people make fun of me, and sometimes directly to my face. I'll get revenge soon enough. fuckers shouldn't have ripped on me so much huh! HA!

Eric Harris: obscene rants from November 1998
(verbatim and uncorrected)

On Tuesday, 20 April 1999, the State of Colorado ('the Centennial State') witnessed the worst mass killing in its entire history. A lengthy dissertation in this book would be a redundant exercise because the tragedy is comprehensively covered elsewhere. However, for our purpose a brief summary is appropriate, because this school shooting has inspired several copycat killers in what has become known as the 'Columbine Effect' – it is the killers' legacy, and it has had, in a disgustingly morbid way, a significant impact on popular culture, too.

The eighteen-year-old Columbine perpetrators were Eric David Harris and Dylan Klebold. Armed with a small arsenal of guns, 99 explosives and 4 knives (not used), they murdered 12 students and a teacher; 21 other people were injured before Harris and Klebold committed suicide after shots were exchanged with the police. Officially, unofficially, and really, who gives two hoots anyway, their motives remain 'inconclusive'. We do know that they had been planning the event for a year. Inanely, they had *hoped* to exceed the death toll of the Oklahoma City bombing (at least 168 deaths, with more than 680 others injured), which occurred on Wednesday, 19 April 1995.

If this was their intention, Harris and Klebold signally failed, however, what they *did* achieve was the introduction of the 'Immediate Action Rapid Deployment Tactic', now used in active shooter situations today. Columbine also resulted in an increased emphasis on school security, with zero tolerance policies. As par for the course, the usual heated debates were once again sparked over firearm control laws and gun-culture high-school cliques, subcultures, and bullying. It also prompted discussions about the moral panic over goths, any types of social outcasts, the use of pharmaceutical antidepressants by youngsters, teenage internet use and violence in video games and movies. A legion of publicly funded psychiatrists and others of their ilk were summoned forth *tout de suite*, to try and figure out upon which planet these two monsters had been living prior to the 'event', what 'dysfunctional social dynamics' had played a part in their worthless lives, etc, etc.

But of course, all of that was in vain; the Columbine horses had already bolted. So how and where did Harris and Klebold acquire their weapons? Because they were under the legal age to buy firearms. Well here we go: the duo having already illegally got their hands on two 9mm guns and two shotguns, Harris somehow acquired the Hi-Point 995 carbine with thirteen 10-round magazines, and the Savage-Springfield 67H pump-action shotgun, which he loaded for bear. Klebold now had a 9x19mm Intratec TEC-9 semi-automatic handgun with one 52, one 32, and one 28-round magazine, and the Stevens 311D double-barrelled shotgun shortened to 23 inches. Harris's shotgun was likewise sawn off to 26 inches.

It's time for you fellow travellers to sit down now and take a *very* stiff drink. For one Robyn Anderson (who, days before the massacre, had gone to a high-school prom with Klebold) had actually bought the carbine rifle and the two shotguns for the murderous pair at the Tanner Gun Show. After the killings, she told police that she had thought that they wanted the firearms for target practice, and that she had no idea what they were actually going to use them for.

Klebold and Harris worked part time at a pizza parlour. Through Mark Manes – a pal of fellow pizza tosser Philip Duran – Klebold bought the TEC-9 on 23 January for $500 at a gun show.

No charges were brought against Robyn Anderson; however, Manes and Duran received prison sentences of six years and four-and-a-half years, respectively. Had the gun laws been abided by, the Columbine killings would never have occurred at all.

Harris and Klebold had also manufactured several improvised explosive devices using instructions downloaded from the internet and *The Anarchist Cookbook*. The ninety-nine devices included nine Molotov cocktails (of which only two proved functional), car bombs, pipe bombs and gunpowder-filled carbon dioxide cartridges (aka 'Crickets'); they built forty-five of the latter, though only eight detonated on the day. They also converted propane gas tanks into bombs. To set them off they used model rocket igniters and ordinary household matches; additionally, they adapted timing devices from clocks and batteries for the car bombs and propane explosives as well as some diversionary devices that they created. Incredibly, Harris had originally planned to use a flamethrower too, and even tried to make napalm for it. The pair attempted to coerce fellow pizza-joint colleague, Chris Morris, into joining them (and storing the napalm at his home), but Morris turned them down, upon which they pretended that it had all been a wind-up.

In the aftermath, and after much work, the FBI came to the somewhat obvious conclusion that Harris was a 'clinical psychopath' and Klebold was 'depressive'. They added that both teenagers were 'victims of mental illness'. Writing up his psychological profile on Harris, Aubrey Immelman, a Minnesota psychology professor, noted: 'Eric Harris's personality, as inferred from his writing, is consistent with the syndrome described by Otto Kernberg (1984) as *malignant narcissism*. The core components of this syndrome are pathological narcissism, antisocial features, paranoid traits, and unconstrained aggression. More narrowly construed,

Eric Harris matches Theodore Millon's (1996) description of *malevolent antisocial.'*

Yep, thank you. We got that in one, Professor Immelman!

Those of you interested in investigating these dark waters further, may wish to visit www.millon.net.taxonomy/sadistic.htm. It's a lengthy read, but well worth it if one wants even to try to understand the malevolent antisocial psychopathology of morally twisted individuals such as Eric Harris.

* * *

It is in the very essence of most humans to want to better ourselves, to excel in our chosen professions or trades, and in our social lives too, because we are social creatures who live in a world where there are ladders to climb, along with a hierarchy. It is like a real-life game of Snakes and Ladders – we climb up, slip, go down a few steps then carry on up, with repeats all the time until those who do persevere hopefully achieve their aims.

It is in our nature that most of us want to find more comfortable places to live, more nutritious food to eat so that we can pass on healthy, strong genes to our offspring.

Let me put it this way. Years ago, I wanted to be a racing car driver. Sadly, my bulk wouldn't permit me to fit into a Massey Ferguson tractor, let alone a Formula One speeding machine. I dreamed of being like Stirling Moss, or emulating Juan Manuel Fangio, who won the World's Driver's Championship five times. Even the President of the United States, Donald Trump, aspires to loftier heights – ballistically higher than we mere mortals could ever dream of. Certainly some of his followers have stated that he was God's choice, or that God's hand was in the 2016 election results. However, Trump is an asshole. That's my humble opinion, for what it's worth. But if he'd come down hard on US gun controls, I might even have invited him round for a cup of tea.

Levity aside, if a child is brought up in a comfortable, secure and loving home, then hopefully he or she gradually grows up into a healthy youth and then a responsible adult, one who wants to emulate their parents and the lessons they learned from them. I have written extensively about this subject in my previous books, but if a child is raised in an unhealthy home environment, one where the parents are non-achievers, are abusive and irresponsible care givers, perhaps alcoholics who let their children become feral, all of society suffers as the result. It seems to me that at least *some* of the mass murder/spree killings we have witnessed arises from a lack of parental control of youths linked to slack gun control laws – both equally irresponsible as far as I can tell.

So we aspire, we seek, we hope, we dream and we look to others who *have* 'achieved'. We seek out role models and many of us witness what the trappings of success can bring to the winners – never to the losers. But total failures wanting to emulate other total failures? How can we even get our heads around this bizarre aspirational wish, this upside-down, inside-out, antisocial mindset?

Well, let's give it a try, shall we? I think that we can go part way there by putting ourselves, as best we can, into the mind of a few mass murderers, then ask ourselves: are there any prizes to be awarded for social ambition here?

So... step forward, our award-losing losers:

Dimitrios Pagourtzis (seventeen): Santa Fe High School Shooting, Texas, Friday, 18 May 2018.

Weapons: 12-gauge Remington 870 shotgun, a Rossi .38-calibre snub-nosed revolver, plus a Molotov cocktail and other explosives

A wannabe Columbine killer – who was often seen wearing a black trench coat, as Harris and Klebold wore – Pagourtzis killed 2 teachers and 8 students and injured another 14, before making a botched attempt to end his own life.

Current status: awaiting trial, facing a life sentence.

Alvaro Rafael Castillo (eighteen): Orange High School Shooting, Hillsborough, North Carolina, Wednesday, 30 August 2006.

Weapons: 9mm Hi-Point 995 carbine and a sawn-off 12-gauge Mossberg 500 pump-action shotgun, which he named 'Arlene'. The name was one that Eric Harris had used for his prized Savage Springfield 67H shotgun. It was taken from one of Harris's favourite characters: Private First-Class (later Lance-Corporal) Arlene Sanders from the four sci-fi novels written by Dafydd ab Hugh and Brad Linaweaver, based on the video game series *Doom*. Their titles are: *Knee-Deep in the Dead*, *Hell on Earth*, *Infernal Sky* and *Endgame*, and Castillo, like Harris, had read them all.

Castillo wasted a lot of money while accumulating a vast collection of Columbine memorabilia, including a black trench coat. He even had a sexual fixation about Eric Harris, of whom he said: 'Eric Harris is just so good-looking. I can't believe he couldn't get a date for the prom. If I was a girl, I would have gone to the prom with him. Does that sound gay, straight or bi?'

Way down in the loser stakes, the bungling Castillo only just managed to kill his father and injure two others.

Current status: prisoner #0973344, Castillo. Life term, Nash Correctional Institution (NC-DPS), Nashville, NC.

Kimveer Singh Gill (twenty-five): Dawson College Shooting, Montreal, Quebec – for the USA does not have monopoly of school shootings – Wednesday, 13 September 2006.

Weapons: Glock 21 .45-calibre pistol, a Beretta Cx4 Storm semi-automatic carbine and a Norinco HP9-1 short pump-action 12-gauge shotgun.

Even further down the listings than Castillo comes Gill. With this small arsenal to hand, he only just managed to kill himself and one other person, although he did injure nineteen others while doing so. More to the point, in his rambling, teeth-grindingly bad online posts, he referred to Harris and Klebold as 'Modern Day Saints', and repeatedly imitated the Columbine mass murderers by writing, 'Heil Heil Heil', including one of Harris's favourite phrases, 'I am God'.

The reader can find photos of him on the internet. One brief glance will tell you that not all of the lights are working inside his head. He had a blog, Vampirefreaks.com. Under his handle 'fatality666' there were more than fifty selfie photos of this halfwit in various poses. In some he is wearing the must-have long black duster (as worn by the Columbine killers) and what appear to be combat boots.

Described by some people as the 'nicest, gentlest person' and 'with a heart of gold', he entertained a fascination for 9/11 conspiracy theories (like millions of others), the war in Iraq, liked Jack Daniel's whiskey (as do I), and was a user of ecstasy (which I am not). As for his motive: it is suggested that this psychotic freak had been bullied at school and was 'stressed'. Oh, bless the dear lad!

Sebastian Bosse (eighteen): Geschwister Scholl-Schule shooting, Emsdetten, North Rhine-Westphalia, Germany, Monday, 20 November 2006.

Weapons: Sawn-off Burgo .22-calibre bolt-action air rifle, a sawn-off Ardesa 'Kentucky' muzzle-loading percussion .45-calibre rifle, an Ardesa 'Patriot' muzzle-loading flintlock black powder .45-calibre pistol, home-made bombs, a knife and a machete.

I hate to be crass here, but this wannabe Columbine killer (whom we met earlier) just couldn't get his act together at all. As I mentioned almost at the start of this book; flintlock black-powder firearms are simply not the way to go, because if you recall it takes at least thirty-five seconds to reload them, so they are entirely unsuited to committing mass murder. As for his .22-calibre air rifle, what more can I say? Perhaps the Bundesrepublik Deutschland has stricter gun control laws than in the USA, who knows?

My fellow travellers may like to hear that several times in Bosse's journal he declared that 'ERIC HARRIS IS GOD!' *But he isn't God*, Herr Bosse... never was, nor ever will be. And we can hardly describe Bosse himself as being modest, shy and retiring when he proclaims: 'It is scary how similar

Eric [Harris] was to me. Sometimes it seems as if I were to live his life again, as if everything would repeat itself.' Then to finish off with a flourish, he adds: 'I am the advancement of REB [Harris]! I learned from his mistakes, the bombs, I learned from his entire life.'

No awards for initiative, Herr Bosse, but you wore the obligatory long black duster (as worn by the Columbine killers) when you wounded five people before killing yourself.

At this point along our road trip into mass murder, please take a look at the pamphlet that came free with your travel pack. It is entitled: *'Christopher does NOT do mitigation of any kind, whether these mass murderers/spree killers had screws loose or not.'*

Why? Because as I have mentioned before, time after time we hear social scientists and psychologists trying to establish a history of mental illness in the killer, as if to excuse them because he, or she, was depressed, or paranoid, or schizophrenic or downright bonkers. But, as we have noted earlier in this book, no early form of intervention can work unless the wannabe killer turns him- or herself into the cops, hands over that arsenal of firearms and says: 'For God's sake, lock me up!' But these mass killers, serial murderers and spree/rampage killers just don't do that, do they? Why? Because they're mentally wired up not to – that's why. These Klebold/Harris wannabes are enjoying themselves too much anyway: buying long, black trench coats; avidly collecting compulsory masturbatory mass-murder and Nazi memorabilia; studying the hallowed words written by these cowardly Columbine monsters, their eyes glued to the videos in which the murderous pair ramble on and on inanely like gibbering apes.

Countless times I have attended court hearings where some killer has an equally half-witted forensic psychiatrist or psychologist on the defence team. In fact, the reader doesn't even have to actually attend any court hearing because one can find numerous YouTube video examples online. You can also find other examples in my book *Talking with Psychopaths and Savages* and the sequel, *Talking with Psychopaths and Savages: Beyond Evil.*

Yes, I have witnessed just about any type of mitigation that an imaginative lawyer can invent in his or her efforts to get their client off the hook. To sway a half-awake jury, or a judge who is bordering on senility and simply wants to get away from the legal smoke-blowing and limp off his bench to his golf club for a round of eighteen holes.

The other issue is simply this: whether the individual was schizophrenic, suffering from multiple personality disorder (MPD), clinically depressed at the time of the incident, or what any other cock-and-bull diagnosis a psychiatrist can pluck out of thin air, they signally fail to refer to the most obvious point: that these killers appeared to live ordinary lives, often holding down responsible jobs before they burst onto the scene. Indeed, one killer was an accountant, another being a property magnate, so make of this what you will! So, perhaps, one should interview the killers who even botched up killing themselves and ask them an easy question: 'If you knew you were going commit mass murder, and you knew that this was a bad thing to do, why didn't you throw your guns into a lake and seek some form of psychiatric help?' I hazard the response might be a glazed expression, some thumb sucking and a lot of 'ums'.

Seung-Hui Cho (twenty-three): Virginia Tech Shooting, Virginia Polytechnic Institute and State University, Blacksburg, Virginia, Monday, 16 April 2007.

This was the deadliest mass shooting/suicide committed by a lone gunman in the USA until it was surpassed by the 2016 Orlando nightclub shooting. (On Sunday, 12 June 2016, the 29-year-old Mateen, a security guard, killed 49 people and wounded 53 others. Cops killed him after a three-hour stand-off.)

Weapons: Glock 19 pistol and Walther P22 pistol.

Another ardent Columbine wannabe. It has to be said that this guy even surpassed the atrocity committed by Klebold and Harris, but 'shamefully' he hasn't received a fraction of the notoriety they did, although several mass killers have paid tribute to him. In one of his video recordings, Cho refers to 'generation after generation, [of] we martyrs, like Eric and Dylan'. He goes on to claim:

> To you sadistic snobs, I may be nothing but a piece of shit. You have vandalised my heart, raped my soul, and torched my conscious [sic] again and again. You thought it was one pathetic, void life that you were extinguishing. Thanks to you, I die, like Jesus Christ, to inspire generations of the Weak and Defenceless people – my Brothers, Sisters, and Children – that you fuck.

Now, almost bursting into song, this Cho chappie adds:

You had everything you wanted. Your Mercedes wasn't enough, you brats. Your golden necklaces weren't enough, you snobs. Your trust funds wasn't [*sic*] enough. Your vodka and cognac wasn't enough. All your debaucheries weren't enough. Those weren't enough to fulfil your hedonistic needs. You had everything.

He sounds a bit pissed off, doesn't he? However, not being prone to exaggeration, he adds:

You had a hundred billion chances and ways to have avoided today. But you decided to spill my blood. You forced me into a corner and gave me only one option. The decision was yours. Now you have blood on your hands that will never wash off.

Somewhat like Harris and Klebold, Cho has attracted a small following of like-minded social failures. Two of them were Vester Flanagan and Wellington Menezes de Oliveira.

Vester Lee Flanagan (forty-one): murders of Alison Parker and Adam Ward, Bridgewater Plaza, Moneta, Virginia, Wednesday, 26 August 2015. Although nowhere in the same dysfunctional league as the Columbine killers and Master Cho, Vester Flanagan was a devotee of Cho, of whom he wrote: 'I was influenced by Seung-Hui Cho. That's my boy right there. He got NEARLY double the amount that Eric Harris and Dylan Klebold Flanagan, shot and killed news CBS affiliate WDBJ Alison Bailey Parker (twenty-four), a journalist with CBS affiliate WDBJ, and photojournalist

Adam Laing Ward (twenty-seven) during a live interview broadcast at the Bridgewater Plaza, Moneta. Eight shots were fired, then there was screaming. When Ward's camera fell to the ground, it captured a shot of Flanagan with a Glock 9mm pistol.

Alison died from gunshot wounds to her head and chest. Adam died from shots to his head and torso. Their interviewee, Vicki Gardner, curled into a foetal ball and pretended to be dead but was shot in the back. She underwent surgery in which a kidney and part of her colon were removed.

The gutless Flanagan fled the scene and after a police chase he shot himself dead in his rented Chevrolet Sonic off Highway 1-66 in Fauquier County. Cops found a wig and six magazines of ammunition in the vehicle.

Although technically a mass shooting, Flanagan's motive was that of a disgruntled former reporter who worked under the name 'Bryce Williams'. Two years earlier, he was summarily fired following complaints about his behaviour from colleagues; thereafter, he vowed that he would make 'headlines'. As police escorted him out of the building that day, he handed the news director a wooden cross and said 'You'll be needing this.' However, it appears that his tipping point was the murder of nine African-Americans in a church in Charleston earlier in 2015. 'I've been a human powder keg for a while... just waiting to go BOOM!!!!' he wrote in a letter. In the mass-murder stakes, more of a 'puff' perhaps?

Wellington Menezes de Oliveira (twenty-four): Rio de Janeiro school shooting, Tasso da Silveira Municipal School, Realengo, Rio de Janeiro, Brazil, Thursday, 7 April 2011.

Oliveira was another devotee of Cho, whom he referred to as 'a brother'. On Thursday, 7 April 2011, this Brazilian shooter killed twelve people then shot himself at the Tasso da Silveira Municipal School, his former elementary school in Realengo, Rio de Janeiro.

Although a good-looking young man, he had been the target of both verbal and physical abuse during his schooldays. He underwent a deluge of constant harassment, not least because he had a withered leg that caused him to limp, and was described as strange by some of his ex-school colleagues. He was called 'Sherman' (a nod to a character from the 1999 romance/comedy *American Pie*), as well as 'Suingue', because of his limp (suingue is Portuguese for 'swing'). To all who knew him, he was kind and friendly, but his tipping point came when he was thrown into a garbage dumpster by students. Thereafter, rage and resentment began to boil inside him.

A couple of days before the atrocity, he recorded a video in which he maintained: 'The struggle for which many brothers died in the past, and for I will die, is not solely because of what is known as "bullying". Our fight is against cruel people, cowards, who take advantage of the kindness, the weakness of people unable to defend themselves.'

He was obsessed by Islam, perceiving as it being the 'only correct religion', and referred to Seung-Hui Cho as 'an icon for those who are oppressed by the majority'. Reports suggest that after entering the school on the day of the killings, he was initially polite and unthreatening. Then, without warning, he took out two revolvers from a bag and opened fire. Of the twelve dead, ten were girls. It has been suggested that de Oliveira only fired at the boys to stun them while he tried his best to kill the girls, whom he considered 'impure beings'. Quickly, police arrived on the scene. He fired at them but missed. He was shot in the abdomen and legs and fell down a flight of stairs, then shot himself dead.

Following this incident, police recovered the murderer's two revolvers, a .38-calibre Rossi Model 971 and a .32-calibre snub-nosed Taurus Model 73, along with some speed-loaders and a bandolier containing eighteen unused rounds. Police managed to trace the owner of the 38-calibre revolver, even though its serial number was nearly completely scratched off. He was a fifty-seven-year-old man who had previously worked alongside Oliveira, and confessed to selling him not only the revolver but the speed-loaders and a large amount of ammunition too..

The Taurus had an even more chequered history. Originally it had belonged to a man who passed away in 1994 but had been stolen, according to his son. The police traced the two thieves, and they confessed that they had sold the revolver to Oliveira, who had told them that he wanted it for protection.

At this point in Wellington Menezes de Oliveira's story, and carefully noting the amount of terrible abuse he suffered at the hands of other students, I am minded not to label him a 'loser', *just yet* – and this implies no allowances for his mass killing. I also ask myself, was he ever truly influenced by Harris, Klebold and Cho, even though he makes some occasional reference to them from time to time? I leave you with his last letter; it's a pretty tall order, too. And he's got a damned nerve, if you ask me:

First of all you should know that the impure ones shall not touch me without gloves, only the chaste ones or those who lost their chastity after wedlock and were not involved in adultery shall touch me without gloves, in other words, no fornicator or adulterer shall have direct contact with me, nor should anything that is impure touch my blood, no impure person shall have contact with a virgin without their permission, those who prepare my burial shall remove all my garments, bathe me, dry me, and drape me completely undressed in a white sheet which is in this building, in a bag that I have left in the primary room of the first floor, after wrapping me in this sheet they shall put me in my coffin. If possible, I want to be buried alongside the grave where my mother lies. My mother is called Dicéa Menezes de Oliveira and she is buried in Murundu cemetery. I need a visit from a faithful follower of the Lord to my grave at least once, I need him to pray in front of my grave asking for God's forgiveness for what I have done imploring that Jesus on his return wake me from the sleep of death for eternal life.

Shhh, now. Enough already, Wellington, we catch your drift. Your almost biblical turn of phrase about being wronged has really caught my readers' attention, but please get to the point...

I have left a house in Sepetiba of which none of my family members need, there are poor institutions, financed by generous people who take care of abandoned animals, I want this space where I spent my last months to be donated to one of these institutions, because animals are very unappreciated beings and need more protection and affection than human beings who have the advantage of being able to communicate, work to feed themselves, therefore, those who take my house...

Wellington, please... stop...

I please ask to have good sense and fulfil my request, by fulfilling my request, you will fulfil the will of the parents who wished to pass this estate onto me and everybody knows this, if you do not fulfil my request automatically you will disrespecting the will of my parents, which will prove that you have no consideration for them, I believe that you all have respect for our parents, prove this by doing what I asked.

Is that it? *Thank you*, Wellington. And here is the good news and some bad news... actually there isn't any good news at all, 'cos lots of heathen, unwashed cops with the kiddies' blood on their hands, are going to throw your body into a black bin liner, cart you off to the morgue where a pathologist is going to examine what's inside your head (wearing gloves, naturally). Then... wait for it... 'cos *no one* is going to claim your body, you're going to be buried in a potter's field, in a hole where even the Lord Almighty won't be able to find you, even if He tried.

There has been much made of Oliveira's state of mind. Various psychologists and psychiatrists have stated that he suffered a schizotypal personality disorder (STPD), which may encompass: strange thinking or behaviour; discomfort in social situations; unusual beliefs; a lack of emotion or inappropriate emotional responses; odd speech that may be vague or rambling; a lack of close friends; extreme social anxiety; and, not unexpectedly, paranoia. It is estimated that STPD occurs in 1–2 per cent of most populations, and may be present in as much as 15 per cent of the US population. It is most common in males.

I think that Oliveira wears all of those hats, but does this give rise to any sort of extenuating circumstances for his dreadful crime? Of course not, and one only has to read his rambling letter above to realise that he could not have cared a damn about the pain and suffering he was about to cause. It was 'me, me, me'. And he was a self-righteous, religious bigot, too.

Pekka-Eric Auvinen (eighteen): Jokela school shooting, Jokela High School, Tuulusa, Finland, Wednesday, 7 November 2007. Auvinen, whom we have met earlier, with his face plucked straight out of the Hitler Youth organisation, found some notoriety when dubbed by the media the 'YouTube Killer'. Another Columbine wannabe, he also compared himself to God, ranted about 'retards', was a Hitler fan, and constantly quoted the Nazi slogan 'Blut und Ehre' ('Blood and Honour'). One only has to take a quick look at him on the internet to envisage 'Sieg Heil' tattooed onto his frontal lobe.

On the morning of Wednesday, 7 November 2007, student Auvinen walked into the Jokela High School, in the municipality of Tuusula, Finland, and fired his SIG Mosquito .22-calibre semi-automatic pistol. He shot to death eight people, wounded thirteen, before turning the gun on himself. He later died in hospital.

Like so many of these teenaged killers, he had written a journal. This he entitled the 'Natural Selector's Manifesto'. A fuller account of this killer's back history is well worth a read on *Wikipedia*. Interestingly, like Michael Ryan, Auvinen had joined a gun club. He had obtained his pistol, along with 500 rounds of ammunition, legally.

> I am ready to die for a cause I know is right, just and true even if I would lose or the battle would be only remembered as evil I will rather fight and die than live a long and unhappy life.
>
> > Pekka-Eric Auvinen, YouTube rant.

There is some debate about Auvinen's motive; some say that he suffered from being bullied and just wanted revenge, which may or may not be so. It seems to be a mixed bag of twisted reasons, however, I am inclined to think that he was more of an extreme right-wing present-day Nazi. Had he lived just prior to World War II, if he had any intelligence at all he would have made an ideal candidate for the SS. His goals came from the pages of *Mein Kampf*, as is apparent from his 'manifesto': to 'eliminate all who I see [as] unfit, disgraces of human race and failures of natural selection . . .', adding, 'It's time to put NATURAL SELECTION &

SURVIVAL OF THE FITTEST back on tracks!' But in everything he dismally failed, which der Führer signally did too, of course.

Matti Juhani Saari (twenty-two): Kuahajoki school shooting, Kuahajoki School of Hospitality, Seinäjoki University of Applied Sciences, Kuahajoiki, Finland, Tuesday, 23 September 2008. The USA does not have it all its own way in the mass-murder stakes. At least Finland has got itself off the starting blocks. Second-year culinary-arts student Saari closely followed Auvinen down the track with what is known as the Kauhajoki School Shooting.

> I saw a guy leaving a big black bag in the corridor and going into classroom number three and closing the door. I looked through the window and he immediately shot at me. Then I called the emergency number ... he fired at me but I was running zigzag. I ran for my life.
>
> I heard constant shooting. He changed another case in the gun. He was very well prepared. He walked calmly.
>
> Jukka Forsberg, school caretaker

The firearm used was a .22 LR-calibre Walther P22 semi-automatic target pistol, and Saari also brought along with him some home-made Molotov cocktails. Altogether, nearly two hundred shots were fired, some into the air, of which twenty rounds were fired into just one of the victims. Ten people died with eleven more injured in this horrific mass murder/arson/suicide event. Saari shot himself in the head and died later in hospital.

By all accounts, Saari appears to have been directly inspired by Auvinen. Videos about the Columbine mass killings appeared on Saari's most-viewed list on YouTube, and his camera pose for his own postings was copycat strikingly similar to photos of Seung-Hui Cho. In Saari, we once again find a Nazi fixation, with an additional crush on the lyrics of songs by the German goth artist 'wumpscut' aka Rudolf 'Rudy' Ratzinger, whose songs are filled with references to child murder and bloodshed.

> Whole life is war and whole life is pain. And you will fight alone in your personal war.
>
> Matti Saari: quoting lyrics from
> Wumpscut's song 'War'

According to his YouTube profile, Saari's main interests included horror movies, guns, sex, beer and computers.

Well, what more could we expect?

Karl Pierson (eighteen): Back to the USA and, as abject losers go, we would have to look long and hard to find a more wretched example than Pierson, who, aged just fourteen, was swotting up on Columbine instead of learning decent social graces. But let's give the lad his due, for he himself acknowledged that he was not completely sane: 'I am a psychopath with a superiority complex,' he wrote in his journal. So full marks, Pierson, for at least giving us an honest psychopathological self-assessment – one that

I am sure will be agreed with by every psychologist and psychiatrist who has ever lived, is practising today, and all those who follow.

> I am full of hate, I love it!
>> Karl Pierson, paraphrasing Columbine killer
>> Eric Harris's love-hate platitude

Pierson's weapons: a legally owned 12-gauge pump-action shotgun with a bandolier of cartridges for it; a machete and three Molotov cocktails. The date of his attack was, suitably, Friday, 13 December 2013. The scene for this 'event' (which lasted ,precisely 80 seconds) was the Arapahoe High School in Centennial, Colorado, of which geeky Karl Pierson was *not* a noted alumnus.. Plenty of others are, though. I could list them, but I won't, simply because the only one who even strikes a match in the dim confines of my brain is Melissa Marie Benoist: the actress in Fox's *Glee* and CBS's *Supergirl*, plus a string of movies over recent years. Melissa Benoist is worthy of further note here, because she portrayed David Koresh's wife Rachael Jones in the miniseries *Waco* (2018) – and we visited the Waco siege much earlier in this book.

To refocus. After fatally shooting his classmate, seventeen-year-old Claire Davis, Pierson tossed a Molotov cocktail which failed to ignite, at which the utterly disgruntled chap shot *himself* dead. I mean, it's the simplest of bombs, consisting of a glass bottle (which is specifically intended to break when it hits something hard, of course) half-filled with petrol and a wick made from a rag stuffed into the neck of the petrol-filled bottle. Light the petrol-soaked rag, throw the bottle and there you go. But Pierson chucks it and it doesn't explode? Correct me if I am wrong, but you have be a moron if you cannot even achieve that.

Pierson's apparent motive. He was bullied at school.

Alex Hribal (sixteen): Franklin school stabbing, Franklin Regional High School, Murrysville, Pennsylvania, Wednesday, 9 April 2014. As the reader is now starting to appreciate, there is a lot to unpack here. And I can assure you that although I might appear to be glib and unsympathetic towards the victims and their grieving next of kin, most certainly I am not. So now we turn to sophomore Alex Hribal, another wannabe prophet of doom according to the Gospel of Harris and Klebold, et al.

This nauseating event took place on Wednesday, 9 April 2014, at the Franklin Regional High School in Murrysville, Pennsylvania. The weapons: a pair of eight-inch kitchen knives, which Hribal used to slash twenty students and a security guard. Four students sustained life-threatening injuries, although happily all of them recovered.

> I can't wait to see the priceless and helpless looks on the faces of the students of one of the 'best schools in Pennsylvania' realise their precious lives are going to be taken by the only one among them that isn't a plebian [*sic*].
>
> Alex Hribal: in a note

I would be nothing and this whole event would never occur if it weren't for Eric Harris and Dylan

Klebold of Columbine High School. They worked hard to achieve freedom in heaven. I admire them greatly because they saw something wrong in the world and moved away [from] the herd of sheep to do something about it. They also possessed three crucial things a person needs in order to become a god: intelligence, ideology, and malice (or cruelty) [...] I became a prophet because I spread the word of a god, Eric Harris.

Alex Hribal: from the same note

Hribal was initially charged as an adult with four counts of attempted murder, twenty-one counts of aggravated assault and one count of carrying a weapon on school property – the latter being the least of his problems. In 2014, he was expected to be transferred to Southwood Psychiatric Hospital in Pittsburgh for further mental evaluation. After a very short preliminary examination, I can only come to the same conclusion as, doubtless, did Southwood's psychiatrists. Something along the lines of a collective: 'F*ck this, he isn't being admitted here, 'cos he's too dangerous and is gonna cause safety concerns... show him the door.'

I mean, you could not make this up if you tried, for and it leaves the movie plot of *One Flew Over the Cuckoo's Nest* in the shade. Because after four years of being bounced from one court to another, with countless mental evaluations and mitigations offered in between, Hribal was diagnosed as having a major depressive disorder and schizotypal personality disorder. He was, according to his attorneys, 'responding to treatment' and 'would continue to favourably respond' if anyone, *anywhere*, could find a mental facility brave enough to admit him. They couldn't.

On Monday, 22 January 2018, Common Pleas Court Judge Christopher Feliciani threw up his hands in exasperation to sling out any further appeals. He'd heard enough already, so he sentenced Alex Hribal to serve 23½ to 60 years in prison, and ordered him to pay $269,000 in restitution – although where he will get the money from is anyone's guess.

* * *

At the end of the day, one can waste hours trawling through the mentally distorted literary garbage these wannabe mass murderers and spree killers spew out into the public domain via their so-called journals and social media video postings. But what do we learn? Nothing of any real value at all when it comes down to it. So one wonders why these sites feel it's of any meaningful social interest to allow this poison to be put up in the first place. Even more to the point, I wonder how the bigwigs at these social media sites would feel if the guy that blasted to death one of their own kith and kin was bragging about it on their platforms, and encouraging others to do exactly the same thing.

If we so wished, we could take stock of all of the opinions offered up by the legions of well-meaning forensic psychiatrists, psychologists, social scientists and anthropologists; and, of course, we citizens are perfectly entitled to form our own opinions too. But does any of this stop mass murder and the rampage killing from continuing? No it does not and, sad to say, it never will.

As base as this might seem, at least serial killers do offer up some use to law enforcement – either post-mortem or while they are incarcerated. For their crimes and *modi operandi* always tell us something about their sickening mindsets, and this assists agencies, such as the FBI's Behavioral Analysis Unit – renamed 'the Behavioral Analysis Unit (5) aka (BAU-5)' – in Quantico, Virginia, in offender-profiling an unidentified killer on the loose and hopefully bringing him, or her, to justice – or kill them – as quickly as possible. At least offender profiling (as seen in the brilliant Netflix series *Mindhunter*) has immense value in predicting what a yet-to-be-apprehended serial killer *might* do next – all, or some of which will reveal his criminal signature. This may hasten his capture, thus saving lives.

Mass murderers and spree killers offer up nothing at all. From nowhere they emerge in an instant: shooting their guns, throwing their Molotov cocktails and stabbing and hacking. Pretty quickly they either blow out their own brains, or the police do it for them, or they end up gibbering like morons in a mental institution or prison. It is true to say that just one them can cause more human destruction in a few minutes than most serial killers could wet-dream of causing in a lifetime.

Scores of mentally lopsided commentators have made the claim that Klebold and Harris have spearheaded a 'revolution.' I suppose it rather depends on one's definition of 'revolution', because it does seem to be over-egging it to even begin to label them as 'revolutionists'. Apparently, these commentators have never read a dictionary, for when used as an adjective, the term 'revolutionary' refers to something that has a major, sudden impact on society or some aspect of human endeavour, for example an attempt to reduce serious injury, or an endeavour to save as many lives as possible – not to kill en masse. Yes, of course if one wants to nitpick one might call them revolutionists as in: cause a revolt; conjure up a social cataclysm or coup d'état; cause havoc, or whip up any other socially negative activity. But when we look at some of the aforementioned mass murderers, we find that the results of their post-incarceration or post-mortem rallying cries have been a tad on the lean side – that many of them have a morbid, often sexual fixation, about paranoid, anti-Semitic Adolf Hitler. Knowing how this coward met his end, one would think that they would know better.

ALEK MINASSIAN (b.1992)

I am a murdering piece of shit. I feel like I accomplished my mission.

Alek Minassian: to Toronto Acting Staff
Sergeant Brad Lloyd, 23 April 2018

At this point we need to move on, because, as we have seen with the cases of David Burke, Andreas Lubitz and Alex Hribal, not all domestic mass murderers use firearms to commit their appalling crimes. And what better example of a 'Homicidal Van Man' is there than Alek Minassian? Minassian was charged with multiple counts of murder in Toronto, Canada, after the van he was driving struck a number of pedestrians. According to the legal papers at the time, Minassian would plead not guilty due to his mental condition, having mowed down 26 people – killing 10 and injuring 16, some critically.

The location: Yonge Street, in the North York City Centre business district in Toronto. The weapon: a white Chevrolet Express van rented from Ryder. In their advertising blurb for this vehicle, Chevrolet states: 'Offering comfortable seating for up to 15 along with advanced safety and entertainment technology...Max available GVWR 9,900 lb, Max horsepower 314 with a Max torque of 373 lb-ft.'

Now, imagine this hefty vehicular hunk travelling at about 40 mph and being rammed into a mass of innocent men, women and children, as happened on Monday, 23 April 2018. Starting at the intersection of Yonge Street and Finch Avenue, the vehicle travelled southwards, ploughing through terrified pedestrians, along Yonge Street to near Sheppard Avenue; there, the van came to a stop on the sidewalk on Poyntz Avenue. This was the deadliest act of mass murder by any means in the city's history. It ended with the driver, twenty-five-year-old Alek Minassian, begging to be shot by police, but at 1.32pm – seven minutes after the first 911 call reporting the incident was made – TPS Constable Ken Lam instead arrested him. Nine pedestrians were killed on the spot and a tenth died later that day, sixteen others were injured, some critically. The ten who died were aged from twenty-two to ninety-four.

As some back history, Minassian had admitted that he is a violent misogynist who was radicalised online after watching a video about the 'incel' online subculture of men unable to find romantic or sexual partners, of which more in the following chapter.

To put Minassian's worthless existence of a mere 25 years into tragically grim perspective, he wiped out a combined total of 494 years of precious life just because he couldn't find a woman who liked him. So I expect that all those who call themselves incels must be very proud of him. To make this case all the more media interactive for my readers, I draw your attention to Minassian's interview with Detective Rob Thomas – it can be easily found on YouTube under the title: 'Alek Minassian confesses in police interview after Toronto van attack'. As David Krajicek succinctly points out in his *Mass Killers: Inside the Minds of Men Who Murder*: 'Minassian's crimes brought new attention to this simmering substrate of mutant masculinity. On his Facebook page just before the murders, he had tipped his hat to an "incel rebellion"', and his attack certainly brought that arid subculture to public notice.'

This book was in editing when, on 9 November 2020, Alek Minassian's trial got under way in a Toronto court. He faced ten charges of murder and sixteen of attempted murder, and entered a plea of 'not criminally responsible' on all counts, on account of his claims that he is autistic. A conviction would have meant a lifetime sentence, and on 3 March 2021 Minassian was duly convicted on all counts, in a verdict that was streamed live on YouTube. The judge, Justice Anne Molloy, deferred sentencing until 2022 to await a decision from Canada's Supreme Court on whether or not convicted criminals can serve sentences for murder consecutively. During sentencing, Justice Molloy consistently referred to Minassian as 'John Doe', rather than by his name, to deny him the notoriety that he so clearly sought. He has now achieved that notoriety, but it is extremely unlikely that he will ever be free to enjoy it.

16

Involuntary Celibates

I've been forced to endure an existence of loneliness,
rejection and unfulfilled desires all because girls have never
been attracted to me. Girls gave their affection, and sex
and love to other men but never to me.

ELLIOT RODGER: LAST VIDEO POSTED ON
YOUTUBE BEFORE KILLING SEVEN PEOPLE, INCLUDING
HIMSELF, AND INJURING FOURTEEN OTHERS, ISLA VISTA,
CALIFORNIA, 23 MAY 2014

The 'incel' subculture of men, mostly heterosexual, mostly white, are united by sexual frustration and a hatred of women. Members of this online community are often characterised not only by misogyny but by a general hatred of mankind (especially sexually active men), against which they harbour seething resentment; additionally, they tend to endorse violence, to be ultra-right-wing, and to be racist. A portmanteau of 'involuntary celibates', the term 'incel' applies to men who define themselves as unable to find a romantic or sexual partner despite their wish for one, a state they describe as 'inceldom'. This chapter attempts to get to grips with their psychopathologies, and we will meet some examples of mass murdering incels shortly. These people 'gather online', as David Krajicek says in *Mass Killers: Inside the Minds of Men Who Murder*, 'and exchange complaints in their own language, often with themes drawn from the hagiographic writings of men [indeed, mass killers] like [George] Sodini and Elliot Rodger, the suicidal virgin who rampaged against young women in 2014 in Isla Vista, California.' What I find mysterious about all this is: if one harbours such a homicidal hatred against women, why would a so-called incel desire one?

Once again I direct readers' attention to Minassian's interview with Detective Rob Thomas. The existence of these can't-get-it-up guys who take their sexual frustrations out on women — actually, on society as a whole — is not a new phenomenon. In fact, as David Krajicek points out in his book on mass murder, 'its roots are primeval. For centuries, lonely-hearted men have used sexual rejection as a motive for murder.' But sexual rejection cannot be their sole reason for committing mass murder, surely, because otherwise countless other guys who have been spurned, or told to get on their proverbial 'bike' by potential romantic/sexual partners would have run amok too. But they haven't.

'Mutant masculinity'? Oh, my, I do love that phrase, I *truly do*, because it sums up these incels in one, as in freaks, lusus naturae, monsters; monstrosities. All in all, that describes every single one of the killers aforementioned in this book, yet many of them sing each other's praises. Revolutionists my left foot.

I expect most of us have experienced some form of rejection in our lives, have we not? And if, once again, you have in mind the urgent need to understand the psychodynamics of what will be going through your mind when you are rejected for any reason whatsoever – be it thrown out of your local darts team, or off a TV baking competition, getting thrashed in *Mastermind*, or that every woman you talk to thinks that you are a creep – then I heartily recommend a really good 'professional' read. It's called *The Pain of Social Rejection*, written by Kirsten Weir and published in the American Psychological Association's magazine *Monitor on Psychology* in 2012 (Vol. 43, No. 4, print version page 50). You can find it here: www.apa.org/monitor/2012/04/rejection..

With my hand on my heart, I really did try to get to the bottom of why incels get so upset when they are rejected by the opposite sex. What I did learn is that women are far better able to handle any form of rejection than men, who often throw their toys out of their cots in a big way. From a layman's point of view, I also learned that Kirsten Weir's well-intentioned and compassionate article will never be read by incels, for several reasons:

1: Most of them are too busy whining to each other in internet forums about their lack of success in striking up a meaningful relationship, when what mates they do have in the real world – if any – are scoring left, right and centre.

2: They have the mental concentration span of a goldfish. And collectively they are comprehensively unable to understand what a 'revolutionist' actually means.

3: And if they did eventually manage to find Kirsten Weir's article online, they'd be as confused as I am right now – feeling rejected by higher intelligence, with me at my wits' end trying to fathom out what all this has to do with mass murder in the first place.

Therefore, in broad non-professional terms, may I suggest that if one feels sexually rejected as these incels do, go get a life or make yourself look more attractive by bleaching your teeth, just as George Sodini did, as readers are about to learn.

17

George Sodini

*All my suffering in this world has been at the hands
of humanity, particularly women.*
GEORGE SODINI: MANIFESTO

Since George Sodini (1960–2009) was hell bent on finding
romance, could he have been the guy for *you*? For he had
been seeking love for many years without any takers. I am
merely asking you this question because my female readers
will be expert at spotting who would or would not make for
an ideal companion by looking at a guy's face – in Sodini's
case, his startlingly white teeth. But what a hunk he was.
This guy pumped iron big time, and he was as fit as any pea-
brain on steroids can be. This mass killer has become a man
to be revered amongst all involuntary celibates who wish to
emulate him, even today. I urge any women who are reading
this to look up George's photos on the internet – you'll find
them easily enough – and give him marks out of ten if you

will, because he has become the 'prototype': the statutory example for every other incel that has followed. Well done, George, you may even have won a prize, although of what sort remains to be determined.

Shall we take a look at how this all came about? It started with Sodini's shooting spree in Collier Township, Pennsylvania, that he kicked off during a female-only aerobic session at the LA Fitness gym at 8.15pm on Tuesday, 4 August 2009. And, although this must seem a deeply insensitive thing to say, in the mass-shooting stakes he didn't exactly hit a high score, recording four deaths (including his own), although nine other people there were wounded. His weapons were two 9mm Glock semi-automatic pistols; a .32-calibre semi-automatic pistol, and a .45-calibre revolver. Those killed were: Heidi Overmier (forty-six); Elizabeth Gannon (forty-nine); and Jody Billingsley (thirty-eight).

Working out in a gym is a great way to keep one's physique in good shape, but bleaching one's teeth is, I think, going a bit too far. Still, Sodini had a lot going for him: he was not unintelligent: he had money in the bank; a new Nissan car; a small house in Scott Township; modest investments; and he was a well-paid systems analyst at the international law firm of K&L Gates, which gave him a good income with money to spare. But as he recorded in his online diary: 'Probably 99 per cent of the people who know me well don't even think I was this crazy,' which completely reinforces what we now already know – that most of these mass murderers do seem perfectly normal until they explode.

The countdown to his killings he'd chronicled online over a lengthy period of time, stating that he hadn't had sex with a woman since July 1990, when he was aged twenty-nine. At the time of the shootings he was forty-eight. 'Who knows why. I am not ugly or too weird,' he wrote, adding 'Last time I slept all night with a girlfriend it was 1982 [...] Girls and women don't even give me a second look ANYWHERE [...] Women just don't like me. There are 30 million desirable women in the US (my estimate) and I cannot find one.' Warming to his theme, 'Mr Desperately Lonely Sodini' railed on:

> Just got back from tanning, been doing this for a while [...] I actually look good. I dress good, am clean-shaven, bathe, touch of cologne – yet 30 million women rejected me – over an 18 or 25-year period. That is how I see it. Thirty million is my rough guesstimate of how many desirable single women there are. A man needs a woman for confidence [...] Flying solo for many years is a destroyer.

Rambling on and on, his narrative becomes even more disjointed:

> Yet many people say I am easy to get along with, etc. Looking back, I owe nothing to desirable females who ask for anything, except for basic courtesy – usually. Looking back over everything, what bothers me most is the inability to work towards whatever change I choose.

There appears to be an interesting misogynistic pathology at work here; note how Sodini plays the 'blame game' card, as in, 'Look how wonderful I am. I am *so* fit, clean and handsome.' Paradoxically, these self-proclaimed losers also exhibit a kind of hyper-masculinity. 'The cultish nature of incels is not an aberration', wrote George Chesterton, in an article for *GQ* (7 November 2018), 'but an extension of male psychological development: a need to control mixed with a sense of humiliation. It's always someone else's fault – in the case of incels, it begins with a belief that genetics has dealt them a bad hand. Damn you, Mother Nature.'

Adam Jukes is a writer and therapist of more than forty years' standing who for half of that time specialised in treating men who abused women. The author of *Why Men Hate Women* and *What You've Got Is What You Want Even If It Hurts*, Jukes is pretty scathing when it come to incels: 'The rage and righteousness against women represent one felt injustice after another,' he says. 'Incels' basic premise of "She won't let me f*ck her" is about as straightforward an Oedipal statement as you can make.' As George Chesterton wrote in the *GQ* article quoted above, 'incels represent the worst in men: how they refuse to accept their own responsibilities and their reluctance to know themselves or admit what lives in their unconscious.'

The Oedipus complex is a term used by Sigmund Freud in his theory of psychosexual stages of development, and while it may be a subject of much interest to some readers seeking some form of mitigation, no matter how small, for incels and their pathological hatred of females, does it rise to the level of an excuse for committing an atrocity such as Sodini's LA Fitness shooting? Of course not.

As for the incel online forums – well, I suppose one might call them upside-down group therapy sessions; a vehicle for a bunch of deadbeats who share a hatred for women, during which they seek the support of others to justify their own individual weaknesses. Of course, real-life group therapy sessions for incels do not exist, because in cyberspace anyone can invent bullshit; in reality they would actually have to meet each other face to face, whereupon they'd finally realise what a bunch of twats they really are.

Leaving aside the Oedipus complex for a moment – for it is, indeed, a heavy subject – maybe there is a much simpler explanation, one which dovetails into Freud's thinking. Having read through a number of Sodini's ramblings, it seems to me that they fit with the rubbish most mass murderers spew out online and in their so-called manifestos, for they are all fixated on themselves. Each of them is totally self-centered; they ignore the needs of others and only do what's best for them. We might also call them egocentric, egoistic, and egotistical – in a word, 'selfish'. The reader will probably know someone who always talks about themselves, makes every issue about them, and are generally all about 'Me, me, me!' Narcissists to a fault. And I would put money on it that any woman whom Sodini did meet sniffed him out in a heartbeat.

We see narcissism writ large throughout Sodini's blog, just as one does when studying the personalities of most mass murderers, for they cannot see the world through another person's eyes. They would rather see it from their blinkered perspective and to protect their own flaws and image with everything they've got. They think the world is all about them. The world, from their point of view, is a place comprising them and perhaps a few other people around them whom they can control. And what gets right up the noses of incels is that they cannot control women, let alone date one. In this regard, their overinflated egos are empty bags of wind, for they have no member of the opposite sex to stroke their feathers. In fact, Sodini said as much himself when he wrote: 'A man needs a woman for confidence' – to kiss his feet, more like? Such egotists are so consumed by their own world and self-image that it is near impossible for other people to measure up to their standards. They maintain a sense of superiority that most commonly leads to them devaluing others – in the cases featured throughout this book, the complete devaluation of human lives.

But they do have a fatal flaw, for the truth is, no matter what sort of success they have, they will always feel inadequate internally. While they may appear confident based on appearances – just like Sodini's fastidious self-presentation – and external achievements, internally, they have fears relating to low self-esteem.

Added to which, narcissists hide who they really are. They will present the best and most captivating part of their personality, but as they are so self-absorbed, they do not want others to see the hidden elements that make them feel secretly insecure. This can lead to them coming across as pretentious and women get a sense about these types of self-absorbed males very quickly. I would suggest that the self-centered, perpetually well-groomed Sodini – the guy always pumping iron at the gym while egotistically admiring his muscles at the same time – got short shrift from all of the females he eyed up there. For him it was payback time for the gals at the gym. And the end of him.

18

Carl Robert Brown

I think Carl was looking for some help … Nine people should still be alive. The fellow needed help so badly.
DONALD FUSSELL, VICE-PRINCIPAL OF DREW MIDDLE SCHOOL, MIAMI, QUOTED IN THE *EVENING INDEPENDENT* (MIAMI), 21 AUGUST 1982

What does one of us Brits do if we have a problem with a lawnmower engine? We either fix it ourselves or we take it in for repair. And if the fix is not quite right, we take it back and tell the engineer to do the job properly then leave, don't we? OK, so what if the grass grows another millimetre in the interim? It's not a big deal. Actually, this can give one the opportunity, and the excuse, to stop off at a pub on the way home and knock back a beer.

However, schoolteacher Carl Brown (1930–82) took an entirely different approach. On Wednesday, 18 August

1982, upon being presented with a bill for about twenty bucks at Bob Moore's Welding & Machine Service Inc. in Hialeah, Florida, he complained that the work was poorly done. His frustration mounted when the traveller's cheque he offered in payment was refused, so he decided to express his unhappiness by going on a homicidal bender: he shot dead eight people and injured another three at the aforementioned workshop the following day. But was Brown worried about his grass growing a little higher? Not exactly, for he wanted to use the lawnmower engine to power his bicycle instead of using his legs. Which makes you wonder: why didn't he just buy a moped?

As he nonchalantly pedalled away from the crime scene en route to Hialeah Junior High School (where he intended to shoot more people, because he was peeved at being suspended from his long-time teaching position), he was, according to some accounts, killed twice – chased, shot and run into by a motorist.

We will return to the tragic shootings momentarily, but it is the chase that intrigues me. For when Mark Kram, who worked at nearby metalwork shop, heard about the killings, he grabbed his .38-calibre revolver and drove off to find Brown, on the way picking up one Ernest Hammett. They finally came across him six blocks away, not far from Miami International Airport. Kram fired off a warning shot intended to whiz straight over the fleeing man's head, but it hit Brown in the back and was to prove fatal. Brown turned around to aim a shotgun at his pursuers, who ran over him before crashing; his body ended up in bushes. Oh, Mr Brown, you really should have planned your getaway more thoroughly –

a sports motorcycle would have been a damned sight quicker than a pedal bike.

Regarding his firearms. On the steaming-hot morning the day after his upsetting experience at Bob Moore's Welding & Machine Service Inc., Mr Brown went to the Garcia Gun Center, where he purchased two shotgun: an Ithaca 37 12-gauge pump-action model and a semi-automatic rifle with mucho ammo. Then, unbelievably, he invited his ten-year-old son to join him, telling the bewildered kid: 'I'm going out to kill a lot of people. You wanna come along for the ride?'. Wisely, the lad declined. Brown's murder victims were: Nelson Barrios (46); Lonnie Jeffries (53); Carl Lee (47); Ernestine Moore (67); Mangum Moore (78); Martha Steelman (29); Juan Ramon Trespalacios (38), and Pedro Vasques (44). The wounded were: Eduardo Lima (30); Carlos Vazquez Sr (42), and Carlos Vazquez Jr (17).

We recall how our homegrown Derrick Bird had been steaming away for months on end before he finally exploded and ran amok. Well, his beefs with his brother, the family solicitor, his diving instructor, and anyone else for that matter, including life and the world in general, were minor when compared with those of Carl Brown. In a nutshell, Brown was way off the wall, and if not as crazy as the proverbial nutty professor, he was educationally qualified as one step removed. So details of some of his back history – his narrative – are called for here. For he was an occupational crisis on a bike; his life was falling apart at the seams, he was becoming mentally unstitched by the day.

Condensing as best I can, up until 1970 Brown seemed to be doing just fine. Having earned a master's degree in

Education, he took a full-time job as history teacher at Hialeah Junior High School in 1962. He married twice and had three children. But his first wife passed away, while according to his second wife their marriage hit the rocks because he declined to get professional help for his deteriorating psychological state.

> [He looked] as if he was eighty years old.
>
> Neighbour of Carl Brown

By the 1970s Brown was mentally going downhill fast. His appearance became unkempt; he started losing weight. Once an outgoing chap, he began to keep himself away from others. It seems that one of his daughters attempted to get him hospitalised, but this required his permission and he refused. So the intervention scenarios mentioned much earlier in this book were attempted but they failed.

I hear large bells ringing here: forty-ish years old; busted marriage because his second wife could not handle his unpredictable moods; in need of psychological help; a teacher of impressionable children. Intervention time is urgently called for.

> We come to school to learn, not to hear his problems.
> How can we learn anything with teachers like that?
>
> Pupil complaining to Hialeah Junior
> High School officials about Brown's
> behaviour in class, in 1977

CARL ROBERT BROWN

At Hialeah Junior High he proved himself to be someone who appeared to hate everyone. The school's principal, Octavio Visiedo, described Brown as 'incoherent' and his classroom as 'total and complete chaos'.

Brown wasted entire class periods babbling diatribes about whatever came to his troubled mind. God, sex, those of a non-white complexion. He had originally been seen as a highly competent teacher whom the pupils and their parents respected, but now they started to bitterly complain about this nonsensical man who was baffling his class with his irrelevant and incoherent soliloquies, in which he claimed to be God's man-on-earth, as the embodiment of Logos, the ancient Greek philosophical concept of cosmic order. That's all very well if the tutor, who is trying to convince his students to complete tasks using logic and reason, is sane; but when a teacher is stark raving bonkers, 'tis no wonder that students often took advantage of this babbling fool and asked him a question that he would take the entire period to answer. 'He was off his rocker,' one student later told the press, adding that, 'he was a moral bigot.'

It is no wonder that as Brown's psychosis worsened, with the signs of paranoid schizophrenia becoming increasingly evident, his professional life began to take the strain. As Brown's mental health deteriorated, so too did his standard of teaching, with lessons becoming less focused and easily thrown off course by a seemingly inane question – a weakness that some pupils were all too keen to exploit. Other students instead preferred to abandon his class altogether and roamed around the school. It wasn't long before this came to the attention of senior members of staff, but despite facing questions as to the productivity of his lessons and his own competence as a teacher, Brown remained indignant, insisting that nothing was at fault.

In the summer of 1981, he was shifted to Charles R. Drew Middle School at 1801 NW 60th Street, Miami. A school which had a mostly African-American student population was not the sort of placement in which a racially bigoted teacher would thrive. So, perhaps unsurprisingly, it was not long before Pat Gray, the school's director of personal control, was forced to pass comment on Brown's behaviour and professional conduct. In an incident that Gray described as demonstrating 'a significant lack of adult judgment, an overtone of sexual fixation, and definite aggression toward students,' Brown had rowed with two black students who were reportedly throwing books at each other. The situation had soon escalated beyond reason, with Brown chasing the students with a stapler while also ranting about his private sexual relationships..

What is perhaps most striking about this episode – and most indicative of his severely compromised mental state – is Brown's complete lack of remorse or regret, as discovered by Pat Gray: 'I found Mr Brown to be incoherent and unable to grasp the severity of the situation at hand. I, also, fear for the safety of the students since during my conference with Mr Brown he demonstrated no regret for his actions pointing to the fact that he is a "man" and any man would have reacted in the same manner.'

It was time for visit to a psychiatrist. Dr Robert A. Wainger examined Brown, concluding: 'Mr Brown is suffering from rather severe anxiety associated with some paranoid and grandiose ideas [...] he also demonstrates a probable thinking disorder.' Wainger continued: 'although he may appear to be rather unusual and disorganised to the people around him, he *does not represent a danger to either*'. How wrong he was.

After twenty years in the profession, Carl Brown was eventually suspended on Wednesday, 3 March 1982. During his final meeting with Pat Gray, Brown apparently said: 'Wainger wants to study me, that's all. I can cure Dr Wainger. I will treat him. I will change his seeds.'

One of the issues that did strike me was Dr Wainger's diagnosis of 'probable thinking disorder'. This may be summarised as any disturbance in cognition that adversely affects language and thought content, and thereby communication, all of which presented themselves in Brown's growing schizophrenic behaviour at both schools. And most certainly in his home life, where he was becoming more erratic and delusional as the months passed by.

It's worth noting at this point that as young man Brown had joined the US Navy and, although he only served for a relatively short time, he was honourably discharged. People who knew him later said that he always carried himself in a militaristic sort of manner. After he had got his master's degree, he gained great satisfaction from helping to educate youngsters. Clearly something had gone wrong inside Brown's head. But what?

According to the NHS, although the exact causes of schizophrenia are unknown, research suggests a combination of physical, genetic, psychological and environmental factors that can make a person more likely to develop the condition. Some people might be prone to schizophrenia, and a stressful or emotional life event might trigger a psychotic episode. However, it is not known why some people develop symptoms while others do not.

Unfortunately, we know little about Carl Brown's personal narrative, so we have no clue as to whether or not genetics, or brain development, or anything else played a part in his deterioration. But we do know that he was under a considerable amount of stress, having lost his job of some forty years, and to him this ended his lifelong relationship with teaching, which may have felt like a form of bereavement. Eventually, it all became too much. As I mentioned at the start of this chapter, a person in a healthy state of mind would have brushed off the issue of an unsatisfactorily repaired mower engine with a shrug of the shoulders. Sadly for Carl Brown and the people he killed, this was the tipping point that finally pushed him over the edge.

We also know that four months after being suspended from teaching, Carl Brown reapplied to get his job back. His request was denied. Two days later, he committed mass murder at the welding shop and he was on his way to Hialeah Junior High, for his deadly mission had only just begun. Most fortunately a firearm was in the hand of Mike Kram who, along with Ernest Hammett, chased the killer down. Had they not done so, then far more innocent people, perhaps children, would have died too.

At the time, this mass murder had the highest body count of any shooting in Florida's history, although it has now long been surpassed . However, back then such was the furore that five weeks after the murders, the Hialeah City Council voted 6–1 to introduce a three-day waiting period to buy rifles and shotguns – presumably to allow time for extra checks. This was a knee-jerk reaction, for just three weeks later the very same council rescinded the ordinance after local gun dealers complained that the law was killing their business. As Krajicek says, 'The short-lived regulation was a herald of the political quagmire that encompassed any attempt to enact a firearms regulation, *however modest*, in the US' (my italics). However, this raises another very important issue: that of maybe well-deserved paranoia.

The pro-gun lobby will say that their side of this firearms control debate proves that someone like the armed Mike Kram did what the police, at that point, were unable to do: bring down a wanton mass murderer and most probably save numerous lives. And I suspect that Kram took no enjoyment at all in killing Carl Brown. He was doing his public duty and no charges were pressed against him.

Then we have to take note of the social dynamics at play: one moment the Hialeah City Council issued their ordinance, then three weeks later cancelled it – ostensibly because it was affecting the sales of firearms in gun shops. As in all cases of mass murder there was, and always will be, a rush by citizens to buy guns, again ostensibly to protect themselves from harm (perhaps citing Kram's prompt action, which *did* save lives). Therefore, the pro-gun lobby has a valid argument, because it all boils down to what the public feel they require to protect themselves. They could not obtain firearms from gun shops, and the Hialeah City Council felt the heat of their complaints. And after all, they are elected officials whose sworn moral duty is to protect their citizens from harm. At the time Carl Brown bought his weapons he had no criminal record at all, thus he was legally entitled to buy just about anything he wanted.

This case is an altogether tragic state of affairs. It raises a lot of other moral issues for which I suspect there can be no definitive answers. Yet perhaps it's fair to extend at least *some* compassion here, because Carl Brown was obviously seriously mentally ill. He is buried at the Winterville Cemetery, 4818-4852 Reedy Branch Road Winterville, Pitt, North Carolina.

Then I look at a similar scenario happening in the UK. Let's imagine that shortly after Derrick Bird ran amok in Cumbria, a public-spirited person – even if his own life is not in peril – effectively took the law into his own hands and shot Bird stone dead, thus stopping his killing spree. Of course, Kram had no idea that Brown was going to a school to kill more people, therefore, hypothetically, the man who shoots Bird would have no idea of his intentions. But in the UK, the man who kills Derrick Bird would almost certainly go to prison, rather than be praised for doing what the police were unable to do at the time – save innocent lives. That said, following a mass shooting in the UK, there is no public panic to inundate gun shops, no pressing need for us to arm ourselves to the teeth. And why not? It's because we do not hand out lethal weapons like sweets, that's why. So, while there are good arguments to be put up by both the pro- and anti-gun lobbies, mass murders are very rare events. In the end, it all comes down to the fact that, should they wish, American citizens are free to buy themselves a small arsenal.

Conclusions

Only the dead have seen the end of war.

<small>ATTRIBUTED TO THE SPANISH-BORN AMERICAN WRITER AND
PHILOSOPHER GEORGE SANTAYANA (JORGE AGUSTIN NICOLÁS
RUIZ DE SANTAYANA Y BORRAS)</small>

Without wishing to appear as if I am at Speakers' Corner in Hyde Park, preaching from atop a stepladder, as any former, or serving professional military person trained to use military-grade firearms will confirm: guns are solely designed to be used for *one purpose* – to maim and kill.

Historians typically recognise Chinese fire lances, which were invented in the tenth century, as the first guns. These bamboo or metal tubes projected flames and shrapnel at their targets. Aside from cannon, the invention in the fifteenth century of the 'lock' – the firing mechanism on the gun – made for the creation of the earliest reliable handguns. The first was the French arquebus, a short-barrelled firearm held at the shoulder and small enough to be handled by one man. The history of firearms is long and fascinating. However, *every single firearm* made since the Chinese fire lances is intended to destroy life, be it animal or human.

The Second Amendment to the United States Constitution declares: 'A well regulated Militia, being necessary to the security of a free State, the right of the people to keep and bear Arms, shall not be infringed.' And how the American peoples have abused those rights ever since; how lawmakers and courts have twisted and massaged and manipulated those 'rights'. Amongst them I quote: United States v. Cruikshank (1876), Presser v. Illinois (1886) and the United States v. Miller (1939), when the Court again recognised that the right to arms is 'individually held' and, citing the Tennessee case of Aymette v. State, indicated that it protected the right to keep and bear arms that are 'part of the ordinary military equipment' or the use of which could 'contribute to the common defence'.

What sort of so-called civilised society could possibly need ordinary military equipment (military-grade high-powered semi-automatic firearms) to protect themselves from their own neighbours? What sort of society is that? I impertinently suggest that the spirit of the Founding Fathers has long since been abused. There would never have been a thought in the minds of these remarkable men that would have condoned the misuse of firearms as witnessed today.

How has all of this judicial wrangling protected US citizens from being victims of mass homicide? Not one bit, for these events are actually on the increase.

With that being said, the American pro-gun lobby has a

valid argument, *inter alia*: why not allow 'responsible citizens' to own firearms for sporting or hunting purposes? I think that's right and fair, but as history has proven time and again, instead of ploughing millions of dollars into a pro-gun lobby president's election campaign (a man who said he could shoot someone and get away with it, remember), perhaps their members' money would be better spent elsewhere, namely to campaign that gun shops do not sell lethal weapons to all and sundry.

There have been many examples in this book highlighting cases where legally owned firearm owners have allowed their kids – often youngsters with serious psychological issues – access to their lethal weapons. These utterly irresponsible parents are either stupid to the nth degree, or should not themselves have owned guns in the first instance, or have never been to a mortuary to see what a firearm can do to an innocent man, woman or child – even a foetus in the womb.

Yes, I may seem to be overdoing it here, but take a look online at post-mortem photos of gunshot victims and you will understand *exactly* what I mean. This mass-murder business is shocking, disgustingly immoral and not something any so-called civilised society should tolerate a day longer.

We have also seen in this book how infectious the mass murders committed by some killers have been, poisoning the minds of other mentally disturbed, angry youngsters who have ready access to firearms. The writing has been on the wall for decades, yet *still* social media platforms allow these wannabe mass killers to 'advertise' their sick intentions for others to praise while venerating the likes of *der Führer* and the Columbine killers as icons of a sort. How perverse is that? Maybe the people who run these media platforms should go and visit a morgue, and imagine if it were their little pride and joy lying there full of holes, grey-faced, ice cold, their last words, 'Mum and Dad, help me please'.

In his excellent book, *Mass Killers: Inside the Minds of Men Who Murder*, David J. Krajicek makes a valid point in this context. For amongst other important issues, he raises the vital one of early intervention. However, I have gone to great pains in this book to try and explain that we can *never know* what is going through a wannabe killer's mind until the dreadful deeds are done. Therefore, perhaps we might use 'intervention' in a different way – for example by putting in place stringent and effective gun controls, or banning semi-automatic weapons from public use altogether. Had that been the case decades ago, and most especially with school shootings, then scores of our young children would be alive today, and not now rotting in their graves under freshly mown, sweet-smelling green grass – flowers well watered by grieving parents' tears.

And it is right and proper to think about our children in my closing words. Specifically for my American readers I say this: throughout my research and during the process of writing this book, I have been in contact with many teachers across 'The Pond'. All of them, without exception, find themselves between a rock and a hard place when it comes down to gun control and school shootings in the USA. And all of them view this most controversial issue through the same end of the telescope as I do. Perhaps it's best summed up in a Messenger text that one very special lady sent to me, dated Wednesday, 8 April 2020:

> I literally hate guns but have seen what happens when they are in the hands of evildoers. Of course I carry a gun for my own protection and the protection of my students. What else CAN I DO?

What a sad state of affairs this is. A very sad state indeed.

Epilogue

*I know it's a movie but I like to think sometimes
I'm the Terminator or something.*

Jake Davison: the Plymouth spree killer, posted on his
YouTube account three weeks before he ran amok

I started researching and writing this book several years ago.

Alas, Rome was not built in a day, and the reader, if he or she so wishes, might want to look further at the mass-murder rates that are exponentially escalating in the USA today, which has made it impossible for me to keep up with the mass-murder epidemic that is plaguing America as I write. Indeed, looking at the current overall homicide statistics, the COVID-19 pandemic has increased stress-related shooting deaths in the US. And, as this book proves beyond any doubt, psychological COVID-related stressors, coupled with easy access to lethal weapons, are a contributory factor in firearm-related deaths across 'The Pond'.

To some extent I understand why this is. People feel disenfranchised. In some states Rebublicans are trying to deny people of colour, among others, the right even *to vote*. So much for this so-called 'Land of the Free'; a country of otherwise good folk who are living in real fear of being shot, even in their own burger joints, schools and places of worship. In this respect the 'Star Spangled Banner' holds aloft *not* 'Hope' but 'Anarchy', as demonstrated by the events of 6 January 2021 in Washington DC: the attack on the very foundation of so-called US democracy, all in the name of a racist, misogynistic, pro-gun lobby, mega-narcissist President.

It was horrendous and sad. Firstly there was shouting, followed by gunshots – three possibly four to begin with. This was when the shooter kicked in the door of a house and randomly started shooting. He ran from the house shooting as he ran and proceeded to shoot at a few people in the Linear Park up from the drive, then he proceeded along Royal Navy Avenue still shooting.

> Sharon (surname withheld for legal reasons):
> to BBC Radio Devon, 13 August 2021, on the
> Plymouth killings

Yet having criticised the America of Donald Trump, are we not at fault ourselves in the UK, as proved by the 12 August 2021 shooting of five innocents – two men; two women and a three-year-old girl with two injured – before twenty-two-year-old heavily bearded incel Jake Davison, following a deadly six-minute spree, shot himself? The incidents happened at around 6.18 p.m., in the Keyham area of Plymouth. In what appears to have started as a domestic argument, Davison first murdered a fifty-one-year-old woman after kicking in her front door. Police believed there may have been a 'familial relationship' here; in fact, the woman was Davison's mother. Thereafter, he walked out into the street, where he immediately shot dead the little girl, then fired at and killed her forty-three-year-old father. In Biddick Drive, he shot and wounded a fifty-three-year-old woman and a man aged thirty-three. Next, he went into a park. Here, he shot dead a fifty-nine-year-old man, before moving to Henderson Place where he shot and seriously wounded a sixty-six-year-old woman who later died in hospital. This total loser then turned the gun on himself.

I have made much about incels (or 'chads' as they are known amongst themselves) in this book, so it is appropriate to draw the reader's attention to the fact that in online videos Davison said that he was socially isolated, struggled to meet women and made references to 'incels' – the misogynistic online groups of involuntary celibate men who blame women for their sexual failings, as we have seen in an earlier chapter.

* * *

I have quoted Davison's view of himself as the Terminator at the head of this chapter, but this amoral, and clearly misinformed, bigot added: '…mass shootings are a *new* phenomena [*sic*] that cannot be directly blamed on guns. Plus there are a lot more guns in Europe and the UK than people think.' Elsewhere in his blog, posting in a group of 'virgins', he complained about being a virgin, stating: 'I can't attract women at all.' 'In his video blogs he used other phrases linked to the incel community', writes Marianna Spring, Disinformation and Social Media Reporter for the BBC. 'He mentions the "black pill overdose". The black pill worldwide view is essentially the belief that if you're unattractive, you don't deserve love and you are destined to fail and become more unhappy every time you pursue it.' (For more about the 'black pill' mentality, see this article on the New America website: https://www.newamerica.org/political-reform/reports/misogynist-incels-and-male-supremacism/red-pill-to-black-pill/.)

According to David Lockwood, Chief Executive of Babcock International, a security and defence engineering company with sites in Plymouth, Davison had worked as an apprentice since August 2020. Posting on Reddit three weeks before the shootings, Davison, who claimed to have got a job as a crane operator, also discussed firearms.

Having been one of the most prominent voices in the incel YouTube community, with his own podcast, he was one of the very few incels prepared to speak to the media after the 2018 Toronto attacks. His YouTube channel has since been taken down.

> Obviously I don't have much hope of attracting a woman in the first place. I've had a couple of negative experiences in relationships and so that has made me feel, like you know…it's hard to move on from my past and start a new relationship.
>
> Jake Davison

This was the first fatal mass shooting in the UK since the Derrick Bird shootings in 2010 (for which see Chapter 13). What is disgraceful is that police had previously confiscated Davison's licensed pump-action shotgun because of some misdemeanor, and then handed it and his shotgun certificate back to him. Something of his character and beliefs can be deduced from a first-rate BBC television documentary, *Inside the Secret World of Incel*, which offers 'A never-before-seen look at the incel community, an online subculture to which multiple mass murders and hate crimes against women have been attributed.' It contains some very shocking language and live footage.

And if that documentary doesn't wake up society to the lethality of firearms, and if the politicians don't come down hard on the side of gun control, then those we elect to keep us safe will have our blood on their hands too.

No nightmares, please!